Do not fear, for I am with you;
I will bring your offspring from the east and gather you from the west. I will say to the north, "Give them up!" And to the south, "Do not hold them back." Bring My sons from afar, and My daughters from the ends of the earth . . .

ISAIAH 43:5, 6, NASB

ISRAEL

THE UNIQUE LAND
THE UNIQUE PEOPLE

Lance Lambert

LIVING BOOKS
Tyndale House Publishers, Inc.
Wheaton, Illinois

Italics in biblical quotations are the author's own.
The following abbreviations are used:

ASV = American Standard Version
AV = Authorized Version
NASB = New American Standard Bible
RSV = Revised Standard Version
RV = Revised Version

This book is the American edition of the book
originally published in England
by Kingsway Publications Ltd.,
under the title *The Uniqueness of Israel.*
The Tyndale House Living Books edition is produced
by permission of Kingsway Publications Ltd.,
Eastbourne, E. Sussex, England.

First printing, Living Books edition, September 1981

Library of Congress Catalog Card Number 81-51463
ISBN 0-8423-1771-6, Living Books edition

Printed in the United States of America

CONTENTS

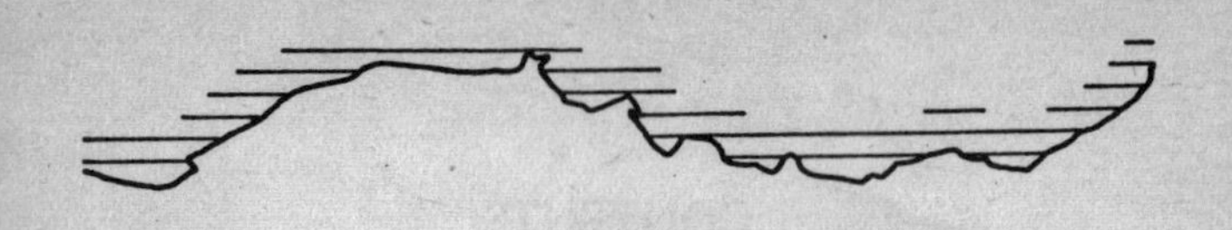

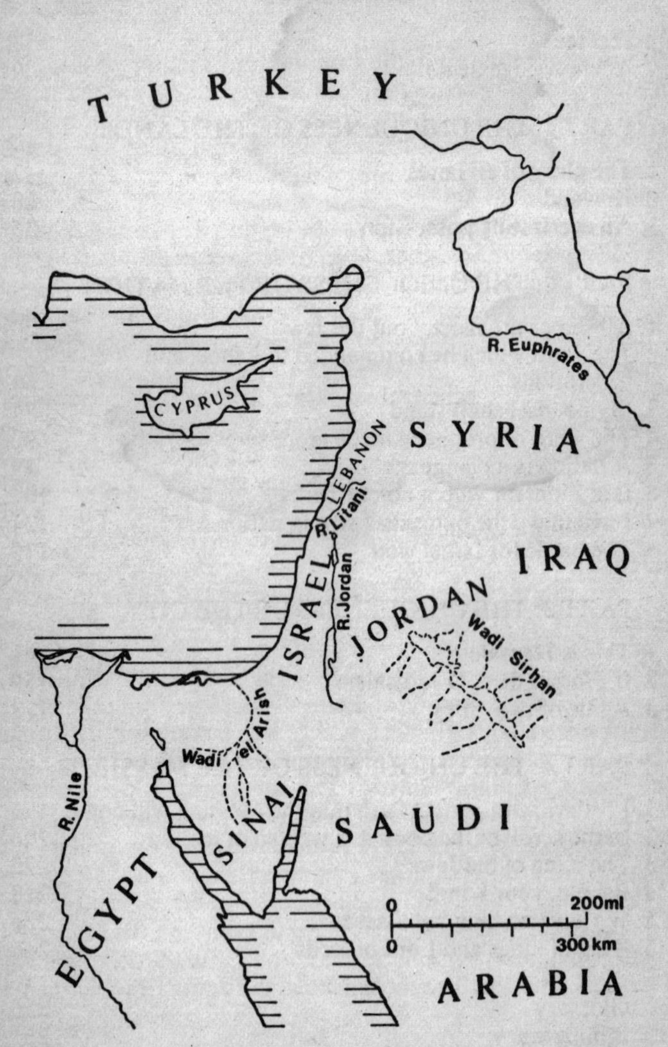

TURKEY
R. Euphrates
CYPRUS
SYRIA
LEBANON
R. Litani
IRAQ
ISRAEL
R. Jordan
JORDAN
Wadi Sirhan
Wadi el Arish
R. Nile
SINAI
SAUDI
EGYPT
ARABIA
0
200ml
0
300 km

PREFACE

It is not without significance for me that I finished the writing of this book on Holocaust Day, the day when Israel remembers in sorrow the systematic murder of six million Jews in Nazi concentration camps. As the sirens wailed and the nation stood for the two minutes' silence, I could not help but wonder at all that had transpired within one short generation. At the time of the second world war the thought of a sovereign Jewish State must have seemed ludicrous, if not impossible. But today I stood in silence amidst the people of that reborn State. The inexorable purpose of God has been fulfilled, although it has been realized through much conflict and bloodshed.

Last night I beheld the solitary and stationary shaft of light which shone into the night sky, piercing, as it were, the heavens. The strength of its clarity, and at the same time the frailty of its solitary beam against the dark night sky, gripped me. It shone into the darkness of the heavens from Yad Vashem, the memorial to the dead of the holocaust in West Jerusalem, and it shone in the darkness to commemorate their death. It was as if the nation were saying, 'We have not forgotten you; out of your suffering and death, we have come.' For Israel was born out of much sorrow. It seemed to me that one beam of light, linking the earth with the heavens, symbolized the history of Israel — light out of darkness. It symbolized not only that which has passed but also that which is yet to come, the glory which is yet to be.

The prayer of my heart is that this book, written out of a sense of my own weakness, and not without much conflict, may also be for some 'light out of darkness'. I am well aware that there are few subjects over which there is so much confusion and controversy as there is over the subject of this book. Some will undoubtedly feel that I have been extremely one-sided in my approach, but I would like to remind all my readers that this is a book about the Jewish people, and I have therefore kept myself within the limitations and the confines of my subject. Others may feel that I have not been critical or forthright enough.

I cannot expect all to agree with my views. I only trust that those who see the matter very differently from me will at least read the book through, and give it serious consideration.

Woven into the very fabric of Jewish existence there is an inescapable uniqueness. Many Jews would love to escape from it, or would at least like to forget it or ignore it, but they find that it is unavoidable. And if that uniqueness is inescapable, so also, thank God, is the destiny. For if the uniqueness of Israel's Messiah gives rise to the uniqueness of the land of Israel, its capital Jerusalem and the Jewish people — their history and final redemption — so too is his glorious destiny for ever bound up with theirs.

This book comes from what I have learnt of the mind and purpose of God for Israel during my own on-going pilgrimage with him. Although I have been a poor learner and follower of the Lord, I have written it as honestly as I know how, by his grace. If the truth which burns in my spirit and in my bones has in some way been clouded by my weaknesses and faults, I ask the forgiveness of my readers. Nevertheless, I have no doubt that it is truth, enduring and invincible, and for that I make no apology.

For this reason the bitter argument and controversy over the subject of Israel leaves me unmoved, for time itself will vindicate the truth. There will come a day more sure and certain than either the sun and the moon, or the seasons of the year, when the Jewish people will be received again by God. That day will be a day of unclouded glory, a day of radiant grace, a day of resurrection power and life for the whole redeemed community. I pray that, in the grace of God, my eyes will see that day, and behold at last the fulfilment of what I believe has been a divinely given burden and travail. But whether I live to see that day or not makes no difference to the certainty of its coming. It is decreed within the changeless counsel of God, and he never fails.

LANCE LAMBERT

ACKNOWLEDGEMENTS

I would like to acknowledge, with deep gratitude, all those who in various ways have contributed to the writing of this book — whether it has been in researching facts, correcting the English, typing the manuscript, or in the making of valuable suggestions. Above all I thank God for their prayer and fellowship.

PART I

THE UNIQUENESS OF THE LAND

A land that I had searched out for them
. . . which is the glory of all lands.

Ezekiel 20:6 (ASV)

CHAPTER 1

THE GLORY OF ALL LANDS

'The glory of all lands' – this was how God described the land of Israel (Ezekiel 20:6, 15, ASV) – a land which he had 'searched out for them'. For many people who visit Israel, this description of the land may be puzzling. For while there are those who are immediately attracted to it, there are also those who are disappointed by it. It does not live up to the conceptions that have formed in their minds over the years. While they appreciate that it is the land of the patriarchs, and prophets, and psalmists, and above all, the land of the Lord Jesus, only a few would describe it as the 'glory of all lands'. Many areas of the world are more scenically beautiful than the land of Israel. There is nothing within her borders, for instance, to compare with the magnificence of the Alps or the Norwegian fjords. For ruggedness and sheer size, the Himalayas and the Grand Canyon exceed anything to be found in her. And her coastline certainly cannot be compared with the idyllic loveliness of the Italian Riviera coast. And yet the land of Israel is unique; there is something about it which is elusive, mysterious and compellingly attractive. It is impossible to put into words what that 'something' is. Many have borne witness to its magnetic quality, and they are by no means only Jews.

The country is, generally speaking, mountainous. Much of the central area of the land covered by Judea and Samaria rises to 3,000 ft (923 m.). In the north, the highest peak is Mount Hermon, rising to 9,232 ft (2,841 m.), and in Galilee, Mount Meiron, 3,963 ft (1,219 m.). In the south, in the Sinai, there are mountains of over 7,500 ft (2,308 m.), the highest being Mount Catherine, 8,700 ft (2,537 m.); while in Edom, in Southern Jordan, there are mountains of over 5,000 ft (1,539 m.).

Within the compass of a very small area this land has a great variety of scenery. From the Mediterranean type of landscape which we find in Galilee and in the north, and also to a certain extent along the Mediterranean coast, it changes to steppe-land east of Jerusalem and around Beersheba, and to desert in the south and in the Aravah. It has some deep valleys. The Jordan Valley is part of the great rift valley which stretches at least 4,000 miles from the mountains of Turkey, Syria and Lebanon to Mount Kilimanjaro in East Africa. At the Sea of Galilee, the Jordan Valley is 656 ft (202 m.) below sea-level, and at the Dead Sea it drops to 1,312 ft (404 m.) below sea-level, the lowest point on the earth's surface. This feature alone makes the land of Israel unique, and has influenced nearly everything within it. It is a land of sharp contrasts and great extremes, of glaring brightness and pitch darkness, of extreme barrenness and great fertility, of difficult mountainous ranges and deep valleys, of fierce heat by day and bitter cold at night, of the most delicate flowers and ugly, tough thorn bushes, of modern paraphernalia and ancient ways.

There are three basic geographical factors which have determined the character of this land: its setting within the Mediterranean zone; its position at the crossroads of three continents and between two oceans; and its situation on the boundary line between the two extremes of the desert and the sown.

Although small in area, the significance of the land of Israel is out of all proportion to its size. During one period of Israel's history, the phrase 'from Dan to Beersheba' was commonly used to describe the whole land. Yet there are a mere 140 miles between Dan in the north, at the foot of Mount Hermon and near the main source of the River Jordan, and Beersheba in the south, near the border between steppe-land and desert (and marking the limits of civilization in olden days). Compared with those large fertile areas, rich in natural resources, which made such a contribution to ancient civilizations, such as Mesopotamia or the Nile Valley and Delta, the land of Israel is small and poor. Yet this little land has figured prominently in the affairs of the world, and its own stormy history provides much evidence for its vital significance and importance.

The land of Israel lies at the crossroads of three continents – Africa, Asia and Europe. The main international highways of the ancient world ran through it. One of those routes, 'the Way of the Sea' (Isaiah 9:1), *Via Maris* to the Romans, connected Egypt with Mesopotamia and Europe. It ran along the Mediterranean coast from Egypt, turned inland to Megiddo, crossed Galilee to Hazor, and then continued to Damascus. From Damascus it forked eastwards to Babylon and Ur, and northwards to Asia Minor (modern Turkey). Another north-south highway was called the 'King's Highway'. It ran from the Arabian Peninsula, through today's Aqaba, to Rabbath-Ammon, modern Amman, and continued to Damascus, where it merged with the 'Way of the Sea', the *Via Maris*.

It was the control of these vital trade routes which caused so much interest in the land of Israel on the part of the super-powers of the day. Every ambitious ruler aimed to bring these routes within his jurisdiction. Thus the land of Israel became the occasion of countless military campaigns and historic battles, for whoever held it subject controlled the vital crossroads of the ancient world. Pharaohs of Egypt, kings of Assyria, Babylonia and Persia; Alexander the Great, Ptolemaic and Seleucid kings; Roman and Byzantine emperors; Arabs, Crusaders, Mamelukes and Turks; or even the British, under General Allenby in the first world war: all fought for the control of this tiny area. The land of Israel was seen as essential to the security and well-being of one side or the other.

The land of Israel is not only set at the crossroads of

three continents; it lies between two seas: the Indian Ocean to the south, extending up the Gulf of Eilat and the Gulf of Suez, and the Mediterranean Sea to the west. It is placed between three deserts: to the east, the Syrian desert; to the south, the Arabian desert; to the south-west, the Saharan desert. This is the most extensive stretch of desert in the world. Indeed, it spreads almost without a break from the Sahara, through Arabia to Syria, and on to southern Iran and Central Asia. All these factors have combined to produce a unique situation within a very small area. They have influenced the climate of the land, its terrain, and its flora and fauna. The powerful forces of sea and desert have both played their part in the little country wedged between them. From the Mediterranean Sea, damp and moist westerly winds bring rain in the winter and some coolness in the long dry summer. From the desert, hot and dry easterly winds bring dust storms and heat waves.

The rainy season in the land of Israel is short. Over 70% of the annual rainfall occurs between November and February. In fact, the entire annual rainfall comes down within forty to sixty days during a season of seven months. This rainfall is described in the Bible as the former rains and the latter rains. Basically Israel has only two seasons, the hot dry summer and the rainy winter season, described by the Talmud simply as 'the days of sun' and 'the days of rain'. The amount of rainfall varies not only from year to year but from area to area. In the Mediterranean zone, for instance, anything between seventeen and forty inches of rain in a year is considered normal. Generally speaking, the further north you go, the wetter the winter is, but as you go south, the rainfall decreases sharply. Eilat, for instance, has an annual average rainfall of half an inch. It is a remarkable fact that Jerusalem and London share the same annual average rainfall of twenty-two inches! The difference is that it all falls in Jerusalem within around fifty days, whereas in London it is spread over some three hundred days.

Rainstorms in Israel are torrential. Visitors to the country are often surprised to see the large dusty wadis, or dried up river courses, in the Sinai, the Negev or the Aravah. It is hard to believe that water ever runs in them. Yet in the rainy season they can become huge and fast-flowing rivers, appearing and disappearing within hours. So localized can the rainfall be in these areas that one wadi becomes a torrent and another wadi a few miles distant remains dry. The ground is dust dry and does not absorb the rain, and this accounts for the very large volume of water in these wadis, since nearly all the rain which falls runs into them. It has been estimated that only 3% of the rainfall in these areas penetrates the surface, while the rest either runs into the sea, or quickly evaporates.

It is this rainy season which makes Israel a paradise of flowers in the months of February and March. For a few weeks the whole land becomes a riot of colour and scent, the air filled with the song of birds and the hum of insects. This annual miracle of resurrection never fails to capture the imagination of all who witness it. To see hills red with anemones and poppies, fields blue with wild lupins or pink with flax, is a sight never to be forgotten. It is no less impressive to see the little clumps of blue iris by the wayside, or pink or white cyclamen amongst the rocks, the solitary beauty of an orchid, or the stately flags in Galilee. The amazing variety and colour of Israel's flowers, which has to be seen to be believed, is the more impressive because so many different species all flower within a very short season. For visitors who have seen the land only in the summer or autumn months it is hard to believe that it is the same country. The wilderness also turns to green and is covered with many kinds of flowers; and even the desert blossoms. It is an unforgettable experience to smell its scent-laden air in February and March.

When the Lord spoke to Moses, he described the promised land as 'a good land, and a large, ... a land flowing with milk and honey' (Exodus 3:8 (ASV), 17;

Numbers 13:27). It was a description which captured the imagination of the people of God. Indeed, for all Bible readers the phrase 'a land flowing with milk and honey' has become synonymous with the promised land and beautifully expresses its fertility. While it was meant to describe the rich and abundant fertility of the land, it was not, however, meant to be a description of a highly cultivated and well tended land, as so many have understood the phrase, but a description of a land uncultivated, a land whose hills were covered with forests, with wild thickets and undergrowth, which in turn produced a wild profusion of flowers. It therefore described the kind of land which provided much grazing ground for both the wild and the domesticated goat, from which people could obtain milk, and the kind of land which provided a profusion of flowers for the bees, from which people could obtain honey. This interpretation is confirmed by Isaiah's words:

> Now it will come about in that day that a man may keep alive a heifer and a pair of sheep; and it will happen that because of the abundance of the milk produced he will eat curds, for every one that is left within the land will eat curds and honey. And it will come about in that day, that every place where there used to be a thousand vines, valued at a thousand shekels of silver, will become briars and thorns. People will come there with bows and arrows because all the land will be briars and thorns. And as for all the hills which used to be cultivated with the hoe, you will not go there for fear of briars and thorns; but they will become a place for pasturing oxen and for sheep to trample. (Isaiah 7:21-25, NASB.)

We need to note that the abundance of milk, and the eating of curds and honey, is linked with the destruction of the vineyards and of the terracing of the hills. The consequence of this destruction would be that the cultivated land would 'run riot' and would become the kind of land in which game would be found, and in which goats and sheep could graze. Certainly this phrase, 'a land flowing with milk and honey', provides us with a picture of a land vastly different from Egypt, or the surrounding desert and steppe-land areas.

The factors which I have described earlier have given rise to the rich variety of animal and bird life, and of plant life, found within the land. In the past this diversity has perplexed naturalists who have sought to classify the confusingly wide assortment of plants, animals and birds of different origins and species found within so small an area. As a general rule, the transition from desert to steppe-land and then to woodland takes place gradually and over a wide extent of country. But in Israel the change is compressed within a small area, and is therefore quite dramatic. In some cases the Mediterranean zone comes right up to the desert without any intervening steppe.

Within the small compass of the land of Israel are five vegetation zones.

(1) The Euro-Siberian zone, representing the kind of vegetation which is found in Europe, Russia and Siberia. This is not a zone such as the other four, which are distinct areas, but represents the Euro-Siberian plants found within the land.

(2) The Mediterranean zone, in which we find conditions similar to those in countries bordering on the Mediterranean Sea.

(3) The Irano-Turanian zone, characterized by the same kind of steppe-land that exists in a wide area from Israel to China, stretching through Iran, Turkestan, and Inner Asia, to the Gobi desert of Inner Mongolia.

(4) The Saharo-Arabian zone, which is pure desert and covers most of the Sahara in Africa, the Arabian Peninsula, and parts of Southern Iran.

(5) The Sudanese zone of tropical vegetation, which in Israel is confined to some small but very interesting enclaves and oases. The second, third, and fourth zones in Israel represent unbroken extensions of their parent regions; the last zone is completely detached, being represented only in oases hundreds of miles away from

their main region. It is unique to find so many vegetation zones within so small an area as Israel.

The geographical position of the land of Israel, linking the three continents, and the rich variety of vegetation zones, make it the meeting ground of plants native to widely differing parts of the earth, plants with such differing origins as Siberia, Western Europe, Inner Asia, North Africa and East Africa. Most of those who are acquainted with the Bible have heard of the 'rose of Sharon' or the 'hyssop which springs out of the wall' or the 'lilies of the field', without paying too much attention to biblical plant life. There are, however, at the present count some 3,000 different species of plants in this small land. This compares remarkably with the 1,800 plant-species of the British Isles, an area two and a half times the size of Israel, or with the 1,500 plant-species of Egypt, an area ten times the size of Israel and including one of the largest and most fertile areas in the Middle East, the Nile Delta. No other land in the world has a wealth of plant life within so small an area as the land of Israel.

For many of these plants, the land of Israel represents the extremity of their distribution. It is the eastern limit for many of the Mediterranean plants; the western limit of a number of the Asian steppe-land plants; the northernmost extremity of African plants, and the southernmost extremity of the Euro-Siberian plants. This is one of the unique features of the land of Israel. Take, for instance, the tropical *Doum* palms north of Eilat, which come from East Africa. There are only three clumps of these palms in Israel, and they represent the northernmost limit in the world of this particular palm. Their nearest relatives are more than a thousand miles away, and no one knows how they came to Israel. Another remarkable example are the Mangrove Swamps in South Sinai. These represent the most northerly point in the world in which these trees, common to the tropics, are found. Yet a further example is the Jujube tree or Christ thorn (*Zizyphus spina-Christi*) which is a tropical tree but which is to be found in almost every part of Israel. Or take the *Moringa* tree, which is a native of Sudan. There are *Moringa* trees to be found at En-Gedi on the Dead Sea, east of Jerusalem.

Sometimes one finds a ravine running east to west, where the southern wall, facing north and therefore cooler, is covered with Mediterranean plants, while the northern wall, facing south and therefore more dry and hot, supports only steppe-loving plants, and on the valley floor between them is an intermingling of both types of plant-life. Anyone who has visited Jerusalem will have been struck by the contrast between the area to the west of the Mount of Olives and the area to the east. In fact, Jerusalem is situated on the dividing line between the Mediterranean zone to the west, and the zones of steppe-land and of desert to the east. It is also striking to come upon some ravine in the desert which has a spring of water and suddenly step from arid desert into tropical and lush greenery. It is a surprise to many when they discover, for instance, the maidenhair fern and even moss happily growing over the rock face in a spring like En-Gedi, a stone's throw from arid desert. It is as great a delight to recognize the bracken so common in Europe in Galilee woodland, or to see the European frog's bit growing side by side with the tropical papyrus in what is left of the Huleh swamp in the Huleh Nature Reserve in Upper Galilee.

Another area of plant life which never fails to fascinate me is the plant life of the desert. Many people tend to feel that the desert is 'dead', until they begin to discover it. Then they find to their amazement that it is teeming with life, and with a life which has adapted itself most remarkably to seemingly impossible conditions. Many desert plants, for example, have concentrated their whole life-cycle into one short season of a few months, in which they germinate, grow leaves, blossom and fruit. In a year of rain, they produce enough seeds for several seasons ahead. Some seeds lie dormant for years awaiting the right conditions to germinate. Some trees and bushes of the desert shed their leaves in rainless years, appearing to the unenlightened to be dead, but in the right conditions they spring back into life. Others drop their leaves in the long hot and dry summer to conserve their life. The desert areas of Israel present us with one more facet of this remarkable land.

It is not only plant life, however, which is remarkable in the land of Israel, but bird life as well. All those familiar with the Bible will have read of the eagle, the raven, the stork, the swallow, or the humble sparrow. At the present count, some 450 species of birds are to be found within Israel. When we consider the larger area of the British Isles with some 460 species, and the vastly greater area of Europe, including European Russia, with 800 species, and the United States with 725 species, we begin to realize what an extraordinary number of birds Israel boasts. There are birds which are resident in the land, such as the Palestinian sunbird and bulbul, or the sparrow; winter visitors from Europe and West Asia, such as the rook or the black-headed gull; summer visitors, mainly from Africa, such as the purple heron; and migrants, passing through Israel twice a year, such as the swallow and the stork. We ought to add to these one further group, those birds which appear in Israel from time to time but which follow no regular path or timetable.

The land of Israel provides highways linking three continents not only for man, but for birds as well. Some of the migrant birds passing through the land of Israel come from the far north of Russia, from Lapland and Greenland, or from East, Central and even South Africa. Thus the land of Israel is literally at the crossroads of their flight paths. African and European migrant birds normally follow the great rift valley, flying along the Gulf of Eilat, the Aravah, the Dead Sea, the Jordan Valley and Galilee; or they follow the Mediterranean coastline of Israel. For some of the birds which come to Israel, as for some plants, it is their southernmost, for others their northernmost limit.

I have always found it a source of great delight to be present in either the spring or the autumn when these feathered flight paths are crowded with traffic! It is a rewarding experience to watch the storks in their thousands using the rising air currents to gain height and then, thousands of feet high, flying either north or south; or to see the swallows skimming over the sea at Sharm esh Sheikh at the southernmost tip of Sinai, knowing that they have just arrived from Africa on their long journey north. It is no less fascinating to see a colony of exotic bee-eaters high up on the Lebanese border, or a flight of nine or ten heavy pelicans in formation, lumbering in from Central Africa.

I never fail to be excited by these birds, whether it is the tiny wren or goldcrest, or the quaint but lovable hoopoe, Israel's national bird, which regularly nests in the Garden Tomb in Jerusalem; or the great lammergeier, the largest of the vultures, with a wingspan often of nine to ten feet, which I saw early one morning flying slowly and majestically up a valley in southern Sinai. The remarkable bird life of this land covers the whole range in size, from the Palestinian sunbird, which is little larger than a hummingbird, to the great eagles, of which the Imperial eagle, Bonelli's eagle, and the short-toed eagle are the most common. In ancient times the range of size was even greater, for the ostrich, the largest of all birds, was a common resident of the wilderness.

The land of Israel is a meeting place for four-footed creatures as well. There are representatives of all the regions found within its borders. The African lion, rhinoceros, hippopotamus, hartebeest, warthog, crocodile, Syrian bear and cheetah, have all died out; but there are still leopards, lynxes and jungle cats, ibex, gazelles and wild goats, hyenas, jackals, wolves and foxes, wild boar, badgers, porcupines and polecats.

The land of Israel is the southernmost limit for the Siberian wolf, which becomes smaller in size the further south it appears. It is not found in Africa at all. Another

European animal which has now penetrated even the Sinai mountains in the far south of Israel is the little dormouse. On the other hand, the coney is an African animal, and Israel and Syria are its northernmost limit. For the leopard, the land of Israel is its westerly limit. Not only are the different continents represented, but sometimes African and Asian species of the same animals exist side by side. For instance, Israel boasts as many as twenty-five species of bat, from all three continents, Europe, Asia and Africa. Many other examples can be seen in the Bible Safari Park, Hai Bar, north of Eilat.

There are animals in this land which cannot survive for long apart from water, such as the wolf, and others which are so adapted to dry conditions that they can live without drinking water, such as the spiny mouse in the Negev. This little creature extracts the maximum use of its body fluids and excretes hardly any water at all. Even the camel and the distinctive black goat of the Bedouin can live without drinking water for up to fourteen days. Recently it has been discovered that this particular goat conserves moisture in the same way as the camel. Even the Bedouin chicken seems to display similar characteristics, and studies are at present being made upon it to determine whether it is a particular species of chicken or a matter of adaptation. There has been, in fact, much discussion over the origin of the goat and the sheep found in Israel. The general consensus of opinion favours the view that both are Asiatic species and not European. The sheep commonly seen in Israel are not the European variety but the distinctive fat-tailed *Awassi* sheep. A number of experts consider that the goat is descended from the wild Cretan goat (the bezoar), which is still found in an area from India to Crete.

The land of Israel can no longer boast of the great abundance of animals she once knew, but she still displays an interesting and striking diversity. Whether it is the diminutive jerboa, the jumping desert rat, the stealthy lynx, the graceful ibex, or the desert fox, the land still abounds with animal life. Indeed Israel, with limited financial resources, is striving to preserve the wild-life of the land. Apart from Jordan, she appears to be the only country in the Middle East making such an effort.

Thus far I have not mentioned either insects or reptiles, both of which abound in the land. The number of invertebrates is almost countless. Certainly their number reaches tens of thousands, the majority of which are insects. These cover the whole range from five species of bee, and four species of hornet, to the many kinds of butterfly, grasshopper and ant; while among non-insects there are at least thirteen species of scorpion, and innumerable kinds of spiders, of all shapes and sizes. One remarkable little creature is unique to Israel – a species of blind fresh water prawn (*typhlocaris*), found only in the warm springs at Tabgha on the Lake of Galilee.

There are more than eighty different species of reptile in the land of Israel, and they too cover a wide variety in shape and size. At one time the African crocodile would have been included, but it died out in the earlier part of this century. They include the tortoise and turtle, of which there are seven species; the lizards, ranging from the chameleon and the gecko to the desert monitor which can grow up to four feet long; and the snakes, of which there are at least thirty-five different species, ranging in size from the ten-inch blind snake to the eight-feet black whip-snake. Some of these reptile species are almost extinct in the rest of the world, while the presence of others is quite remarkable.

Even this brief survey of the natural life of Israel must include one further area of uniqueness: the coral reef of the gulf of Eilat. This is one of the three richest coral reefs in the world. They contain a vast variety of tropical fish and organisms connected with coral. To see them is to enter another world of incredible colour, shape and beauty, for they include the whole range of the highly diversified world of the Indo-Pacific coral reef.

Another striking fact is that since the Suez Canal was

opened more than a century ago, there has been a remarkable invasion of tropical marine organisms from the Red Sea into the Mediterranean, over 200 species in fact. By 1973 some thirty Red Sea species of fish alone had been counted, fish which have emigrated to the Eastern Mediterranean and which have gained commercial importance for fishing. This provides a further illustration of the way in which this region is the meeting place not only of continents but of seas as well! So real is this invasion that future specialists in this area will have to view the Eastern Mediterranean as a distinct sub-region of the Mediterranean proper, characterized by an admixture of some 20% Indo-Pacific marine fauna.

I am not a zoologist, or a botanist, or an ornithologist, and write only as a layman and amateur in these fields, but the natural life of the land of Israel enthrals me. Its amazing variety must strike anyone who begins to investigate it. Add to this the remarkable range of scenery within so small an area, and it becomes the cause for greater wonder. I find it unique – whether it is the granite mountains of the south Sinai with their strikingly different colours – black or yellow or red – and their varying shapes and forms, their sills and dykes, changing in interest with every hour of the day according to the direction and intensity of the sun's rays; or whether it is the Jordan rift valley, the lowest point on the earth's surface, with its summer warmth even in winter, especially at the Dead Sea. You can shiver in Jerusalem's cold, and within hours be sunbathing 4,000 ft below Jerusalem on the shore of the Dead Sea. Within hours, you can drive from the green and cool, wooded mountainous area around Safed in the Upper Galilee, to the shimmering heat and arid atmosphere of the lower Jordan Valley. Or you can leave the warmth of Tiberias on the Lake of Galilee in winter, and be skiing on the snow-covered slopes of Mount Hermon, some 9,000 ft above the lake. Although the mountains of this land are by no means the highest or the greatest in the world, to stand upon their summits gives a most remarkable sense of elevation. To look down from Mount Scopus upon the Dead Sea and the Jordan Valley never fails to excite me with the sense of being on top of the world! It is the same with Mount Tabor in Galilee. Although rising to only 1,929 ft, its steepness and isolation give the surrounding country the quality of a relief map. Whether viewing the Plain of Armageddon to the south, the Lake of Galilee to the east, the Mediterranean Sea to the west, or the mountains of Lebanon to the north, one has the feeling of standing upon a summit which is at least four or five times greater than its true height.

When the Lord described the land of Israel as 'the glory of all lands' (Ezekiel 20:6), the Hebrew word used for 'glory' is not the usual term, but one which means 'beauty' or 'honour' as well as 'glory'. It is the word used also for 'gazelle'. To me this so aptly describes the land of Israel, for the beauty and the glory of the gazelle are indeed unique. It is 'the glory of all lands', and the more we explore it and seek to understand it, the more accurate we discover the words of the Lord to be.

CHAPTER 2

HIS LAND

The land of Israel is unique in another and more deeply significant way. God speaks of it as 'my Land'. This is as remarkable as it is singular. For instance, in Leviticus 25:23 he says:

> The land, moreover, shall not be sold permanently, for the land is Mine. (NASB)

This is not the only time that the Lord refers to the land of Israel in this way. For example, in Isaiah 14:25, he says:

> I will break the Assyrian in *my* land, and upon *my* mountains tread him under foot;

and, in Jeremiah 2:7 –

> I brought you into a plentiful land ... but when ye entered, ye defiled *my* land, and made mine heritage an abomination. (RV)

Furthermore God still refers to the land as his even in the last days – Ezekiel 38:16 –

> ... it shall come to pass in the latter days, that I will bring thee against *my* land, that the nations may know me. (RV)

And yet again, in Joel 3:2 –

> I will gather all nations ... and I will execute judgment upon them there for my people and for my heritage Israel, whom they have scattered among the nations: and they have parted *my* land. (ASV)

The divine affection and care for the land is stated simply and lucidly in the inspired words of Moses recorded in Deuteronomy 11:11-12 –

> But the land, whither ye go over to possess it, is a land of hills and valleys, and drinketh water of the rain of heaven: A land *which the Lord thy God careth for*, the eyes of the Lord thy God are *always upon it*, from the beginning of the year even unto the end of the year. (RV)

When we understand this it is no cause for wonder that Hosea (9:3) refers to it as 'the Lord's land', saying: 'They shall not dwell in *the Lord's land*' (AV); or that Joel (2:18) calls it 'his land', saying: 'Then the Lord became jealous for *his* land'; or that the Psalmist triumphantly exults in Psalm 10:16 – 'The Lord is King for ever and ever: the heathen are perished out of *his* land' (AV); or prays in Psalm 85:1 – 'Lord, thou hast been favourable unto *thy* land: thou hast brought back the captivity of Jacob' (AV). These examples are enough to prove that the land of Israel stands in a unique relationship to the Lord. Nowhere in the Bible does he refer to anywhere else as 'my land'.

Every part of the earth is God's by right. The Lord himself declared this in Exodus 19:5 – '... all the earth is mine'. The Psalmist echoes it:

> The earth is the Lord's, and the fulness thereof; the world, and they that dwell therein. (Psalm 24:1, AV.)

Furthermore, we know that the earth is waiting for the final restitution of all things. Our ascended, glorified Messiah is the guarantee of this. For however forcefully the authority of God may have been usurped by the powers of darkness, or however deeply the world may lie in the clutches of the evil one, the uttermost parts of the earth are destined to come back to God through the finished work of the Lord Jesus. The nations may rage against God and his purpose, but it will make no difference to the final outcome.

God himself has clearly stated this in one of the greatest of the messianic Psalms:

> Yet I have set my king upon my holy hill of Zion. I will tell of the decree: the Lord said unto me, Thou art my son; this day have I begotten thee. Ask of me, and I will give thee the nations for thine inheritance, and the uttermost parts of the earth for thy possession. Thou shalt break them with a rod of iron; thou shalt dash them in pieces like a potter's vessel (Psalm 2:6-9, RV).

Yet another messianic Psalm declares that

> He shall have dominion also from sea to sea, and from the river unto the ends of the earth .... all nations shall serve Him. (Psalm 72:8, 11, AV.)

All this will be fulfilled when 'The kingdom of the world has become the kingdom of our Lord and of his Christ' (Revelation 11:15).

Nevertheless the glorious truth that the whole earth belongs to God and will one day be restored to him does not diminish the fact that he speaks of the land of Israel as *his* land. This makes it unique.

The land of Israel is the land where God spoke to man and revealed himself. It is supremely the land of the Bible. It is true that both Mesopotamia and Egypt were also lands in which God revealed himself to chosen men, but it was always in relation to *this* land, in order to bring them into it. We are told, for instance, in Acts 7:2-3, that:

> The God of glory appeared unto our father Abraham, when he was in Mesopotamia ... and said unto him, Get thee out of thy land ... and come into *the land which I shall shew thee.* (RV)

and that the Lord said to Moses, in Exodus 3:8 –

> And I am come down to deliver them out of the hand of the Egyptians, and *to bring them ... unto a good land* ... unto a land flowing with milk and honey. (RV)

It is from the land of Israel, and not from Mesopotamia and Egypt, that the imagery of the Bible is drawn. There are, of course, some general similarities common to the whole of the Middle East, but it is from the mountains and valleys of the land of Israel, from its climate and the rich variety of its natural life, that the illustrations and lessons of the Bible are taken. The richness of biblical imagery is directly related to the richness of the natural life of this land.

It is the country of the patriarchs: the land of Abraham, of Isaac, and of Jacob and his sons. It is the land in which God met with them and worked miracles on their behalf; the land which he promised to them and to their descendants for an everlasting possession. To this day there are places in the land for ever linked with their names: Beersheba, Shechem, Bethel, Hebron.

It is the country of Moses and Joshua. Moses was born in Egypt, spent the first forty years of his life there, and a further forty years in the Sinai Wilderness, and never actually entered the promised land, yet from the moment the Lord appeared to him, the land of Israel was his land. Even the mighty wonders and signs which God worked in Egypt through Moses and Aaron, in order to deliver a slave people from Egyptian power, had this land in view. For forty years God led them through the wilderness by the pillar of cloud and fire, feeding them with manna and quenching their thirst with water which came miraculously out of the rock, in order to bring them into it. This was the land where the River Jordan parted, and the nation passed over as on dry ground; where the walls of Jericho fell down; and where at Gibeon and Aijalon the sun and the moon stood still for a day. It was in this land that the people of Israel experienced the power of God, enabling them to possess it, or, when alienated from God through sin and unbelief, knew defeat.

It is the country of the judges. At the Spring of Ein Harod in Galilee, the Lord whittled down Gideon's army from 32,000 men to 300, and then led them to victory. At

Mount Tabor, also in Galilee, Deborah the prophetess inspired Barak to defeat Sisera. In the Vale of Sorek and at Gaza (then in Philistine territory) the sad story of Samson was played out. In Shiloh in Samaria the young Samuel obeyed the Lord's voice, and went on to become a key figure in biblical history.

This is the land where kings ruled, the country of David and Solomon; of good kings such as Jehoshaphat, Hezekiah and Josiah, and of evil kings such as Ahab, Ahaz and Manasseh. Wherever you travel in this country there are reminders, in the rebuilt cities and towns and in the ancient ruins, of places which figured so prominently in their reigns.

It is the land of the Psalmists – David, Asaph and the sons of Korah; and the land of the prophets – like Elijah, Isaiah and Hosea. It was in this country that they lived and died, and it was of this country that they repeatedly spoke. And surely the feelings of those in exile, whether prophets like Ezekiel and Daniel or leaders like Nehemiah and Ezra, were most beautifully expressed by the Psalmist when he wrote:

> By the rivers of Babylon, there we sat down, yea, we wept, when we remembered Zion. Upon the willows in the midst thereof we hanged up our harps. For there they that led us captive required of us songs, and they that wasted us required of us mirth, saying, Sing us one of the songs of Zion. How shall we sing Jehovah's song in a foreign land? (Psalm 137:1-4, ASV.)

This country is also the land of the New Testament. It witnessed the preaching of John the Baptist, heralding the coming of the Messiah. To this day you can visit Ein Kerem, by tradition his birthplace; or see the ravines and great open wastes of the wilderness of Judea where he lived; and the River Jordan near Jericho where he baptized.

Supremely, the land of Israel is the land of Jesus. Wherever we tread in this country, we tread where Jesus trod. It was in Bethlehem that he was born, and in Nazareth that he was brought up. There he spent the first thirty years of his life, becoming a carpenter by trade. He made Capernaum on the north shore of the Lake of Galilee his base during the three years of his public ministry. As far as we know, he never left this land. From the way he spoke about it and its natural life, we understand how much he loved the land. He spoke of reading the weather signs, of the lilies of the field which 'toil not, neither ... spin', and the birds of the air which 'sow not, neither ... reap, nor gather into barns', of the foxes and their 'holes'. The shepherd and his sheep, the farmer ploughing, sowing and reaping, the vinedresser and his vineyards were all part of the scene he loved. From its hills and valleys, its seasons and moods, its plants, its flowers, its animals and birds, he drew his parables and his illustrations. Above all, he loved its people. Their common life and experience was the source of many of his stories. It was, simply, *his* land.

For it was in this land that 'the Word became flesh and dwelt among us' and the first disciples beheld 'his glory, glory as of the only begotten of the Father, full of grace and truth' (John 1:14, AV). This was the land which saw the love of God incarnate, 'the heart of God revealed'; which heard his matchless words, and witnessed his signs and miracles. It was here that he gave the blind their sight, and caused the deaf to hear, the dumb to speak, and the lame to walk. This land became the scene where the leper was healed, and the dead raised to life; where God restored the outcast, and received the sinner.

It was on one of the mountains of this land, perhaps Tabor or Hermon, that Jesus was transfigured in glory; on a hill above the Lake of Galilee he preached the 'sermon on the mount' and fed the five thousand; on one of its lakes, the Lake of Galilee, he calmed the storm and walked on its waters.

It was a quiet garden in this land which heard his strong crying and witnessed his tears and agony in prayer. At the foot of one of its hills he was crucified, nailed to a tree that had once grown within it. In a grave, newly hewn out of one of its rocks, his body was gently and sorrowfully laid. It was also in this land, thanks be to God, that he rose from the dead on the third day, the glorious Victor over sin and death and hell, to become the everlasting Saviour of all who put their trust in God through him. Then from one of its mountains, the Mount of Olives, he ascended to the Father, to sit down at his right hand for ever. Truly, the land of Israel is the Lord's land.

This country is also unique because all the final great events of world history prophesied in the Bible will take place either in relation to it or actually within its borders. Here the last great battles will be fought. On the mountains of Israel the whole armed confederacy of the north will be destroyed (Ezekiel 38-39), and on the plain of Armageddon in Galilee the final battle of human history will be fought (Revelation 16:13-16). And it will be in this land that the Spirit of grace and supplication will be poured upon the Jewish people with the most glorious results (Zechariah 12:10). Nor is that the end of the story, for it is to this land that the Messiah will return. His pierced feet will once again stand upon the Mount of Olives. He does not come first to the lands of the super-powers, or to lands of riches or culture. He returns to his own land – the land of Israel.

All of this makes Israel unique. Many lands can boast of great wealth and natural resources, of vast military might, or of a highly sophisticated culture. But none can boast that it is 'his land'. In this, the land of Israel stands alone.

CHAPTER 3

AN EVERLASTING POSSESSION

A further fact which makes the land of Israel unique is that it is the subject of divine promise. No other land on earth has ever been promised by God to one particular people. It is true, of course, that God watches over the destinies of all the nations, controlling their rise and fall, and their part in world history. He says, for instance, in Amos 9:7 –

> Have not I brought up Israel out of the land of Egypt, and the Philistines from Caphtor, and the Syrians from Kir? (ASV)

Nevertheless, the fact remains that to no other nation on the earth has God *promised* a particular land. Furthermore, his promise is both categoric and dogmatic.

The promise was first made to Abraham:

> And the Lord said to Abram ... 'Now lift up your eyes and look from the place where you are, northward and southward and eastward and westward; for all the land which you see, I will give it to you and to your descendants forever. And I will make your descendants as the dust of the earth; so that if anyone can number the dust of the earth, then your descendants can also be numbered. Arise, walk about the land through its length and breadth; for I will give it to you. (Genesis 13:14-17, NASB.)

We ought to note carefully the words 'all the land which you see, I will give it to you and *to your descendants forever*'. The promise is clear, no matter what some may say or feel. It is not just a promise to Abraham's son or grandson, to Isaac or to Jacob, nor even to Abraham's great-grandchildren. The promise is specific: 'I will make your descendants as the dust of the earth.' It is a promise, therefore, which is operative as long as there is a Jewish people.

Further, the promise is to 'you and your *descendants after you throughout their generations for an everlasting covenant*'. And again: 'I will give to you and to *your descendants after you*, the land of your sojournings, all the land of Canaan, for an *everlasting possession*' (Genesis 17:7-8, NASB). The promise was confirmed to Isaac:

> Sojourn in this land and I will be with you and bless you, for to you and to *your descendants* I will give all these lands , and I will establish the oath which I swore to your father Abraham. And I will multiply your descendants as the stars of heaven, and *will give your descendants all these lands*; and by your descendants all the nations of the earth shall be blessed. (Genesis 25:3-4, NASB.)

The promise was confirmed not only to Isaac but also to Jacob:

> And the land which I gave to Abraham and Isaac, I will give it to you, and *I will give the land to your descendants after you*. (Genesis 35:12, NASB.)

Centuries afterwards, Moses told the children of Israel before they crossed Jordan to possess the land:

> See, I have placed the land before you; go in and possess the land which the Lord *swore to give to your fathers*, to Abraham, to Isaac, and to Jacob, *to them and their descendants after them*. (Deuteronomy 1:8, NASB.)

The Psalmist sums up this whole matter in emphatic words:

> He is the Lord our God: his judgements are in all the earth. He hath remembered his covenant for ever, the word which he commanded *to a thousand generations* ; The covenant

> which he made with Abraham, and his oath unto Isaac; And confirmed the same unto Jacob for a statute, to Israel *for an everlasting covenant* : Saying, Unto thee will I give the land of Canaan, the lot of your inheritance. (Psalm 105:7-11, RV.)

It is extremely important to note that God's promise to Abraham would be fulfilled 'in Isaac' and not 'in Ishmael'. Genesis 17:20-21 says of Ishmael, 'I will make him a great nation. *But My covenant I will establish with Isaac*' (NASB). For this reason the promise made to Abraham is confirmed by God to Isaac and not Ishmael, to Jacob and not Esau. Moses clearly understood this, as did the Psalmist. The New Testament repeats the statement: 'What saith the Scripture? Cast out the handmaid and her son: for the son of the handmaid shall not inherit with the son of the free woman' (Galatians 4:30, RV).

It is sometimes said that Ishmael, the father of the Arab peoples, as well as Esau and others, were also the seed of Abraham and therefore qualify for the fulfilment of the divine promise made to him. The word of God is clear and specific: Ishmael was certainly the seed of Abraham, but he does not qualify for the covenant and the promise. It is the same with the other sons of Abraham by Keturah (Genesis 25:1-6). God did make certain other promises regarding Ishmael, which have been and are being fulfilled. For instance, God told Abraham: 'And also of the son of the handmaid will I make a nation, because he is thy seed' (Genesis 21:13, ASV); and to Hagar he said: '... for I will make him a great nation' (Genesis 21:18, RV). Notwithstanding, these promises were made at the same time that God pointed out to Abraham that 'through Isaac your seed shall be named' (Genesis 21:12, NASB). Earlier, the Lord had been even more specific: 'And as for Ishmael, I have heard thee: behold, I have blessed him, and will make him fruitful, and will multiply him exceedingly; twelve princes shall he beget, and I will make him a great nation. *But my covenant will I establish with Isaac* ...' (Genesis 17:20-21, RV).

It is clear from these Scriptures that whatever claims the Arabs – and the Palestinian Arabs in particular – may make upon the Holy Land, those claims have to be based upon political, historical or practical grounds and not upon Scripture. As far as the word of God is concerned, the land has been specifically promised as an everlasting possession to the descendants of Abraham through Isaac and Jacob. There are, of course, some Christian Arabs who were originally of Jewish stock, who became Christians during the early centuries of this era, and never left the land. It is also true of some Muslim Arabs. These have all intermarried with the stock of Ishmael, especially the latter. The nearest the Bible comes, however, to Arab claims on the land is contained in the phrase: 'he shall dwell over against all his brethren' (Genesis 16:12, ASV). The AV rendering is: 'he shall dwell in the presence of all his brethren'; which NASB translates: 'he will live to the east of all his brothers.' The meaning of the Hebrew is that Ishmael and his seed will live in proximity to Isaac and his seed. This they have done for nearly 4,000 years, and even when the Jewish people were dispersed into the whole world for 1,900 years, there were always sizable Jewish communities in Arab lands. Nevertheless, the Holy Land is promised not to the seed of Ishmael but to the seed of Isaac, even though it is prophesied that Ishmael and his seed will 'dwell over against all his brethren'. Certainly there is enough land in the Middle East for both Jew and Arab to live side by side in peace. By the mutual sharing of resources and technological knowledge great areas of the Middle East, at present barren and waste, could be reclaimed and developed to the benefit of not only the two communities but of the whole world. Sooner or later the seed of Abraham through Ishmael and the seed of Abraham through Isaac will have to live together in peace and to the mutual benefit and welfare of each other. Then that ancient prophecy of Isaiah will be fulfilled which says:

> In that day shall Israel be the third with Egypt and with Assyria, a blessing in the midst of the earth; For that the Lord

> of hosts hath blessed them, saying, Blessed be Egypt my people, and Assyria the work of my hands, and Israel mine inheritance. (Isaiah 19:24-25, RV.)

The Scriptures give no other example of particular land or territory being promised to a particular nation. Even the words of Deuteronomy 2:5 ('I have given mount Seir unto Esau for a possession') simply record the fact that the Lord had apportioned Esau a particular area. This statement may come into the same category as that of Amos 9:7, which refers to the Lord leading the Philistines and the Syrians to their lands. According to Deuteronomy 32:8, the Lord watches over all the nations and determines their course and their national boundaries; 'When the Most High gave the nations their inheritance, when He separated the sons of man, He set the boundaries of the peoples ...' (NASB). The land of Israel is, however, unique in this respect: it is the subject of divine promise. God has promised this land categorically to a particular people, to that nation which is descended from Abraham, through Isaac and Jacob. The Lord put this simply and lucidly in a prophecy in the Book of Jeremiah:

> Thus speaketh the Lord, the God of Israel, saying, Write thee all the words that I have spoken unto thee in a book. For, lo, the days come, saith the Lord, that I will turn again the captivity of my people Israel and Judah, saith the Lord: and *I will cause them to return to the land that I gave to their fathers*, and they shall possess it. (Jeremiah 30:2-3, RV.)

Once again:

> And there is hope for thy latter end, saith the Lord; and thy children shall come again *to their own border.* (Jeremiah 31:17, RV.)

And the Lord restates this through the prophet Ezekiel (20:42):

> And you will know that I am the Lord, when I bring you into the land of Israel, into the land which I swore to give to your forefathers. (NASB)

These promises are not conditional but absolute; they are not only for the immediate seed of Abraham, Isaac and Jacob, but we are told that, when their descendants have become like the dust of the earth for multitude, the promises will still be operative.

I most seriously question the view that this promise of God has been cancelled by the New Covenant. To me, it casts doubt upon the literal veracity of God's word. If God says that he has confirmed this 'to a thousand generations', and 'for an everlasting possession', and yet again that he has given the land 'for ever', I am confused when I am told that God did not mean it. Indeed, in my estimation such a view makes God guilty of speaking gross untruth, or at the least, of uttering misleading statements.

There are those who teach that the land of Israel was only promised to the children of Israel and the Jewish people until the time of Christ. This argument is often based upon Paul's words in Galatians 3:16 –

> Now to Abraham were the promises spoken, and to his seed. He saith not, And to seeds, as of many; but as of one, And to thy seed, which is Christ. (RV)

The Hebrew word translated 'seed' in the AV and 'descendants' in the NASB in passages such as Genesis 3:15; 13:15-16; 15:18; 17:7-8; 26:3; 35:12, etc. means 'sowing', 'seed' or 'offspring'. The word may be taken as either collective or singular, rather like the use of the English words 'sheep' or 'fish'. It would be quite wrong to take the 'seed of Abraham' as referring *only* to Messiah or Christ. God said that Abraham's seed would be as 'the dust of the earth: so that if any man can number the dust of the earth, then may thy seed also be numbered' (Genesis 13:16), and as numerous 'as the stars of the heavens and as the sand which is upon the sea shore' (Genesis 22:17).

As is so often the case with the Bible the use of the term 'seed' covers a number of fundamental matters. First it refers to Abraham's need of a physical heir in a physical land in and through whom the promise will be fulfilled. Whatever else is intimated in the promise, this fact is unmistakably clear from the context. Secondly, it refers to the numerous descendants of Abraham through Isaac and Jacob. The promise is apparently operative while there are such descendants. Thirdly, it refers to the Messiah, who is the key to the ultimate realization of the purpose of God and the basis for the fulfilment *of its every phase.*

At a first reading of these words from Galatians 3:16 –

> He saith not, And to seeds, as of many; but as of one, And to thy seed, which is Christ

it might seem that the apostle was categorically ruling out the first two interpretations, but I do not think that he was. Paul took for granted that the Galatians realized from the wording of the promises to Abraham that they were related to the abundance of his descendants and their connection with the land of Israel. It was the reference to the Messiah in these promises which was not immediately clear, although fundamental to the whole, and so Paul draws attention to it. Yet the apostle's main point in Galatians 3 is not the fact that it contains a wonderful reference to the Messiah, fundamental to the whole purpose of God as are his coming, his person and his finished work; it was that once a covenant is made by man it cannot be arbitrarily set aside, nor can qualifying conditions be added to it at a later date. Note verse 15:

> Brethren, I speak in terms of human relations: even though it is only a man's covenant, yet when it has been ratified, no one sets it aside or adds conditions to it. (NASB)

He then states, in verse 17, that a covenant made by God must be even more certain and immutable:

> What I am saying is this: the Law, which came four hundred and thirty years later, does not invalidate a covenant previously ratified by God, so as to nullify the promise. (NASB)

The point which he was making so emphatically was that the giving of the law could not invalidate the covenant and the promise which had been made some 400 years earlier. By the same token, therefore, if the land of Canaan has been promised to Abraham's descendants 'for ever', as an 'everlasting possession' to 'a thousand generations', then the coming of the Messiah has in no way set aside that covenant, nor added any new conditions to it. The promises within it stand for ever and the person and work of the Messiah, Jesus, are the basis both of their being made and of their fulfilment.

Peter's reference to the promised 'seed' in Acts 3:25 should help to clarify this matter further. In his message to the Jewish people who had gathered in the Temple area following the remarkable healing of a lame man outside the Gate Beautiful, Peter spoke to them concerning their rejection of Jesus as the Messiah. Even so he still refers to them as 'the sons of the prophets, and of the covenant which God made with their fathers, saying to Abraham, "And in your seed all the families of the earth shall be blessed."' (NASB) He went on to remind them that God having raised Jesus from the dead sent him to them firstly in order to bless them and turn them from their wicked ways. Peter obviously did not think that the covenant with Abraham was now no longer valid for the Jewish people because of their rejection of the Messiah. Whereas he saw that the promised 'seed' referred to the Messiah Jesus, he saw also that all the promises made to Abraham were for the Jewish people not only until Messiah's first appearing but even thereafter, although they had rejected him. They were still Abraham's sons and the land of Israel rightfully belonged to them and not to the Romans. It seems clear from the manner in which Peter spoke in this same message of 'the restoration of all things, whereof God spoke by the mouth of the holy prophets that have been from of old' (Acts 3:21) that he believed that the kingdom would be restored to a saved and completed Israel (see also Acts 1:6-7). God has not terminated so much as one of the promises made to Abraham.

Likewise also Stephen in his famous defence before the Sanhedrin quoted God's promise to Abraham that the land of Canaan would be given to his seed after him. By the way Stephen interpreted the promise it is clear that he understood the word 'seed' as referring to the Jewish people (see Acts 7:4-6). Note 'his seed' verses 5, 6; 'Joseph's race' verse 13 (RV); 'our race' verse 19 (RV, RSV).

The covenant and the promise made to Abraham, and confirmed to Isaac and Jacob, had the Messiah in view. He is the key to all history and, most particularly, to the history of his elect and redeemed people. He is also the key to Jewish history. In some mysterious way he encompasses the whole of it, and will finally redeem it from all futility. In him the history of the Jews is interpreted and through him their destiny will be fulfilled. He stands at the heart of both of their exile from the land and of their return to it; both of their being cast away and of their being received again. The final chapters of Jewish history will be written through him.

The finished work of the Messiah as the Passover lamb has a retrospective effect and action as far as the Jewish people is concerned. Although they have been led back to the land in unbelief, the basis upon which God acts over them, and for them, is the Messiah's work on the cross. Furthermore, Abraham has become 'the father of all who believe' (Romans 4:11). All who have truly believed, and have been born again, have become sons of Abraham through faith and 'Abraham's seed' (Galatians 3:29; cf.

Romans 9:7-8). They have been introduced to the true Israel of God, as wild olive branches grafted in to the natural olive tree. This Israel, saved through the finished work of the Messiah Jesus, will inherit the whole earth; 'For the promise to Abraham or to his descendants that he would be heir of the world was not through the Law, but through the righteousness of faith' (Romans 4:13, NASB). While all is given to us, whether Jew or Gentile, through the grace of God, living, God-given faith is the key to inheriting the promises. Nevertheless, God has not cast off the Jewish people for ever. There will come a day of restoration, and the basis for that restoration is and will be the Messiah and his finished work. The glorious fact is that God's purpose has not been frustrated through their fall but fulfilled. When the fullness of the Gentiles has come in, that is, God's plan to redeem men and women from every nation, then that partial hardening which has befallen Israel will be removed, and in this way all Israel will be saved.

For those who have been born again of God's Spirit it is right to understand the spiritual typology of the promised land, remembering the words of the apostle Paul: 'Now these things happened unto them by way of example; and they were written for our admonition, upon whom the ends of the ages are come' (1 Corinthians 10:11, RV). Yet there is also the literal side to these promises. To discount that is to do damage to the full meaning and significance of God's word. The land has been promised to the descendants of Abraham through Isaac and Jacob for an everlasting possession and that promise has never been annulled.

If however we are clear on the promise itself, what was the extent of the land of promise? In Genesis 15:18-21, the Lord said to Abraham:

> To your descendants I have given this land, From the river of Egypt as far as the great river, the river Euphrates: the Kenite and the Kenizzite and the Kadmonite and the Hittite

and the Perizzite and the Rephaim and the Amorite and the Canaanite and the Girgashite and the Jebusite. (NASB)

Exodus 23:31 and Joshua 1:2-4 mention approximately the same area. In Numbers 34:1-12 we are given a more specific definition of borders. There has been much discussion about the identification of the river of Egypt. Is this the Nile? In Exodus 23:31 and Joshua 1:2-4 it is not mentioned. In Hebrew there are two words translated 'river'. The one used in Genesis 15:18 signifies a normal river; the other used in Numbers 34:5 signifies a seasonal river, i.e. a watercourse, dry except in the rainy season: in Arabic, a *wadi.* Almost certainly 'the river of Egypt' mentioned in Numbers 34:5 is to be identified with the Wadi-el-Arish just east of El Arish. This boundary is generally considered by Talmudic scholarship and by modern Jewish sources to be the south-western limit of the promised land.

At all events the land promised by God to Abraham and to his descendants for an everlasting possession lies between the River Nile and the River Euphrates! It most certainly includes the area of modern Israel.

The connection of the Jewish people with this promised land goes right back to the times of Abraham, Isaac and Jacob. Few other peoples have had such a long association with their national territory as the Jewish people. Israel today is the only country in the Middle East whose people still live in the same area, who still speak the same language which their ancestors spoke, and who still maintain traditions and memories lasting at least some 4,000 years.

Even in the long periods of exile and dispersion, the Jewish people have never forgotten their homeland; it haunted their exiled existence. They lived not according to the seasons of the lands into which they had come, but according to the seasons of a land which they had lost. They lovingly remembered its geographical features; they even prayed for rain or dew at the time of the year when drought had been a problem in Israel, no matter if they were living in a land of continual and abundant rainfall! It did not matter how cold was the clime in which they lived, it was the date palm, the olive tree, the pomegranate and the vine which were still inextricably part of the cycle of their life. Even in the furthest parts of the earth, and in areas as different from the land of Israel as it was possible to be, they lived as if they were still there.

It was for this reason that Benjamin Disraeli once wrote:

> The vineyards of Israel are no more, but the eternal law enjoins upon the sons of Israel to celebrate the grape harvest; a race which persists in celebrating the grape harvest despite having not grapes to gather, will have its vineyards again.

In all the years of exile, the Jewish people never ceased to pray for the redemption of the land of Israel. It was a common theme running throughout the daily prayers, the festival prayers, and the prayers on especial days and occasions.

In later chapters, I will again take up this matter of the land and the nation. What I want to emphasize just now is that the land of Israel is unique because it is promised land. God himself promised it to a certain people. It is an interesting fact of history that whenever the land has been divorced from the Jewish people, it has become desolate and ruined. God had warned his people that this would be so:

> And I will make the land desolate so that your enemies who settle in it shall be appalled over it. You, however, I will scatter among the nations and will draw out a sword after you, as your land becomes desolate and your cities become waste. (Leviticus 26:32-33, NASB.)

Yet whenever the Jewish people have come back, the land has been tilled again, and vineyards, orchards and gardens have once more been planted. This has never been more true than in our own day. It has been the fulfilment of Ezekiel's ancient prophecy:

> But ye, O mountains of Israel, ye shall shoot forth your branches, and yield your fruit to my people Israel; for they are at hand to come. For, behold, I am for you, and I will turn unto you, and ye shall be tilled and sown ... And the land that was desolate shall be tilled, whereas it was a desolation in the sight of all that passed by. And they shall say, This land that was desolate is become like the garden of Eden ... Then the nations that are left round about you shall know that I the Lord have ... planted that which was desolate: I the Lord have spoken it, and I will do it. (Ezekiel 36:8-9, 34-35, 36, RV.)

Before, however, the land could become 'like the garden of Eden', a high price in human life had to be paid. The modern-day reclamation of the land of Israel was costly and involved much sacrifice and suffering. Many of the early pioneers succumbed to disease, particularly to malaria. In some areas, a number of attempts to reclaim the land failed, either through the death or the illness and discouragement of the pioneers, before success was finally achieved. The turning of malarial swampland or arid wilderness into fertile arable land has been no small feat of endurance and sacrifice. Yet it has come to pass in this century. Isaiah had prophesied long ago:

> The wilderness and the solitary place shall be glad; and the desert shall rejoice, and blossom as the rose. It shall blossom abundantly, and rejoice even with joy and singing; the glory of Lebanon shall be given unto it, the excellency of Carmel and Sharon .... (Isaiah 35:1-2, RV.)

It is an amazing fact that not only have areas of land been reclaimed which were fertile in times long past, but even areas of desert which had never before yielded fruit, such as in the Negev, or in the Aravah, or in the Sinai, have now been or are in the process of being reclaimed.

The re-afforestation of the land is no less remarkable. In this respect, the land has suffered deeply from its various conquerors during the course of its long history.

So often, for various reasons of their own, they cut down the forests, but made no attempt to replant them with new trees. The result has been soil erosion over large areas of the hill country. The goats and sheep of wandering beduin tribes did the rest. The Turks dealt the final blow in the period of the first world war, when they cut down the last remnants of the forests to keep the railways running! With the coming of the British in 1917, a scheme of re-afforestation was launched, but encountered many difficulties. It was the determination and vision of the Jewish pioneers and settlers which finally made the scheme a reality and, after 1948, the re-afforestation of the land became a national priority for the new State of Israel. It was recognized to be vital in re-establishing the ecological balance in the land.

Thus, in 1948-49, there were some 13,000 acres of forest; by 1963 this had risen to 92,000 acres, and by 1978 to 285,000 acres. In 1948 there were some 4,388,000 trees in Israel; in 1978 the figure stood at approximately 130,000,000. In the hills of Judea, just west of Jerusalem, 6,000,000 trees alone were planted in a forest called 'the forest of the martyrs', one for every Jew who had died in Nazi concentration camps. There could have been no more beautiful way than this to remember those who died through human wickedness. The success of the re-afforestation scheme has been very largely due to the energetic endeavours of the Jewish National Fund.

The first tree to be introduced in those schemes was the eucalyptus tree from Australia. Originally brought in to help in swamp drainage, it was discovered that it did equally well in dry regions. From 1917 onwards coniferous trees, such as the pine and the cypress, were widely planted, especially in the rocky hill country where erosion had made fruit farming impossible. These trees tend to retain any existing soil and to create new soil. Thus, on every level, the land is being reclaimed, and where a century ago there were only arid and eroded hills, today there are miles of forest.

We cannot call this re-afforestation of the land of Israel unique in itself, for there are examples of it elsewhere in the world. What is unique is the fact that it is the descendants of those who lived in this land thousands of years ago who have taken up the task in this last century. After some 1900 years of exile, the Jewish people have come back to the land promised to them by God.

Furthermore, of no other land has the Lord prophesied saying:

> But ye, O mountains of Israel, ye *shall shoot forth your branches*, and yield *your fruit* to my people Israel ... and ye shall be *tilled and sown* ... I the Lord have ... planted that which was desolate: I the Lord have spoken it, and I will do it. (Ezekiel 36:8-9, 36, RV.)

This has come to pass in our day: the Lord had spoken it and the Lord has done it. For 'God is not a man, that he should lie, neither the son of man, that he should repent: hath he said, and shall he not do it? or hath he spoken, and shall he not make it good?' (Numbers 23:19, RV).

PART II

THE UNIQUENESS OF THE NATION

And what one nation on the earth is like
Thy people Israel. . . ?

2 Samuel 7:23 (NASB)

CHAPTER 1

ALL THINGS ARE MORTAL BUT THE JEW

In the annals of world history, there is nothing to compare with the history of Israel and her remarkable survival.

Her history began with one man – Abraham – to whom God appeared some four thousand years ago, and it has continued to this day. The cord which links the whole into one continuous history has never been broken. The transformation of Abraham's family into a people while in Egypt, the moulding of a nation in the wilderness under Moses, and then the possession of the promised land under Joshua, is one continuous story. The same unbroken cord runs from the beginning of the Kingdom under David and Solomon, its division into Judah and Israel, on to the Babylonian exile, and the return of the faithful remnant a generation later. It continues through the Maccabean period, with its glorious story of Jewish heroism and emancipation, and on through the occupation and oppression of the Roman period, for ever linked with the birth and death and resurrection of the Messiah Jesus. We follow that unbroken cord beyond the fall and dispersion of the Jewish people in A.D. 70 and the destruction of Jerusalem and the Temple, and with it the loss of Jewish statehood, so clearly predicted by the Lord Jesus. That history continues through the Talmudic era, with its great rabbis and sages, and nineteen hundred years of exile, right up to the re-creation of the State of Israel in 1948.

The story has many faces with many moods. Sometimes it is the story of bloody persecution and violent hatred, as in the period of the Crusaders in the 11th-12th centuries, or of the Inquisition in the 15th and 16th centuries, or of the pogroms in the late 19th and early 20th centuries, or the Nazi era of the 1930s and 40s. Sometimes it is the story of the mysticism and yearning of the Kabbalist era (15th-16th centuries), or the story of great piety and unabashed emotion, as in the Hasidic era (18th century), or the story of deep learning and sacrificial good works, which emerged so often from a common experience of abject poverty. Sometimes it is the story of the fiery zeal and the patriotism of Zionism, the story of Zionist pioneers and Jewish freedom fighters prepared to pay with their lives for the ideal of a Jewish homeland.

Her history covers the whole gamut of human life and experience, from the high peaks of divine vision and self-sacrifice to the deepest valleys of sinful iniquity and treacherous disobedience. At times it is the story of living faith and selfless purity, of noble ideal and example, and at other times it is the story of civil war, factional jealousies and inner dissension, of inter-rivalry and corruption in high places, of narrow-minded bigotry and blind prejudice. It reaches the heights in its record of devotion to God's word and purpose, and plumbs the depths in its record of the rejection and crucifixion of the Messiah. However the story is told, it is the story of one people, the Jewish people, and of one nation, Israel.

The pages of that history are crowded with patriarchs and prophets, kings and 'sweet singers', reformers, pioneers, and martyrs, sages and rabbis, statesmen and freedom fighters, the good and the bad, the saint and the sinner. Above all, at the very heart of that history, invisible at times but yet underlying the whole, is the story of the Messiah Jesus. Although not recognized or understood by many of the Jews, he is *the* key to Jewish history, the key to the fulfilment of its yearnings and aspirations, to its anguished sorrow and failure, and to its divine and irrevocable destiny.

Furthermore, this history has not yet been completed. In 1948, Israel took the platform in world affairs, and has remained there ever since. In war after war, battling against tremendous odds, this little nation has triumphed again and again; its history is still being written! The most glorious chapters of its history are still in the future, but no matter what, they *will* be written, for the hand of God is in it.

God has dealt with no nation as he has dealt with the Jewish people. In their 4,000-year-long history, they have been exiled from their land twice, and have been restored to it twice. The first of these exiles we call the Babylonian captivity, and it began in 607 B.C., in the reign of Jehoiachin. It lasted seventy years. Technically it was seventy years of captivity, but fifty years of actual national exile. In fact, during the first twenty years, only the royal family and certain aristocratic families were deported from the land to Babylon. It was in 587 B.C., during the reign of King Zedekiah, that the whole nation was deported there and only the poorest of the poor were left. The second exile commenced in A.D. 70, and was on a much larger scale than the first exile. The Romans slaughtered some 600,000 Jews at that time, and enslaved some 300,000 more, deporting them all over the known world.

No other nation in the history of mankind has twice been uprooted from its land, scattered to the ends of the earth and then brought back again to that same territory. If the first exile and restoration was remarkable, the second is miraculous. Israel has twice lost its statehood and its national sovereignty, twice had its capital and hub of religious life destroyed, its towns and cities razed to the ground, its people deported and dispersed, and then twice had it all restored again.

Furthermore, no other nation or ethnic group has been scattered to the four corners of the earth, and yet survived as an easily identifiable and recognizable group. The nation of Israel is comprised of some eighty-seven different nationalities. From the Far East to the Far West there is hardly a nation that has not had Jewish citizens within it. The remarkable fact is that the Jewish people has been able to survive as *a people*, instead of being absorbed and assimilated into the large Gentile majorities among whom it was scattered. We must remember that we are not considering a period of one generation, or even one century, but nearly 2,000 years. In this long era, the Jewish people have remained the Jewish people. Benjamin Disraeli (1804-81), twice Prime Minister of Great Britain, referring to disparaging remarks about his Jewish ancestry, retorted:

> Sir, you are proud of your ancient descent; but in the veins of the meanest Jew there flows blood compared to which the blood of the proudest noble is ditch water. For when your ancestors were in a pagan tribe, mine were standing as priests in the Temple of God. [Quoted in *Decision* magazine.]

While absorbing much of the culture and ways of those nations among whom they lived, speaking their languages, taking their place as subjects or citizens in so far as they were allowed to do so, they have survived as Jews. No other ethnic group has the same story. For, when we consider this long passage of time, the persecution the Jewish people have so often encountered and the pressures upon them to surrender their identity and be absorbed into the nations among whom they were living at the time; and when we consider also the fact that they were a scattered people, not all concentrated in one area at the same time, we have to recognize that the survival of the Jewish people is without parallel.

Many other peoples, much more powerful and influential in their day than the Jewish people, have long ago vanished. It is impossible today to identify Assyrians or Babylonians. They have disappeared among other nations and peoples. Even the Celtic peoples have remained recognizable to this day only because they migrated together as a tribe across the face of the earth. Originating somewhere between the Baltic and the Black Sea, they moved into eastern and central Europe, and finally to the British Isles. Where they remained together in large numbers during their slow migration, they have survived, but where they were weak and more scattered they have long since been absorbed by the native population. The Jewish people ought also to have disappeared since they never moved together en masse, but, in spite of being scattered throughout the earth, they have survived as a distinct and recognizable people.

In 1899, Mark Twain wrote an essay which he entitled 'Concerning the Jews', and brought it to a remarkable conclusion. We must remember that this was long before the Balfour Declaration of 1917, let alone the re-creation of the State of Israel in 1948. He wrote:

> If the statistics are right, the Jews constitute but one per cent of the human race. It suggests a nebulous dim puff of star dust lost in the blaze of the Milky Way. Properly the Jew ought hardly to be heard of; but he is heard of, has always been heard of. He is as prominent on the planet as any other people, and his commercial importance is extravagantly out of proportion to the smallness of his bulk. His contributions to the world's list of great names in literature, science, art, music, finance, medicine and abstruse learning are also way out of proportion to the weakness of his numbers. He has made a marvellous fight in this world, in all the ages; and has done it with his hands tied behind him. He could be vain of himself, and be excused for it. The Egyptian, the Babylonian and the Persian rose, filled the planet with sound and splendour, then faded to dream-stuff and passed away; the Greek and the Roman followed, and made a vast noise, and they are gone; other peoples have sprung up and held their torch high for a time, but it burned out, and they sit in twilight now, or have vanished. The Jew saw them all, beat them all, and is now what he always was, exhibiting no decadence, no infirmities of age, no weakening of his parts, no slowing of his energies, no dulling of his alert and aggressive mind. All things are mortal but the Jew; all other forces pass, but he remains. What is the secret of his immortality?

At about the same time Leo Tolstoy wrote an essay in a similar vein which he entitled 'What is a Jew?' In it he wrote:

> This question is not at all so odd as it seems. Let us see what peculiar kind of creature the Jew is, which all the rulers and all the nations have together and separately abused and molested, oppressed and persecuted, trampled and butchered, burned and hanged, and, in spite of all this, is yet alive ... the Jew is the emblem of eternity. He whom neither slaughter nor torture of himself for years could destroy; he whom neither fire nor sword, nor inquisition was able to wipe from off the face of the earth; he who was the first to produce the oracles of God; he who has been for so long a time the guardian of prophecy, and who has transmitted it to the rest of the world – such a nation cannot be destroyed. The Jew is everlasting as eternity itself.

There can be only one answer to Mark Twain's question, 'What is the secret of his immortality?' *The secret of Jewish immortality is God himself.* In the book of Malachi God declares: 'For I the Lord change not; therefore ye, O sons of Jacob, are not consumed.' (Malachi 3:6, RV.) A famous rabbi of the 12th century, Rabbi David Kimchi, commenting on this verse says:

> You were not consumed as were the other peoples who have left no trace behind and have ceased being nations. You have not disappeared, nor will you. You will always be distinguished from the others as a nation alone on earth. Even though you have been driven into exile and banished into every corner of the earth, your name has survived everywhere. The hurt that I have given you was in consequence of your sins. Just as I shall not change, so shall you not be consumed; and in the latter days, you will regain your ascendancy and will be supreme over all the nations of the earth.

I believe that the Lord Jesus was referring to this 'immortality' of the Jewish people when he said: 'From the fig tree learn its lesson' (Matthew 24:32, RSV). The lesson we are to learn is surely not merely about the coming of summer, but concerns the Jewish people, their land, statehood and destiny. The fig tree which the Lord judged the previous day (see Matthew 21:19; Mark 11:13-14, 20-21) must have been very much in their minds when he said, 'From the fig tree learn its lesson.' He used that fig tree as a parable. The events immediately before and after that incident relating to it were all connected with the Jewish leadership and establishment of the day. Together they constitute the Lord's final confrontation with them. Somewhere, on the upper slopes of the Mount of Olives, overlooking the Temple and the city, Peter, James, John and Andrew came to him privately and said: 'Tell us, when will these things be, and what will be the sign of Your coming, and of the end of the age?' (Matthew 24:3 NASB; cf Mark 13:3-4). He then gave them a bird's-eye view, as it were, of all that would happen, and summed it up with the words: 'From the fig tree learn its lesson.' It would be remarkable if those disciples did not think immediately of the fig tree which the day before and that very morning had so gripped their attention. (See chapter 10 of my book *Battle for Israel* for a fuller treatment of the fig tree.)

That Jesus thought of the fig tree as representing the Jewish people is shown by another parable:

> There was once a man who had a fig-tree growing in his vineyard. He went looking for figs on it but found none. So he said to his gardener, 'Look, for three years I have been coming here looking for figs on this fig-tree, and I haven't found any. Cut it down! Why should it go on using up the soil?' But the gardener answered, 'Leave it alone, sir, just one more year; I will dig round it and put in some manure. Then if the tree bears figs next year, so much the better; if not, then you can have it cut down.' (Luke 13:6-9, Good News Bible.)

The Lord Jesus was clearly referring to himself and to the three years of his messianic ministry. He found no fruit among the people of God at that time, only a barren formalism. In the parable a year of grace was given to the barren fig tree; in fact between the death and resurrection of the Messiah (A.D. 30) and the judgement that fell upon the Jewish people (A.D. 70), a whole generation elapsed. It was a generation that was given every evidence to enable it to believe, but it remained barren, and therefore divine judgement was inevitable. Thus began the second and most terrible exile in Jewish history.

The Messiah said: 'From the fig tree learn its lesson: as soon as its branch becomes tender and puts forth its leaves, you know that summer is near' (Matthew 24:32 RSV). The obvious lesson of the fig tree is that when we see the things coming to pass which he has enumerated in the preceding verses, we shall know that his coming is near. The profound lesson of the fig tree is that the Jewish people will still be there at the end of the age to witness the Messiah's return. Judged because of fruitlessness, the fig tree had withered from its roots and died; yet at the end of the age that same fig tree would be there, its branches tender and full of sap, full of leaf and the promise of fruit. In telling the disciples to learn the lesson of the fig tree it was as if the Lord Jesus were warning them not to take the destruction of Jerusalem and the Temple, the termination of Jewish statehood and the scattering of the nation, as the end of the Jewish people. It would not be their end. It would be the beginning of a long era of anguish, suffering and persecution such as that people had never known before. Yet they would miraculously survive, and at the end the same fig tree would be there as at the beginning! But with this difference: instead of dying away, it would be in the full vigour of life.

This lesson of the fig tree is underlined by what the Lord Jesus went on to say as recorded in Matthew 24:34: 'This generation shall not pass away, till all these things be accomplished' (ASV). The NASB and the New International Version give an alternative rendering in the margin: 'This race will not pass away until all these things take place.' The Greek word commonly translated 'generation' in our English versions had a generalized and rather indefinite meaning. Primarily, it meant a begetting, rather than that which is begotten. Then it came to mean a family and thus a generation, that is, people born at the same time. It also had the wider meaning of race, that is, people born of the same origin and possessing the same characteristics.

The usual interpretations of this verse have always left me unsatisfied. One interpretation is that the words 'this generation' refer to those who were alive at that time, the generation represented by Peter, James, John and Andrew. According to this view, Jesus meant that all the predictions he had made, including that of his coming again, would be fulfilled in the lifetime of that generation. I cannot accept the explanation that this gross error was due to the fact that his understanding was limited by his humanity. Such an explanation means that the Lord Jesus could be guilty of making wild, misleading and even stupid statements. I could never accept that. Neither does it help me to be told that I must look on the credit side and recognize that so much of what he predicted, as recorded in Matthew 24, Mark 13 and Luke 21, was fulfilled in A.D. 70, in the terrible events surrounding the destruction of Jerusalem and the Temple. The fact remains that what he prophesied was not exhaustively and accurately fulfilled in that year. It may have had its 'first fulfilment', but if that were the final fulfilment, then I would find it very difficult to trust the accuracy and reliability of the words of the Lord Jesus. If, as some suggest, he was wrong upon so fundamental a matter as his own return, upon what other matters could he also be wrong?

Another interpretation which has gained wide acceptance in many Christian circles is that the words 'this generation' refer to that future generation during which the fig tree would burst into leaf. According to this view, the generation which would witness the fulfilment of the preceding predictions, in particular the re-creation of the Jewish State, would live to see his return. There may be more to commend this view, but one wonders why our Lord spoke of *'this'* generation instead of the far more accurate *'that'* generation. If he had said 'that generation will not pass away' there could have been no doubt whatsoever as to his meaning.

There may be some truth in both of these views. But do they adequately interpret the words of the Lord Jesus? It seems to me that the alternative rendering 'This *race* will not pass away until all these things take place' has much to commend it. The Lord may have deliberately used this word to cover all three interpretations, for the first fulfilment of much of what he predicted did come within the lifetime of that generation, and it may also be true that the generation which has witnessed the re-creation of the Jewish State will witness his coming again. For me, however, the most satisfying interpretation is the third. The generation to whom he was speaking would witness the termination of the Jewish State and Commonwealth, and the dispersion of the nation into the rest of the world. It would witness the destruction of Jerusalem, the capital of the State and centre of its national life and aspirations. The Temple, the hub and heart of the spiritual life of the Jewish people, would be razed to the ground before the eyes of that generation; not one of its stones would remain upon another. All this would come to pass in the life of that generation, as in fact it did, in A.D. 70. *Yet they were not to draw any false conclusions.* That *race* would not disappear but would survive. Indeed, the Jewish people would do far more than survive, they would triumph. From all the nations into which God scattered them, they would be gathered back to the very land from which they had been dispersed. The Jewish State would rise again from the ashes, and Jerusalem would once more become its capital.

The Jewish people indeed have not only survived, they have survived with a vengeance! In thirty years this little nation of 3,500,000 people has become the touchstone of world politics. Israel is debated in the United Nations and discussed in world capitals. Nearly every day it is mentioned in the news on the radio and television, or written about in the newspapers. Giant planes of the Israeli National Airline, El Al, fly the major routes of the world, bearing the Israeli national colours and with the national emblem, the star of David, emblazoned on their tails. Forty years ago there was no Israel; today no one is in doubt about her existence. The Lord Jesus had said to those disciples, 'From the fig tree learn its lesson.' The fig tree once barren, judged and dead from its roots, would still be there at the end, renewed from its roots, with fresh vitality and the promise of fruit.

CHAPTER 2

THE WORD WHICH HE COMMANDED TO A THOUSAND GENERATIONS

Divine prophecy makes Israel unique amongst the nations of the world, for no other nation has been the subject of such detailed prophecies as the Jewish people.

This fact, as most of my readers will know, has been the focal point of much heated controversy. Some say that there are no prophecies concerning the future of the Jewish people other than those which predict judgement. As far as God is concerned, so the argument runs, there is no future for the Jewish people; when Jewish statehood was terminated, and Jerusalem and the Temple razed to the ground in A.D. 70, he finished with them as a nation. According to this view, God has finally turned away from the Jewish people *as a nation*, being no more interested in them as a distinct people than in the British or the French or the Russians. It is asserted that the purpose of God for the Jewish people has been fulfilled in the emergence from it of Christianity and the church, and God is now essentially interested only in individuals and their salvation, and in that spiritual kingdom to which he has called them. But this is surely a dangerous half-truth. There can, of course, be no discussion over the necessity for every human being to know personally the saving power and grace of God. Scripture is perfectly clear about this fundamental truth. John 3:16 declares 'God so loved the world, that he gave his only begotten Son, that *whosoever* believeth in him should not perish, but have everlasting life' (AV). Jesus told Thomas, 'I am the way, the truth, and the life: *no man* cometh unto the Father, but by me' (John 14:6, AV); and Nicodemus, 'Verily, verily, I say unto thee, Except a man be born again, he cannot see the kingdom of God' (John 3:3, AV).

Nevertheless, the word of God also plainly declares that the living God is the God of all the nations and rules over them, determining their rise and their fall. In Psalm 46:10, God says: 'Be still, and know that I am God: I will be exalted among the nations, I will be exalted in the earth' (RV). The Psalmist says: 'Say among the nations, The Lord reigneth: the world also is stablished that it cannot be moved: he shall judge the peoples with equity' (Psalm 96:10, RV). Jeremiah describes the Lord as 'King of the nations' (Jeremiah 10:7, RV). Daniel declares that 'the Most High ruleth in the kingdom of men, and giveth it to whomsoever he will' (Daniel 4:17, 25, 32, RV). This statement indeed provides us with a key to the book of Daniel, for its main object is clearly to reveal that God rules over all human history, and determines its course. Human history is not merely a matter to do with economics, politics and human personalities. Behind its course there are great spiritual beings. See Daniel 10:13, 18-21; 12:1. They are there called 'princes', 'chief princes' and 'kings', but they are not to be confused with earthly rulers. These are angelic beings fallen and unfallen. They include the spiritual powers and rulers of the darkness of this world, the hosts of wicked spirits in the heavenly places mentioned in Ephesians 6:12. Or again, Ephesians 2:2 speaks of 'the prince of the power of the air . . . the spirit that now worketh in the children of disobedience' (RV). Daniel 10-12 is like a window into that invisible world which lies behind all that is seen, revealing to us that the history of the nations is essentially a spiritual matter. The angelic armies of the Most High are involved in much conflict with these fallen angelic principalities and powers in the realization of God's purpose.

In the light of all this I have to ask myself a vital question: 'Is this simply the realm of fairy stories and ancient myths, or was it, and is it still true? Was it only in the ancient world that God took such an interest in the nations? Has he changed, having grown old and weary?' The answer, of course, is that the Lord neither slumbers nor sleeps; he does not faint nor become weary. Today he rules as he has always ruled over the nations, reigning over the super-powers and determining their rise and fall. It is said of the Lord Jesus that he is 'ruler of the kings of the earth' (Revelation 1:5, RV). This statement is empty unless it means that he rules over the governments of the world and their leaders. Through the Lamb slain, God is calling out a people from 'every tribe, and tongue, and people, and nation,' ... to be 'an elect race, a royal priesthood, a holy nation, a people for God's own possession' (Revelation 5:9; I Peter 2:9; RV). This is his *supreme* purpose. But this does not contradict the fact that he rules over the nations, working all things according to the counsel of his own will. The basic but profound truth is that he rules the nations with that end in view. However materialistic or rationalistic the outlook of the present age, Scripture reveals that this world is essentially spiritual. The church closes its eyes to this fact at great risk to its spiritual well-being and health. For, just as the Lord introduced Daniel to the ministry of intercession in this conflict, so the Lord would bring us into it. (See Daniel 9.) The vital call of the true church is to ensure that his kingdom comes, that his will is done on earth as it is in heaven.

This 'ruling in the kingdom of men' is not something impersonal, vague and far off. Some Christians consider that while God may rule the nations in a general way, he is not too concerned with their affairs. Yet see just how close an interest he took, for instance, in the affairs of Assyria. It was the Lord's concern for Nineveh, the capital of Assyria, that caused such a problem for Jonah! God is not different today. He takes a detailed interest in the nations, whether they are small and newly emerging, or great and long established. Moreover, if this is true, surely God pays special attention to the Jewish nation. Paul alluded to this when he said, 'as touching the election, they are beloved for the fathers' sakes' (Romans 11:28).

For those who believe that there are no prophecies in the word of God concerning the future of the Jewish people, and that God's purpose for them as a nation has ended, the re-creation of the State of Israel in 1948 is a serious embarrassment. The history of Israel since then, with its four wars in thirty years, with the reunification of Jerusalem under Jewish sovereignty, has increased that embarrassment. For those who cannot recognize the hand of God in the re-creation of the Jewish State and the many deliverances and triumphs it has experienced, there can be only one answer: 'Israel is a political accident,' they declare, 'the result of a highly organized and well financed political movement known as Zionism'; 'the State of Israel is the creation of super-power politics at its worst, and has nothing whatsoever to do with the Word of God.' What can we say in answer to this? Only that while there have been some wild and exaggerated interpretations of prophecy concerning Israel, and some seriously unbalanced theories propounded, the fact remains that there is a hard core of Scripture which cannot be explained away.

In prophetic Scripture there are both literal historical fulfilments and abiding spiritual values to be considered. Take Isaiah 62, for example. The abiding spiritual value contained in these verses is the appeal of the Lord for those who will be 'the Lord's remembrancers' in the realization of his purpose (Isaiah 62:6, RV), for those who will intercede until his heart's desire is achieved for the redeemed, for the bride, for his Zion. For me, this is the deepest and most important meaning of the prophecy. The literal meaning of the prophecy is surely related to the restoration of Jerusalem,, whether in the first or in the second exile. Furthermore, when we consider the literal meaning of prophecies, we must remember that they have often more than one fulfilment. For example, the prophecy in Joel 2:28-32 was fulfilled on the day of Pentecost, according to Acts 2:16-21. Yet from a careful noting of the prophecy, we realize that certain features were not fulfilled on that day but refer to the time of the end. Note verses 30-31: 'and I will show wonders in the heavens and in the earth, blood, and fire, and pillars of smoke. The sun shall be turned into darkness, and the moon into blood, before the great and the terrible day of the Lord come' (RV). As we progress, we shall discover further examples. It is confusion over this point which has led many to false or inadequate interpretations.

It might be helpful to make one further general observation about prophetic Scriptures and their fulfilment. To some Christians, it seems as if those who believe that Israel is the fulfilment of God's prophetic word handle the Scriptures illogically, if not deceitfully. The heart of the problem appears to be that certain verses are taken as fulfilled in some event or another, while the preceding or succeeding verses are ignored. When we consider, however, the way in which the New Testament states that certain Scriptures have been fulfilled, we have the same problem! The logical, 'tidy' western mind tends to become confused and perplexed by this. Take for instance Matthew 2:14-15:

> And he arose and took the young child and his mother by night, and departed into Egypt; And was there until the death of Herod: that it might be fulfilled which was spoken by the Lord through the prophet, saying, Out of Egypt did I call my son. (RV)

Matthew states that the flight of the holy family into Egypt and their return is the fulfilment of a prophecy in Hosea 11:1: 'When Israel was a child, then I loved him, and called my son out of Egypt' (RV). Some Bible students find this hard to understand, since neither the general context of this chapter in Hosea nor even the complete verse itself seems to refer to the Lord Jesus. Basil F. C. Atkinson, commenting on this passage in *The New Bible Commentary*, writes: 'In the original context the passage refers to the redemption of Israel from Egypt by Moses. There was a hidden meaning implanted in the passage by the Holy Spirit, which is here brought out by the evangelist.' In my mind, I have no doubt about this 'hidden meaning' which was fulfilled in the return of Jesus from Egypt, since I believe in the authority and inspiration of God's word. What I find instructive is the way in which the Holy Spirit uses the prophetic word he has inspired.

There is a further example in the same chapter, Matthew 2:17-18. Matthew states that the massacre of all children under two years of age in Bethlehem was the fulfilment of Jeremiah 31:15. From the earliest times Rachel captured the imagination of the Jewish people and came to represent Jewish motherhood with all its aspirations and longings. Rachel is, of course, buried at Bethlehem. It is interesting to note the way the Holy Spirit takes the one verse, Jeremiah 31:15, and disregards the succeeding verses 16-17.

We have yet another example in Matthew 1:23. There it is stated that the birth of Jesus was the fulfilment of Isaiah 7:14: 'Therefore the Lord himself shall give you a sign; behold, a virgin shall conceive, and bear a son, and shall call his name Immanuel' (RV). This prophecy in Isaiah 7:14 seems to stand on its own when one considers the context, yet no true believer would question its fulfilment in the birth of the Lord Jesus.

These few examples may help to explain more about the mystery of prophecy. None of us wishes to be involved in wild and unbalanced interpretations of the prophetic word, but neither do we want to become prey to the kind of mind which rejects everything that it cannot explain away rationally, or cannot readily and fully understand.

Now I would like to draw attention to some of these prophecies concerning Israel. Take, for instance, Deuteronomy 28:64-67, where we find recorded the solemn and awesome words of Moses:

> Moreover, the Lord will scatter you among all peoples, from one end of the earth to the other end of the earth; and there you shall serve other gods, wood and stone, which you or your fathers have not known. And among those nations you shall find no rest, and there shall be no resting place for the sole of your foot; but there the Lord will give you a trembling heart, failing of eyes, and despair of soul. So your life shall hang in doubt before you; and you shall be in dread night and day, and shall have no assurance of your life. In the morning you shall say, 'Would that it were evening!' And at evening you shall say, 'Would that it were morning!' because of the dread of your heart which you dread, and for the sight of your eyes which you shall see. (NASB)

No words could more adequately describe Jewish life, whether during the first exile to Babylon in 587 B.C., or the second exile into the whole world which began in A.D. 70 and lasted until the mid-20th century. It is remarkable that words so ancient in origin should be so accurate in describing what came to pass all those centuries later. The anguish, the insecurity, the impermanence of Jewish life in exile is poignantly summed up in these phrases: 'there shall be no resting place for the sole of your foot'; 'there the Lord will give you a trembling heart, failing of eyes, and despair of soul'; 'your life shall hang in doubt before you'; you 'shall have no assurance of your life'; 'the dread of your heart which you dread'. All the Jewish experience of suspicion, hatred and discrimination, of bigotry and persecution during those exiles, are found within these prophetic words of Moses, and even more so in his declaration: 'You shall become a horror, a proverb, and a taunt among all the people where the Lord will drive you.' (Deuteronomy 28:37, NASB.)

In 2 Chronicles 7:19-22 we have the prophetic words of Solomon:

> But if you turn away and forsake My statutes and My commandments which I have set before you and shall go and serve other gods and worship them, then I will uproot you from My land which I have given you, and this house which I have consecrated for My name I will cast out of My sight,

> and I will make it a proverb and a byword among all peoples. As for this house, which was exalted, everyone who passes by it will be astonished and say, 'Why has the Lord done thus to this land and to this house?' And they will say, 'Because they forsook the Lord, the God of their fathers, who brought them from the land of Egypt, and they adopted other gods and worshiped them and served them, therefore He has brought all this adversity on them.' (NASB)

It is amazing to consider that this prophecy has been fulfilled in detail twice. Twice the Jewish people have been uprooted from the land, and the Temple destroyed.

It is also interesting to note Deuteronomy 30:1-10. There the Lord promises that if they would return to him, then, although their 'outcasts are at the ends of the earth, from there the Lord your God will gather you, and from there He will bring you back. And the Lord your God will bring you into the land which your fathers possessed, and you shall possess it' (verses 4-5, NASB).

These prophecies were fulfilled in both exiles of the Jewish people from the land of Israel, and also in the return from Babylon in 536 B.C. Over the second return from exile which this century has witnessed there is much controversy. But leaving the controversy aside for a moment, one fact is plain: no other nation has been the subject of such specific prophecies, promises and warnings.

In a previous chapter, I have spoken of the uniqueness of the land of Israel as divinely promised (Part I, chapter 3). In all history there is no other record of land being promised specifically by the living God to a particular people. The words of the Lord to Abraham are highly significant:

> Now lift up your eyes and look from the place where you are, northward and southward and eastward and westward; for all the land which you see, I will give it to you *and to your descendants forever* (Genesis 13:14-15, NASB).

This promise is confirmed in Genesis 17:8 where God says:

> And I will give to you and *to your descendants after you*, the land of your sojournings, all the land of Canaan, for an *everlasting possession*; and I will be their God. (NASB)

What we need to underline is that this promise of a particular land being given to a particular people is *for ever*. It is to be for an *everlasting* possession. The psalmist is emphatic:

> He has remembered His covenant forever, the word which He commanded *to a thousand generations* [lit. forty thousand years!], the covenant which He made with Abraham, and His oath to Isaac. Then He confirmed it to Jacob for a statute, to Israel as an *everlasting* covenant, saying, 'To you I will give the land of Canaan as the portion of your inheritance' (Psalm 105:8-11, NASB).

No human argument can destroy the simple fact that God himself has made a specific promise to a particular people. It is unique. From this specifically promised land the people have twice been scattered by God among the nations of the earth, and then have been twice brought back to that same land to repossess it. Whatever men may say, God is true, and his word endures for ever.

Then again, God said to Abraham:

> I will make you a great nation, and I will bless you, and make your name great; and so you shall be a blessing; and I will bless those who bless you, and the one who curses you I will curse. And in you all the families of the earth shall be blessed (Genesis 12:2-3, NASB).

This promise of God to Abraham has been remarkably fulfilled. It is impossible to measure what has come to the whole world through Abraham's seed. Speaking of the Jewish people, that 'great nation' which has come out of Abraham, the apostle Paul declares in Romans 9:3-5 –

> For I could wish that I myself were accursed from Messiah for my brethren, my kinsmen according to the flesh: who are Israelites; to whom pertaineth the adoption, and the glory, and the covenants, and the giving of the law, and the service of God, and the promises; whose are the fathers, and of whom as concerning the flesh Messiah came, who is over all, God blessed for ever. Amen. (AV margin, reading 'Messiah' for 'Christ'.)

It does not matter how we view this subject. It has been through the Jewish people that the revelation of the one true and living God has come to the rest of the world. They created no vast empire; they left us no pyramids or sphinx; they are not famous for their architecture, and they built no great metropolis. They gave us the knowledge of God. Through them has come the word of God to the world, the promises of God and the revelation of his eternal purpose. In them alone of all the nations of the earth, the saving grace and power of God was made known. Above all it was through them that the Saviour, the Lord Jesus, the Messiah, came, born of the royal line of King David. Nor was the divine promise to Abraham only fulfilled through the rising and faithfulness of the Jewish people. By the grace of God it was also fulfilled through their fall.

In Romans 11:12, the apostle Paul asks:

> 'If their stumbling turns out to be the enriching of the world, and their reverse the enriching of the Gentiles, how much more enrichment will their full restoration bring?' (F.F. Bruce's translation.)

The purpose of God to use the Jewish people to bless the whole world has been fulfilled, for through their fall the salvation of God has come to the ends of the earth. From every tongue and tribe and nation, there are those who have been redeemed through the precious blood of the Lamb, who have been born anew of the Spirit of God, and who have been brought into the commonwealth of Israel.

CHAPTER 3

MY COUNSEL SHALL STAND

> Fear not; for I am with thee: I will bring thy seed from the east, and gather thee from the west; I will say to the north, Give up; and to the south, Keep not back; bring my sons from far, and my daughters from the end of the earth. (Isaiah 43:5-6, RV.)

This prophecy is one of many that has had a literal fulfilment in our day. If, as it is often stated, this prophecy was fulfilled in the return from Babylon in 536 B.C., I should like to know when they returned from the *south* and from the *west.* When the main body of the people returned it was from Babylonia, from the *north* and from the *east.* Then again, when were his sons brought 'from far' and his 'daughters from the ends of the earth'? We are told that in Isaiah's day, the 'end of the earth' was Armenia and the Caucasus Mountains, and I have no argument with that. Nevertheless I see the far greater fulfilment of this prophecy in our own generation. In this century God has brought back the Jewish people to the promised land from the far east to the far west, from the far north to the far south. They have been gathered back literally from the ends of the earth. They have come back to Israel from Manchuria and China, from Australia and New Zealand, from Russia and Siberia. They have returned from Scandinavia, from Britain and from all the European countries. From North Africa, from South Africa they have been gathered back. They have returned from North America and from South America. They have been brought back from India and from south-east Asia, from Persia and from Iraq. From at least eighty-seven countries they have returned to the land promised for ever to Abraham and his descendants. I do not doubt that this prophecy was *partially* fulfilled in thc return from Babylon. But in the second return from exile during the course of the present century, it has been fulfilled far more literally.

One of the largest Jewish communities in the world, some three million people, exists within the Soviet Union. Knowing the scarcely concealed antagonism of the Soviet Union towards Israel since the early fifties, no one could have conceived that that huge monolithic system would ever allow any of its Jewish citizens to emigrate to Israel. Yet God has said: 'I will say to the north, Give up.' The Soviet Union has allowed thousands of its Jewish citizens to emigrate to Israel. It is a fulfilment of God's word. There will surely be a yet greater exodus of Russian Jews in the years ahead, for God's word still stands.

At the end of the war in 1945, there were just over two million Jews who had either escaped from or survived Nazi concentration camps. It was natural for those survivors to believe that the whole world would open its arms to them and receive them. They thought that the fact that they had survived the most terrible onslaught on Jewish life and existence in their long history, and that they were witnesses to the butchering of six million Jews in the most horrific circumstances, would touch the heart of the anti-Nazi and free world. Nearly one half of the world's Jews had been affected directly by the Nazi fury. Of the nine million Jews of Europe, two thirds had died. It had been no small attempt at genocide. Whereas before it had been countries or regions which had been affected by anti-Semitism, this was the greatest area of the world ever affected at one time. From the Atlantic to the Ural Mountains, from the Arctic to the Mediterranean, a coldly thought-out plan catered for the systematic liquidation of tens of thousands of Jews each day, until Europe would be 'cleansed from all Jews'. It was aptly named the 'final solution of the Jewish problem'. Even the disposal of the remains of the murdered was provided for – human hair was to be used for upholstery, human fat melted down into soap, human ashes used for fertiliser; gold fillings from the teeth were to be extracted and melted down into gold bars.

Those survivors would be scarred in body and soul for the rest of their lives. They were the remnants of great and historic Jewish communities that had been liquidated by Nazism. In many cases, they were the only members of large families to survive. They naturally thought that the heart of the world would be filled with compassion for them. In fact, no one wanted them. For example in 1946 the United States Congress would allow only 4,760 of those Jewish survivors to enter its borders. It was the same story all over the world. Those Jewish survivors, renamed 'displaced persons', were herded back into the very concentration camps in which they had witnessed the destruction of the majority of European Jewry. Although the camps were cleaned up, provided with proper medical facilities and food, it was for many the supreme horror of the second world war. It dawned on them finally that the world did not want them. Then into their hearts came the words of Theodor Herzl. The Jewish people would never be safe and would never receive respect or dignity until they had a state of their own. He had said about the Jewish State: 'It is no fairy tale, if you will will it.' It was there that the Jewish State was born! For, into those emaciated bodies and grief-stricken hearts was born the determination that the Jewish nation must rise again. Ages before, Jeremiah had prophesied:

> I will restore health unto thee, and I will heal thee of thy wounds, saith the Lord; because they have called thee an outcast, saying, 'It is Zion, whom no man careth for' (Jeremiah 30:17, RV margin).

For some 1900 years, no one cared for Zion. The Jewish people had been, if not openly hated, very often only tolerated. Certainly, those survivors experienced what

Jeremiah had meant. It was as if some divine, invisible, magnetic force began to draw them back to the land promised to Abraham and to his descendants for ever. Jeremiah had also prophesied:

> Thus says the Lord, "A voice is heard in Ramah, lamentation and bitter weeping. Rachel is weeping for her children; she refuses to be comforted for her children, because they are no more." Thus says the Lord, "Restrain your voice from weeping, and your eyes from tears; for your work shall be rewarded," declares the Lord, "and they shall return from the land of the enemy. And there is hope for your future," declares the Lord, "and your children shall return to their own territory" (Jeremiah 31:15-17, NASB).

This was partly fulfilled when they returned from Babylon. However, it has had an even greater fulfilment in our own day. Many Jewish people 'were no more', but the survivors did 'return from the land of the enemy ... to their own territory'. The survivors of the concentration camps came from the north and from the west. In their thousands, they began the long journey home. For them, Europe was no longer home. They had no home in the whole earth but Palestine. By one means or another, they stole out of those camps and began the trek over the mountains of central Europe and down to the Mediterranean coast. Old and young travelled together, weak through years of malnutrition and ill treatment. Some lame, some blind, all bearing for ever the scars of Nazi inhumanity, they made the long and arduous journey. When they reached the Mediterranean coast, they boarded anything which floated, anything that would transport them to British Mandated Palestine. The simple fact of sailing in vessels flying the Israeli flag, however unseaworthy the vessel and however congested the conditions, had an incredible effect upon those survivors. For the first time in some 1,900 years they were travelling under their own flag and amongst people to whom the name 'Jew' was not a dishonour but a distinction.

The trickle of human beings became a flood. Unarmed,

they faced the might of the British empire. The British government was unsympathetic, and instructions were issued that none of the 'illegal immigrants' was to be admitted. Thousands were interned in Cyprus or turned back to Europe; a handful were allowed to settle in Palestine. However, the tide of those desperate, determined and homeless Jewish survivors became so strong, and the British authorities' measures so unpopular with world opinion, that finally, in 1947, the British government gave back the Mandate to the United Nations. It was a battle the government could never have won, for unbeknown to them they were withstanding the hand of God. The British empire and the word of God had come into collision, and the word and purpose of God, as ever in the history of man, prevailed. Whatever other economic and political factors were involved, it is a point worthy of note that from that time the eclipse of the British empire began. The age-old promise to Abraham still holds for his seed: 'I will bless them that bless thee, and him that curseth thee will I curse' (Genesis 12:3, RV). God confirms this solemn promise with the words in Isaiah: 'For that nation and kingdom that will not serve thee shall perish; yea, those nations shall be utterly wasted' (Isaiah 60:12, RV).

In Jeremiah 31:7-9, God says:

> Thus saith the Lord, Sing with gladness for Jacob, and shout for the chief of the nations: publish ye, praise ye, and say, O Lord, save thy people, the remnant of Israel. Behold, I will bring them from the north country, and gather them from the uttermost parts of the earth, and with them the blind and the lame, the woman with child and her that travaileth with child together: a great company shall they return hither. They shall come with weeping, and with supplications will I lead them: I will cause them to walk by rivers of waters, in a straight way wherein they shall not stumble: for I am a Father to Israel, and Ephraim is my firstborn. (RV)

Anyone who witnessed the return of these survivors to the promised land must recognize the accuracy of Jeremiah's words. With the great multitude who returned there were many on stretchers, many who were blind or lame, conditions due for the most part to malnutrition and brutal ill-treatment in Nazi concentration camps. In not a few cases, the lameness and blindness was the result of experimental operations performed upon them without anaesthetics, by Nazi doctors and surgeons. Amongst that great company who returned were those who were pregnant, and those who had given birth on the arduous journey. Certainly they all came back with much weeping.

Moreover, it was not only the survivors of the concentration camps who came back this way: it was also true of the great influx of Jewish refugees from Arab lands between 1947 and 1951. Whole communities returned, including the old, the infirm, the sick and the pregnant. Jeremiah's words were a literal description of their return to the promised land.

Even the World Zionist Organization recognizes that it was not wholly due to their influence that so many returned to Israel at that time. There was infinitely more to it than political agitation. The hand of God was behind it. Take for example the Yemenite Jews. That colourful community had its origin in the Solomonic era (9th century B.C.) and has existed in an unbroken tradition from then until modern times. Living a feudal existence in the Yemen, the vast majority had never seen a car, or an aeroplane, or a telephone, or any of the gadgets of modern civilization. Yet, in 1948, without warning, some 43,000 Yemeni Jews left behind their homes and their livelihood, and trekked across the Arabian peninsula into the then British Colony of Aden. It was a source of acute embarrassment to the British government which had had enough involvement with the problem of Jewish immigration to Palestine, and wanted no more to do with it. So they set up camps for these Yemeni Jews while they investigated the cause of their sudden movement, and considered what action to take. Centuries before, the Lord had declared: 'I will say ... to the south, Keep not back; bring my sons from far ...'(Isaiah 43:6, RV). It is a striking fact that the Muslim Yemeni authorities allowed the Jewish community to leave, for they recognized the hand of God. They said: 'God expelled the Jews from their land, and God has been appeased and has restored their land to them. Who are we then to challenge the Divine Will?'

When the Jewish Yemeni leaders were asked why they were leaving the Yemen, they replied that the time had come for them to go home to Israel. A prophet amongst them many centuries before had predicted that at the end of the times, before the coming of the Messiah, they would all be transported back to the promised land on the wings of a great silver bird. It was in fact precisely what happened. The British government permitted the whole Yemeni community to be airlifted by Dakota aircraft to Palestine in an operation named 'Operation Magic Carpet'. Between June 1949 and June 1950, 43,000 Yemeni Jews were airlifted to Israel. Today there remain in the Yemen only a few Jewish families.

This airlift was only exceeded in magnitude by the airlift of the large Iraqi Jewish community in 1950. In ancient and medieval times, it was a community unsurpassed for learning, wealth and influence. In an airlift named 'Operation Ali Baba' 113,000 Iraqi Jews were transported to Israel.

Isaiah had prophesied saying: 'Lo, these shall come from far: and, lo, these from the north and from the west; and these from the land of Sinim' (Isaiah 49:12 RV). The location of 'the land of Sinim' has been the subject of much discussion. Some scholars suggest Egypt or Phoenicia. But the great authority Gesenius considered it to be China, and in modern Hebrew Sinim means 'the land of the Chinese'. There were Jews trading in Khotan, in Sinkiang (Chinese Turkestan), before the 8th century A.D., and in Canton, South China, in the 9th century A.D. In the 9th and 10th centuries there was a sizable Jewish Chinese-speaking community in Kai-feng, the provincial capital of Honan. The synagogue and Jewish cemetery remain to this day and some 250 people still live there, although their Jewishness has been lost through intermarriage. The famous traveller Marco Polo, who visited China towards the end of the 13th century, reported various decrees made by the Chinese authorities which mentioned the Jews by name. This indicates that a sizable number of Jews was resident at that time in China. In 1937 there were about 10,000 Jews living within her borders. By 1941-42 the number had risen to 25-30,000 – due largely to refugees from Nazism. Many of these Jews returned to Israel from China, as well as from central Asia. From far and near, from east and west, from north and south, God has drawn them back to the promised land.

The words of the Lord are recorded by the prophet Micah:

> "In that day," declares the Lord, "I will assemble the lame, and gather the outcasts, even those whom I have afflicted. I will make the lame a remnant, and the outcasts a strong nation, and the Lord will reign over them in Mount Zion from now on and forever." (Micah 4:6-7, NASB)

It is quite remarkable that this great multitude should have been forged into a strong nation. They have been drawn from the four corners of the earth, speaking literally dozens of languages, coming from at least eighty-seven different nations and from cultures as widely differing as the Canadian from the Yemeni, many of them bearing – in mind if not in body – the scars of their exile affliction. Truly, the Lord has made 'the lame a remnant, and the outcasts a strong nation'. The newly-born Israel has survived four wars in thirty years and triumphed over the overwhelming odds arrayed against her. Describing the Jews in exile, the Lord said: 'They have called thee an outcast, saying, It is Zion, whom no man careth for' (Jeremiah 30:17, RV margin); describing those who have returned from exile, he says: 'I will make ... the outcasts a strong nation' (Micah 4:7, NASB).

All this is summed up in Ezekiel 34:11-16:

> For thus saith the Lord God: Behold, I myself, even I, will search for my sheep, and will seek them out. As a shepherd seeketh out his flock in the day that he is among his sheep that are scattered abroad, so will I seek out my sheep; and I will deliver them out of all places whither they have been scattered in the cloudy and dark day. And I will bring them out from the peoples, and gather them from the countries, and will bring them into their own land; and I will feed them upon the mountains of Israel, by the watercourses, and in all the inhabited places of the country. I will feed them with good pasture, and upon the mountains of the height of Israel shall their fold be: there shall they lie down in a good fold, and on fat pasture shall they feed upon the mountains of Israel. I myself will feed my sheep, and I will cause them to lie down, saith the Lord God. I will seek that which was lost, and will bring again that which was driven away, and will bind up that which was broken, and will strengthen that which was sick: and the fat and the strong I will destroy; I will feed them in judgement. (RV)

A further example of fulfilled prophecy in our day is found in Isaiah 61:4:

> Then they will rebuild the ancient ruins, they will raise up the former devastations, and they will repair the ruined cities, the desolations of many generations. (NASB)

It is often stated that this prophecy was fulfilled on the return from Babylon. There is no doubt at all that when they returned from Babylon they did rebuild the ancient ruins and repair the ruined cities. That exile lasted seventy years: in fact, it was a captivity of seventy years, and an exile of fifty years. One could hardly call that the 'desolations of *many generations*'! At the most it was the desolations of two generations. However, if this prophecy refers to the return from the second exile, then it most certainly has been fulfilled in an exhaustive manner. It has been the desolations of forty-seven generations that have been repaired by those who have returned.

All over Israel the fulfilment of this prophecy is to be found, in the cities and towns and settlements. There are many examples – Bet Shemesh, Rehovot, Lod, Beersheba, Arad, Bet Shean, Tiberias, Ashkelon, Ashdod,

Gath, Lachish, En-Gedi. These have all been rebuilt, either on the ruins of the former cities or beside them. Other nations have not rebuilt their ancient towns and cities. We do not find, for instance, in Egypt, the rebuilt cities of Memphis, Rameses or Thebes or, in Iraq, the rebuilt cities of Nineveh or Babylon. It is true only of Israel because God said it would be so. In Isaiah 58:12 this is put in a slightly different way, but it is the same thought:

> Those from among you will rebuild the ancient ruins; you will raise up the age-old foundations; and you will be called the repairer of the breach, the restorer of the streets in which to dwell. (NASB)

In Amos 9:14-15 God says:

> I will bring again the captivity of my people Israel, and they shall build the waste cities, and inhabit them; and they shall plant vineyards, and drink the wine thereof; they shall also make gardens, and eat the fruit of them. And I will plant them upon their land, and they shall no more be plucked up out of their land which I have given them, saith the Lord thy God. (RV)

It is often claimed that this prophecy was fulfilled in the return from Babylon. But such a claim disregards the words, 'And I will plant them upon their land and they shall *no more be plucked up* out of their land which I have given them.' When Amos recorded God's promise, the greatest exile and dispersion of the Jewish people was yet to be: not an exile lasting seventy years, but an exile lasting 1,900 years. If then it was fulfilled in the return from Babylon, the Lord made an emphatic and categoric promise knowing full well that he would not keep it. This would mean that God is an exaggerator, if not a liar. However, the Lord neither exaggerates nor does he lie. His word is reliable and accurate. This ancient prophecy has had its exact fulfilment in our day.

Isaiah prophesied: 'They shall build the old wastes, they

shall raise up the former desolations' (Isaiah 61:4, RV), and, as we have seen, Amos prophesied in similar vein: 'they shall build the waste cities, and inhabit them.' But he goes on to say: 'and they shall plant vineyards, and drink the wine thereof; they shall also make gardens, and eat the fruit of them.' No one who visits Israel today could be in any doubt that the Jews who have returned have indeed planted 'vineyards and drink the wine thereof', and have made 'gardens and eat the fruit of them'.

The claim is often made by those unsympathetic to the State of Israel that the early Zionist pioneers around the turn of the century swindled simple Arabs out of valuable and fertile land. This claim does not tally with the facts. There may have been one or two such cases, but they were the exception. It was very often malarial swamplands, arid waste lands, or desolate eroded areas from which all fertility had long since departed which were sold to the pioneers, and for high prices. Furthermore, they were often sold by absentee landowners living in Beirut or Damascus or Baghdad or Cairo. Many were amused that anyone should want to buy such land, believing that once they settled on it, they would die like flies, and in the end the land would come back into Arab hands. In fact, those early Jewish settlers did die like flies. They died of malaria, black fever, yellow fever and dysentery. But when they died others took their place, and when those died, still others took their place. Eliezer Ben Yehuda has recorded in his journal how he sat with the last settlers of a little settlement called Hadera as they lay dying of yellow fever. He noted that their whole concern was for the continuation of the settlement: who would take over the pioneer work? In the end, others did come and take it over, and today Hadera is a thriving modern city. Those early Zionist pioneers endured until slowly the malarial swamplands were drained and the desert began to blossom like the rose. They endured at tremendous cost to life and limb, until the orchards and gardens, the vineyards and fields of modern Israel took shape.

It is remarkable that most travellers to Palestine in the days of the Turkish empire in the 19th and early 20th centuries were at one in their judgement that Palestine was a waterless wilderness. In their journals, diaries and books, they remarked on its desolation and neglect, on its 'atmosphere of past glory and present dereliction', on its 'monotony of stagnation, devoid of life and movement'. Even Theodor Herzl considered the 'promised land' a desolate, waterless wilderness.

Anyone visiting Israel now would find it hard to recognize the land from that kind of description. From almost any vantage point in Galilee today, there are only fields and orchards and woods to be seen. It is the same across the Sharon plain, with its great citrus groves and fields. Even in the south, in the Negev and in the Aravah, verdant areas stand out in contrast to the white-yellow desert. These are the later pioneer settlements. Ezekiel prophesied concerning this:

> But ye, O mountains of Israel, ye shall shoot forth your branches, and yield your fruit to my people Israel; for they are at hand to come. For, behold, I am for you, and I will turn unto you, and ye shall be tilled and sown: and I will multiply men upon you, all the house of Israel, even all of it: and the cities shall be inhabited, and the waste places shall be builded: and I will multiply upon you man and beast; and they shall increase and be fruitful: and I will cause you to be inhabited after your former estate, and will do better unto you than at your beginnings: and ye shall know that I am the Lord. Yea, I will cause men to walk upon you, even my people Israel; and they shall possess thee, and thou shalt be their inheritance, and thou shalt no more henceforth bereave them of children. (Ezekiel 36:8-12, RV.)

And again, in verses 32-36:

> Not for your sake do I this, saith the Lord God, be it known unto you: be ashamed and confounded for your ways, O house of Israel. Thus saith the Lord God: In the day that I cleanse you from all your iniquities, I will cause the cities to be inhabited, and the waste places shall be builded. And the land that was desolate shall be tilled, whereas it was a desolation in the sight of all that passed by. And they shall

> say, This land that was desolate is become like the garden of Eden; and the waste and desolate and ruined cities are fenced and inhabited. Then the nations that are left round about you shall know that I the Lord have builded the ruined places, and planted that which was desolate: I the Lord have spoken it, and I will do it. (RV)

In Isaiah 61:5, God says:

> And strangers shall stand and feed your flocks, and aliens shall be your plowmen and your vinedressers. (RV)

In the return from Babylon, we do not have any record of aliens or foreigners, non-Jews, returning with the Jewish remnant to help in the restoration of the nation and of the land. It is true that, in the days of Moses, when the people of God left Egypt, a mixed multitude went with them. However, Nehemiah records how careful he was not to allow any Gentiles to take part in the restoration work, and Ezra was even more adamant on this matter. We know that it was a small remnant of the vast number of Jews in exile who returned, about sixty thousand, but there is no mention of any Persians or Babylonians among them. It is however a remarkable fact that, since 1948, large numbers of Gentile young people have gone to assist in the recovery and restoration of Israel. It is a wholly new phenomenon in Jewish history! Never before in Jewish history have so many non-Jewish young people wanted to support and assist them. Furthermore this help has been very largely to do with the agricultural side of Israeli life. These 'foreigners' have become herdsmen, vinedressers and ploughmen! The prophecy has been accurately fulfilled.

Another example of prophecy fulfilled in our day is found in Zephaniah 2:4-7 –

> For Gaza shall be forsaken, and Ashkelon a desolation: they shall drive out Ashdod at the noonday, and Ekron shall be rooted up. Woe unto the inhabitants of the sea coast, the nation of the Cherethites! The word of the Lord is against

you, O Canaan, the land of the Philistines; I will destroy thee, that there shall be no inhabitant. And the sea coast shall be pastures, with cottages for shepherds and folds for flocks. And the coast shall be for the remnant of the house of Judah; they shall feed their flocks thereupon: in the houses of Ashkelon shall they lie down in the evening; for the Lord their God shall visit them, and bring again their captivity. (RV)

When the people of God returned to the land from exile in Babylon, they did not return to Ashkelon. From its beginnings until New Testament times, it remained a basically Gentile city. In its early history, it was one of the five Philistine city states. In the Persian period, the time of the return from exile, it was under the control of Gentile Tyre. Later, it became an important centre of Greek civilization and maintained its independence from Jewish control, even during the glorious Maccabean era. In the reign of Herod the Great, under the Romans, it was not included in his territory, although since it was his birthplace he beautified it.

Zephaniah's specific prophecy was never fulfilled on the return from the first exile in Babylon. So when was it fulfilled? Some Jewish immigrants settled in the Ashkelon region from 1949 onwards, but it was in 1955 that Ashkelon was granted city status. A garden city had been planned with funds set aside for that purpose in 1952 by South African Jewry. By 1975 it had a population of 47,900 – and it has continued to increase in number since then. Today Ashkelon is a very pleasant and totally Jewish modern seaside resort. In the town square, in the Afridar quarter, the words of Zephaniah are to be found engraved in Hebrew upon a piece of stone (2:7, quoted above).

Ashdod, like Ashkelon, was one of the five Philistine city states. During the period following the return from the Babylonian exile it was in fact the Philistine capital. Only in the late Maccabean period (100-63 B.C.) did it become a Jewish town; and it remained so till the second century A.D. In 1956 the modern city of Ashdod was founded with a population of 200 people! It was planned that Ashdod should become a major port and industrial area. By the early sixties extensive work was already under way, and by 1975 the population had reached 52,500. It continues to increase. It is the same with Gath, the home town of Goliath. During the last decade, Gath has developed into a sizable modern Jewish city (with a population in 1975 of 21,500) and is the centre of the Israeli textile industry.

Gaza alone has not been 'forsaken' in the sense that it is still a large and totally Arab city. It was abandoned by the Egyptian Army in 1967 and has since then been under Jewish rule. One of the oldest cities in the world, it has always been a Gentile city. Now, however, there are thriving Jewish settlements all around Gaza.

The name Palestine is derived from the Hebrew for Philistia, *Peleshet*, or Philistines, *Peleshtim*. It was originally an adjective in Greek derived from the Hebrew, and we find it mentioned first in the writings of Herodotus (484-25 B.C.) as 'Palestinian Syria' or 'Philistinian Syria'. The word he used in the Greek was *Palaistinē*. Subsequently it was shortened and became a noun – Palestine. It seems that the first time it was officially used to designate the territories of the former Israel, or Judea, was by the Roman Emperor Hadrian, after the Jewish revolt under Bar Kochba in A.D. 135. Hadrian's policy was to eradicate every trace of a connection between the Jewish people and the promised land. He renamed Jerusalem 'Aelia Capitolina', and renamed Judea 'Provincia Syria-Palaestina', as part of this policy. In the 4th century A.D. the Christian Byzantine rulers divided the land into three provinces, Palaestina Prima, Palaestina Secunda and Palaestina Tertia. Thus the name Palestine has come into English from the Hebrew, through Greek and Latin. In modern Arabic, Palestine is 'Filustin', and a Palestinian is a 'Falastin'. I am saddened when Christians refer to the promised land as Palestine, for it is not the land of the Philistines but the land of Israel. It is interesting to note that the angel who appeared to Joseph in a dream said:

> Arise and take the young child and his mother, and go into the *land of Israel.* (Matthew 2:20, RV.)

He did not say 'go into Judea' or 'go into the Roman province of Syria'; he described it as 'the land of Israel'.

The Lord also speaks in the Zephaniah prophecy of the 'remnant of the house of Judah' (2:7). The name 'Jew' is derived from Judah. Thus we have here mentioned the two antagonists in the area: the Palestinian and the Jew. Whatever the rights or wrongs of the Palestinian case (and, in the end, some just solution has to be found for the Palestinian as well as the Jew), it is predicted here that the Palestinian will go out and the Jew will come in.

What shall we say in the light of all this fulfilled prophecy?

In Isaiah 46:9-11, the Lord says:

> I am God, and there is none like me; declaring the end from the beginning, and from ancient times things that are not yet done; saying, My counsel shall stand, and I will do all my pleasure: ... yea, I have spoken, I will also bring it to pass; I have purposed, I will also do it. (RV)

That which he has spoken and purposed, he has brought to pass. His counsel has stood and will stand for ever.

CHAPTER 4

THE WORD OF PROPHECY MADE MORE SURE

All the prophecies in the two previous chapters have been from the Old Testament. But in the first chapter, I referred to Matthew 24:32-34. Are there any more prophecies in the New Testament concerning the Jewish people and their future? Although I see the Old and New Testaments as two parts of one whole, it is a sad fact that many Christians view any evidence taken from the Old Testament as inconclusive, outdated and suspect. Does the New Testament provide any more evidence? I believe it provides incontrovertible evidence. Take, for instance, Acts 1:6-7 –

> They therefore, when they were come together, asked him, saying, Lord, dost thou at this time restore the kingdom to Israel? And he said unto them. It is not for you to know times or seasons, which the Father hath set within his own authority. (RV)

In the moments before his ascension to the right hand of the Father, those Jewish disciples were asking him whether or not he was going to give back to Israel her sovereignty. At that time they had home rule under Roman government. Now if there were no future for the Jewish people, and no possibility of a *sovereign* Jewish State, one wonders why the Lord did not take the opportunity to refute the idea once and for all. Why did he not point out to them that God's purpose for the Jewish people had been completed and that the church had been substituted for Israel? He could have made clear to them in a sentence or two that the kingdom would never be restored to Israel. Instead, the Lord answered them in a remarkable way:

> It is not for you to know times or seasons, which the Father hath set within his own authority. But ye shall receive power, when the Holy Ghost is come upon you: and ye shall be my witnesses both in Jerusalem, and in all Judaea and Samaria, and unto the uttermost part of the earth. (Acts 1:7-8, RV.)

He did not deny that, at some point in time, Jewish sovereignty would be restored. In fact, the very way in which he answered their question implies that it would be restored; but the time and season was wholly within the authority of God. Long before that took place, the Holy Spirit had a work to do, beginning in Jerusalem with the disciples themselves, and continuing from there through all the nations of the earth.

The point is further underlined by the apostle Paul:

> Now if their fall is the riches of the world, and their loss the riches of the Gentiles; how much more their fulness? (Romans 11:12, RV.)

All are agreed concerning the *fall* and the *loss* of the Jewish people. That is a fact of history recognized even by Judaism. But what kind of exegesis is it which emphasizes the words 'their fall' and 'their loss' and completely ignores the words in the same sentence 'their fulness'? Since there have been a *fall* and a *loss* of the Jewish people, then there will also be a *fullness* of the Jewish people. Furthermore, if their fall and loss involved not only a spiritual but a political fall and loss, surely their fullness will be likewise not only a spiritual but a political restoration and fullness as well? In the same vein we read in Romans 11:15 –

> If the casting away of them is the reconciling of the world, what shall the receiving of them be, but life from the dead? (RV)

If we all agree that there was a 'casting away of the Jewish people', what shall we say about the phrase 'the receiving of them'? Note carefully, therefore, these inspired words '... how much more their fulness?' and '... what will the receiving of them be but life from the dead?' This hardly suggests that God has finished with the Jewish people. On the contrary, it clearly implies that there will be a fullness, a receiving of them which will be 'life from the dead'. We have the same theme again in verses 25-29.

> For I would not, brethren, have you ignorant of this mystery, lest ye be wise in your own conceits, that a hardening in part hath befallen Israel, until the fulness of the Gentiles be come in; and so all Israel shall be saved: even as it is written, There shall come out of Zion the Deliverer; he shall turn away ungodliness from Jacob: and this is my covenant unto them, when I shall take away their sins. As touching the gospel, they are enemies for your sake: but as touching the election, they are beloved for the fathers' sake. For the gifts and the calling of God are without repentance. (RV)

This chapter is far from teaching that there is no future at all for the Jewish people. How do we understand the word '*until*'? 'A hardening in part hath befallen Israel, *until* the fulness of the Gentiles be come in; and so all Israel shall be saved.' It can mean only one thing, and that is that the hardness which has befallen the Jewish people will remain *until* the purpose of God to save an innumerable multitude out of the nations has been fulfilled. *Then* it will be removed, with the most glorious results for the Jewish people. This interpretation is further reinforced by those wonderful words: 'The gifts and the calling of God are irrevocable' (RSV). This glorious statement is primarily connected with the calling of the Jewish people. 'As touching the gospel, they are *enemies* for *your* sake: but as touching *the election*, they are beloved for the fathers' sake,' the apostle writes, inspired by the Holy Spirit. It seems transparently clear that the Lord's purpose for the Jewish people is to be fulfilled through both their fall and their restoration. Their gifts and their call have not been revoked. Moreover, this matter concerns divine love, which will neither give up nor let go.

It comes to many Christians as a considerable shock to realize that the church of God is described as 'their own olive tree' (verse 24). However far we might have strayed from this truth, it makes no difference to the fact. No matter how many Gentiles have been saved by the grace of God, they are still wild olive branches grafted into the natural olive tree. Verses 17-18 make this point even clearer:

> But if some of the branches were broken off, and thou, being a wild olive, wast grafted in among them, and didst become partaker with them of the root of the fatness of the olive tree; glory not over the branches: but if thou gloriest, it is not thou that bearest the root, but the root thee. (RV)

The glorious fact is that God has never surrendered his heart's desire to save a people, saved by his grace and born of his Spirit, in complete union with himself. It was the calling of the Jewish people that they should be the means by which the knowledge of God, the word of God and the salvation of God should come to the whole earth. In this the Jewish people failed; but the purpose of God did not fail. By their fall salvation is come to the whole world. Nor does God forget them, for he describes the church, those redeemed from every nation, as the Jewish people's 'own olive tree'. (See also Romans 9:6-8, 24-28; 11:1-5; Ephesians 2:11-15; 3:6.) In the end, when his purpose for the Gentiles is nearing completion, he will remove the veil from the Jewish heart, and thus all Israel – the whole elect people of God, the 'olive tree' with both its 'natural' and 'wild' branches – will have been saved.

In Luke 21:20-24 we have a clear and specific prediction which the Lord Jesus made concerning the Jewish people. It is highly significant.

> But when ye see Jerusalem compassed with armies, then know that her desolation is at hand. Then let them that are in Judaea flee unto the mountains; and let them that are in the midst of her depart out; and let not them that are in the country enter therein. For these are days of vengeance, that all things which are written may be fulfilled. Woe unto them that are with child and to them that give suck in those days! for there shall be great distress upon the land, and wrath unto this people. And they shall fall by the edge of the sword, and shall be led captive unto all the nations: and Jerusalem shall be trodden down of the Gentiles, until the times of the Gentiles be fulfilled. (RV)

In A.D. 66-70 the Roman armies, under the leadership of Titus, laid siege to Jerusalem. That siege ended with the most terrible carnage, the destruction of the Temple and city, and the scattering of the nation. Was that judgement upon the Jewish people final, or not? I say that it was not a final and irrevocable judgement upon them because of the force of the words 'and Jerusalem shall be trodden down of the Gentiles, *until* the times of the Gentiles be fulfilled'. Once again, the word '*until*' surely indicates that there is a time-limit set to the destruction of Jewish statehood and the loss of Jewish sovereignty, and the world-wide dispersal of the Jewish people. To those who reply by declaring that it does not imply the re-creation of Israel and the regathering of the Jewish people, but refers generally to the end of the age and the coming of the Lord, I would ask why the Lord Jesus mentioned the Gentiles when he said: 'Jerusalem shall be trodden down by *the Gentiles* until the times of *the Gentiles* be fulfilled.' Would it not have been more accurate, and certainly less misleading, if he had said, 'Jerusalem shall be trodden down until the purpose of God has been fulfilled'? The reference to the Gentile nations implies, in my estimation, that the national sovereignty of the Jewish people would one day be restored.

In Matthew 23:37-39, we read the words of the Lord Jesus:

> O Jerusalem, Jerusalem, thou that killest the prophets, and stonest them which are sent unto thee, how often would I have gathered thy children together, even as a hen gathereth her chickens under her wings, and ye would not! Behold, your house is left unto you desolate. For I say unto you, Ye shall not see me henceforth, till ye shall say, Blessed is he that cometh in the name of the Lord. (AV)

The occasion of these words was the final confrontation, in the Temple, between the Messiah and the Jewish establishment of the day. For two days, the various religious parties had made trial of him, by asking trick questions with the sole objective of trapping him, and it had ended in one of the most fearful and solemn denunciations found in the Bible. The Lord Jesus had never before referred to the Temple as 'your house', but had always called it 'my Father's house'. As he left the Temple for the last time, he said: 'Behold, your house is left unto you desolate. For I say unto you, Ye shall not see me henceforth, till ye shall say, Blessed is he that cometh in the name of the Lord.' Sadly, many Christians emphasize the first part of the verse, as if that were the whole statement. They read it as: 'Behold, your house is left unto you desolate. For I say unto you, Ye shall not see me henceforth.' But Jesus did not finish there. He went on: 'Ye shall not see me henceforth *till* ye shall say, Blessed is he that cometh in the name of the Lord.' Once again we need to note the force of the word 'till'. Furthermore, 'welcome' in modern Hebrew is '*baruch haba*', which is literally 'blessed is he that comes'. If you want to be traditional in the orthodox manner you say, '*baruch haba ba Shem Adonai*,' which means 'welcome in the Name of the Lord', literally 'Blessed is he that comes in the Name of the Lord'. This predicted welcome of him by the Jewish people does not tally with the view that, being under the final and irrevocable judgement of God, they will wail and mourn at the sight of him, cringing in the caves and in the holes of the earth. On the contrary, the words of the Lord Jesus certainly suggest that, in the end, the Jewish people's estimate of his person and work will be completely reversed. Instead of fearing, rejecting, or hating him, they will recognize him, receive him, and welcome him in the name of the Lord. One wonders what kind of biblical exposition it is which equates a people saying 'welcome in the Name of the Lord' with their final damnation.

It is to this change of heart that the prophet Zechariah alludes:

> I will pour upon the house of David, and upon the inhabitants of Jerusalem, the spirit of grace and of supplication; and they shall look unto me whom they have pierced; and they shall mourn for him, as one mourneth for his only son, and shall be in bitterness for him, as one that is in bitterness for his firstborn. In that day shall there be a great mourning in Jerusalem, as the mourning of Hadad-rimmon in the valley of Megiddon. And the land shall mourn ... all the families that remain, every family apart, and their wives apart. In that day there shall be a fountain opened to the house of David and to the inhabitants of Jerusalem, for sin and for uncleanness. (Zechariah 12:10 – 13:1, RV.)

This is a most remarkable prophecy. First, it declares that the spirit of grace and supplication will be poured upon the house of David, and the inhabitants of Jerusalem, at some stage during the last great battles over Jerusalem and Israel, and before the final battle of the age when the Messiah returns. (See Zechariah 12:1-9, and compare it with Zechariah 14:1-9.)

Secondly, note carefully that they will 'look *unto* me whom they have pierced', (RV, ASV). In my estimation, this is a much more accurate rendering than the AV rendering, 'they shall look upon me whom they have pierced', or the NASB rendering, 'they will look on Me whom they have pierced'. The Hebrew word translated 'upon' in the AV, and 'on' in both the NASB and RSV, means literally 'to', 'unto', 'by', 'towards' or 'in the direction of'. (The same construction is in Psalm 2:7, where it is translated 'to me'.) This word is quite different from that earlier translated 'upon' in the same sentence of Zechariah 12:10: 'upon the house of David and upon the inhabitants ...'. It is also instructive to note the remarkable change of pronoun in this one sentence, although the same person is meant: 'they shall look unto me ... they shall mourn for *him* ... be in bitterness for *him* ....' Some hold the view that Revelation 1:7 is a commentary upon this verse.

> Behold, he cometh with clouds; and every eye shall see him, and they also which pierced him: and all kindreds of the earth shall wail because of him. Even so, Amen. (AV)

Certainly it is true that every eye will see him, including the Jewish people. But they were not alone in the responsibility for the death of the Messiah: the Gentile authorities were equally responsible. The wording of Zechariah's prophecy seems to suggest that it is a spiritual awakening to the person of the Lord Jesus, and not a physical seeing of him at his second coming.

Thirdly, we should note carefully the reference in these verses to 'mourning':

> and they shall mourn for him, as one mourneth for his only son, and shall be in bitterness for him, as one that is in bitterness for his firstborn.

This verse does not breathe the atmosphere of the dreadful finality of God's judgement and wrath such as we find in Revelation 1:7. On the contrary, this prophecy suggests that as a result of the Spirit of God's being poured upon the Jewish people, they will begin to recognize the significance of the person and work of Jesus. Then, in deep and utter repentance, they will be saved. The prophecy suggests the godly sorrow which works repentance unto salvation, and not the sorrow of the world which works death (2 Corinthians 7:10). In the same way that countless numbers of Gentiles have discovered the 'fountain opened for sin and uncleanness' so too, through the finished work of Messiah, the Jewish people will experience the saving grace and power of God. (See Zechariah 13:1.) This mourning will end not in judgement, but in salvation! This is not shallow mourning, but mourning 'for him, as one mourneth *for his only son* ... as one that is *in bitterness for his firstborn*'. It speaks of a broken-heartedness that will lead to glorious salvation.

From Zechariah 12:11 it appears that this mourning will be national and official:

> In that day shall there be a great mourning in Jerusalem, as the mourning of Hadad-rimmon in the valley of Megiddon.

This is a reference to the great national mourning over the death of King Josiah. (See 2 Chronicles 35:24-25.) This national mourning over the death of the Lord Jesus will be an event not only without parallel in the history of the Jewish people, but an event unique in world history. No nation has ever nationally mourned an action which took place around two thousand years before – an action which it has come to recognize as the key to its whole history and destiny. Yet this is what Zechariah prophesies will happen with Israel.

Furthermore, this repentance will not be a matter of a few hours, but will last for some time.

> And the land shall mourn, every family apart; the family of the house of David apart, and their wives apart; the family of the house of Nathan apart, and their wives apart; ... all the families that remain, every family apart, and their wives apart. (Zechariah 12:12-14, RV.)

Those acquainted with Jewish mourning customs know that they are no light or brief matter. For seven days the life of the chief mourners is disrupted, and for thirty days life for them is abnormal. Some hold the view, based on Isaiah 66:8, that the whole Jewish people will be born again in a single day. This prophecy of Zechariah appears to be at variance with such a view, and is one of the reasons why I feel that I cannot subscribe to it.

It therefore seems to me that the word of God provides concrete evidence, not only in the Old Testament but also in the New, for both the political and national restoration of the Jewish people, as well as for their spiritual restoration. Such prophecy makes Israel unique among the nations of the world.

CHAPTER 5

A NATION IS ITS LANGUAGE

If prophets of the Old Testament were to stand today in any busy street in Tel Aviv, or Haifa, or Jerusalem, they would hear Hebrew spoken, a Hebrew that is still essentially the language they spoke. It is true that they would have some trouble in understanding modern pronunciation and grammar, but it would be a problem which they could soon overcome. Obviously they would also have problems with new Hebrew words as, for example, the word for 'car', or 'aeroplane', or 'television', but I have no doubt that their alert minds would soon add these new words to their vocabulary!

Jeremiah prophesied:

> Thus saith Jehovah of hosts, the God of Israel, Yet again shall they use this speech in the land of Judah and in the cities thereof, when I shall bring again their captivity: Jehovah bless thee, O habitation of righteousness, O mountain of holiness. (Jeremiah 31:23, ASV)

It is true that the Hebrew word translated 'this speech' refers primarily to what he went on to say and not to the Hebrew language. Nevertheless, the Hebrew word used does signify the content of what is spoken, the speech, rather than the act of speaking itself. Whether or not it be right to see in Jeremiah's words a deeper meaning, predicting the renewal of Hebrew on the return from exile, it is an incontrovertible fact that Hebrew has been reborn and that its rebirth is unique in the story of the nations.

A hard battle has been fought in this century by some numerically small peoples to keep their languages alive, for instance the Welsh language, or Irish, or Basque. Yet these never ceased to be used as the languages of the home. The battle has been fought, not for their resurrection, but for their survival. Even the newly emerged nations of Europe during this century, such as the Norwegians, Finns, or Czechs, never entirely lost their languages. Their languages were never totally submerged by other more widely spoken ones, although they were in danger, and when those peoples gained or regained their sovereignty, the preservation of their languages was assured.

Hebrew, however, has had a different story. For some 1,700 years it was no longer the spoken language of every day. Some historians argue that, in fact, it had ceased to be used for as long as 2,400 years, since the language which the Jewish people spoke on the return from Babylon in 536 B.C. was not Hebrew but Aramaic. Aramaic is, of course, related to Hebrew, but still another language. From 536 B.C. until A.D. 70 it was the official and colloquial language of the Jewish people, and only faded out towards the end of the third century A.D. Aramaic was the language which Jesus and the apostles used. As for Hebrew, that became a sacred language, the language of the Temple and the synagogue, the language of liturgy and prayer, the language for worship and for the study of the Holy Scriptures. In this sense, it resembled Latin, which also died as an everyday language, while surviving in the worship and liturgy of the Roman Catholic Church.

Then a miracle took place! After some 2,400 years, Hebrew was reborn and became the spoken language of a modern nation. Never before in all history has a language which has ceased to be spoken been reborn after centuries of disuse. Yet Hebrew is again the language of the home and of the street, of the market and of the Knesset. It has become the viable language of college and university, of news media and of books and magazines. Out of the ashes it has risen again to become the language of a contemporary nation.

How did this miraculous rebirth come to pass? Strangely enough, it was not the result of an educational movement, or a university programme. In fact, there had been an attempt to revive the use of biblical Hebrew for secular literary purposes by the Haskalah movement (1750-1880), but it failed completely to adapt the language to modern life and thought. Later, even the Zionist movement did not, at the beginning, throw its whole-hearted support behind the attempt to revive Hebrew. Its revival is due almost wholly to the vision and endeavour of one man, Eliezer Ben Yehuda.

He was born Eliezer Perlman in 1858 in Luzhky, Lithuania. Very early in his sad and lonely life, a love of learning and literature developed within him. As a teenager he read *Robinson Crusoe* in Hebrew (a product of the Haskalah movement), and that made him realize that the language could be used for secular purposes. Those ideas, which then began to form in his mind, were to lead him into a costly life-long struggle. At that time, some of the orthodox were outraged at the use of Hebrew for secular purposes. In their eyes it amounted to blasphemy.

In 1879 he was a student at the Sorbonne in Paris. After the Russo-Turkish war, the Balkan nations were struggling for liberation. The thought came to him that if freedom was the right of those nations, why should it not also be the right of his own people, the Jewish people? It was then that he had a vision that was to transform his whole life and, in the end, consume it. Describing what happened, he wrote:

> In those days it was as if the heavens had suddenly opened and a clear incandescent light flashed before my eyes, and a mighty inner voice suddenly sounded in my ears – 'the renaissance of Israel on its own ancestral soil.'

He changed his name from Eliezer Perlman to the Hebrew name of Eliezer Ben Yehuda. Yehuda was the Hebrew translation of his father's Yiddish name, Leib. It also means 'Judah' or 'Judea'. 'Eliezer, Son of Judah' was a fitting name for the one who for ever afterwards in Jewish history would be called 'the father of modern Hebrew'. In 1880 he wrote to the girl who later became his wife:

> I have decided that in order to have our own land and political life, it is also necessary that we have a language to hold us together. That language is Hebrew, but not the Hebrew of the rabbis and scholars. We must have a Hebrew language in which we can conduct the business of life. It will not be easy to revive a language dead for so long a time. [Robert St John, *Tongue of the Prophets (1952), page 40.*]

The task which confronted him was the rebirth of a language dead for many centuries. It was to cost him everything, but he lived to see his vision realized; to see General Allenby's published proclamation about martial law in Jerusalem printed first in Hebrew; to see Hebrew proclaimed as one of the three official languages of Palestine. Ben Yehuda wanted to revive Hebrew in its more melodious Sephardic pronunciation rather than in the awkward Ashkenazic pronunciation. It was given to him, before he died, as it is granted to few pioneers, to hear the melodious sound of that reborn Hebrew in the streets, market places and schools of Palestine.

From an early age he had suffered from tuberculosis, and his great fear, from the moment that his life's work became clear to him, was that he might die before he could finish it. He wrote of being like a man 'working with a few hours to live'.

In 1881, Ben Yehuda emigrated to Palestine. Deborah Yonas, his fiancée, joined him, and they were married en route. They decided to set up a Hebrew-speaking home to show the Jewish world that it could be done. From the moment they boarded the ship, they vowed never to speak any other language but Hebrew, and indeed, their children grew up hearing and speaking only Hebrew.

He devoted his time to teaching the language, speaking for the Zionist cause, and editing a succession of Hebrew language newspapers, none of which had a circulation during those early years of more than 200 copies. He used his newspapers as a vehicle for introducing and testing new words in Hebrew. He wrote in a simple and popular style, championing the new pioneer settlements, fiercely defending the use of Hebrew as a colloquial language, and incessantly attacking the Halukkah system whereby money was sent from overseas to support the Jewish communities. In his view this system hindered the hard work of the resettlement and reclamation of the land by turning many Jews into 'parasites' living on charity. The orthodox communities were outraged by Ben Yehuda's progressive views. They stoned his office; they denounced him to the Turkish authorities for treason; they placed him under a rabbinical ban of excommunication; they even refused to bury his wife in the Ashkenazic cemetery, when she died of tuberculosis in 1891, leaving behind her five children.

None of this opposition unnerved him. He worked on, and later married Deborah's sister, Hemda. In 1883 he founded *Tehiyyat Israel* (Revival of Israel) with its five principles – work on the land, revival of spoken Hebrew, creation of a modern Hebrew literature, education of the youth in a patriotic and humanist spirit, and active opposition to the Halukkah system. Its members covenanted to 'speak to each other in Hebrew in society and meeting places and in the streets and market places and not be ashamed'.

For Hebrew to be a viable language catering for everyone, from engineers to artists, from shepherds to surgeons, thousands of new words were needed. For every idea and innovation in the last two thousand years, a new word had to be found. Ben Yehuda was painstaking in his approach. Two factors governed his work: the language should be kept 'pure' and there should be no harsh or grating sounds. His first action was to discover if the word had once existed in Hebrew. This would involve combing through hundreds of books. Sometimes these 'lost' words would be found by accident. If he failed to find the wanted word, it could take anything up to ten years to create one. The sister languages of Hebrew – Arabic, Aramaic, Coptic, Ethiopic – provided him with many of the needed words. This research involved working in English, French, German and Russian. If he needed to make a new word, he would take a Hebrew base and develop it. For example, for the new word for 'dictionary', he took the Hebrew for 'word', '*millah*', as his base, and created '*millon*'. These new words would then be launched through the newspaper and the people would, in the end, either accept them or reject them.

It was about this time that he began to gather material for a Hebrew dictionary. This was published after his death, as the definitive dictionary of the Hebrew language. It now numbers seventeen volumes. He realized the need to standardize pronunciation, if the language was to be properly taught. So in 1890 he founded a language committee (*Va'ad ha-Lashon*) to be the supreme tribunal to pass on new words and settle disputes.

Ben Yehuda had a continual struggle because of lack of funds. His family continually lived near the poverty line. Hemda went to Europe to raise funds for the first volume, and was successful, but it cost them dearly in time and energy. For many years this became the pattern – Eliezer researched in the libraries of Europe, while his wife sought financial support for the work.

The story of the rebirth of Hebrew has its humorous side. Ben Yehuda's study overflowed with small pieces of paper, sometimes no larger than a postage stamp, upon which he had written in his neat, minute handwriting. These notes sometimes represented years of research. No one was allowed to tidy his study for fear of destroying this work. Hemda became more and more concerned about the mess in his study, and when she saw a mouse appear from under the mountain of old books and paper, she felt it was time to take action. 'Eliezer,' she said, 'unless something is done about your study, the bugs and mice will eat your lovely language!' 'One living Hebrew word,' he replied with great seriousness, 'is stronger than any bug or mouse! It will fight for its life and survive all its enemies.' Nevertheless he did invest in some large wooden chests in which all the pieces of paper were stored. Nothing else would have induced him to take such action than the thought of the Hebrew language being devoured!

One day a friend was greatly perturbed to find Eliezer rummaging through one of those wooden chests, overflowing with tiny pieces of paper, with an oil lamp precariously perched on top. 'Is this the way to treat the treasury of the Hebrew language?' the friend asked. 'You might start a fire which will not only burn down your home but reduce Hebrew to ashes!'

On another occasion, he lost one of the tiny pieces of paper on which a new word had been written. It had taken years of research. The whole house was turned upside down in the search to find the missing word, but without success. Eventually, it came to light – in the turn-up of Eliezer's own trousers!

No other language has hung on so slender a thread for its revival. It was virtually the life of one man and his family upon which the rebirth of Hebrew depended.

One day a group of Jewish women came to Hemda. They were going to give a concert in Jerusalem and wanted a Hebrew word for 'concert' in order to advertise it. Not long before, Eliezer had found a Hebrew word, *tizmoret*, and had introduced it in his newspaper. Unfortunately a rival group picked up the word from his newspaper and used it to advertise their own concert! Eliezer locked himself away and, from ancient Hebrew literature, discovered another word for them, *manġina*. Thus, in modern Hebrew, there are two words for 'concert'!

On another occasion, a wealthy English Jew offered Ben Yehuda a sizable cheque if he would telegraph back a suitable Hebrew word for 'sport'. Ben Yehuda, however, would not be hurried. It was some years before he finally announced the word *mil'ab*, based on the Arabic root 'to play'. In the Ben Yehuda family it came to be known as the most expensive word in Hebrew! It has since fallen into disuse.

There was one last battle to be won. In 1913 wealthy German Jews financed the building of the Technicum (now called the Technicon) in Haifa. It transpired that German was to be the language of the curriculum. Ben Yehuda led the fight against its use. It was his contention, backed by a life-long struggle, that 'a nation is its language, no less than its sweat and blood'. Teachers abandoned their class-rooms to support his stand; emergency schools were organized. Eventually peace was made, but the language war had been decisively won. From that time onwards, it would not be French, German, English or Yiddish that would be the language of the Jewish people, but Hebrew.

Although Eliezer Ben Yehuda 'lived, slept and died' Hebrew, he was not narrow in his heart or mind in his view of Zionism. In his second appeal issued about 1897, he declared:

> This must be a movement of all Jews, whether they are extremely orthodox in their religious beliefs or have adopted the 'assimilation' position, or even if they have embraced Christianity.

Towards the end of his life, he changed the motto on his study wall. Formerly it had read 'The day is short, the work to be done so great.' Now he changed it to 'The day is long, my work is blessed.' He had travelled a long way. Due to the vision and efforts of this one man, suffering from a then incurable disease, and assailed on all sides, Jews now spoke, wrote and read a revived national language. There was a Hebrew press and a flourishing Hebrew literature. The census in 1916 revealed that 40% of the Jewish population spoke Hebrew as their first language.

At this time he found his own personal fulfilment. Sitting in a synagogue with tears trickling down his face, he listened to the official pronouncement signifying the end of the longest Jewish exile, in the melodious Hebrew he had fought for and won.

In 1922 he died, and three days of national mourning were declared. Thirty thousand people followed the coffin to its last resting place on the Mount of Olives.

In 1948 Hebrew was declared the official language of the State of Israel. Since then Israeli scholars have carried on Ben Yehuda's work. On the one hand they have been much more careful in adopting new words and on the other hand have been more tolerant about the introduction of foreign words, especially those which are international terms. Some words which Ben Yehuda created have dropped out of usage, but his main work has proved to be foundational. That it is today a language used for everything from football to nuclear physics is owed largely, under God, to one man, Eliezer Ben Yehuda. I say 'under God' for, in my opinion, there is no adequate explanation for the miracle of the rebirth of Hebrew other than that God was behind it. The story is without precedent in the history of mankind. It provides us with yet another facet of the uniqueness of this nation.

CHAPTER 6

IT IS ZION, FOR WHOM NO ONE CARES

> Thou shalt arise, and have mercy upon Zion: for ... the set time is come. For thy servants take pleasure in her stones, and have pity upon her dust. So the nations shall fear the name of the Lord ... (Psalm 102:13-15, RV).

Do these words of the psalmist have any reference to the literal restoration of the Jewish people to their land, or do they have only a spiritual meaning? What does Zion signify?

The name Zion is used frequently in the Bible, and it is clear from even a superficial reading that the way it is used is deeply significant. We read of 'Mount Zion', of the 'stronghold of Zion', of 'Zion ... the city of the Great King'; of the 'inhabitants of Zion', of the 'daughter of Zion', of the 'children of Zion'. We are told that the Lord 'loves the gates of Zion', that he has 'founded Zion' and that he calls it 'My holy hill of Zion'; that he has 'chosen Zion', that he 'dwells in Zion', that he is 'great in Zion', that he 'fights for Zion', that he is 'jealous for Zion', that he will 'roar from Zion', that 'out of Zion, the perfection of beauty, he hath shined forth'. We are told that 'the Redeemer will come to Zion', that he will 'save Zion', that he will 'build Zion', that he will 'comfort Zion', that he will 'reign in Zion'; and that the 'ransomed of the Lord shall return, and come with singing unto Zion; and everlasting joy shall be upon their heads: they shall obtain gladness and joy, and sorrow and sighing shall flee away' (Isaiah 51:11, RV).

It will help us to understand a little of the profound significance of the name Zion if we recognize that it is used in four ways. First, it is used of an actual mountain, Mount Zion. Take, for example, Psalm 78:68 –

> [He] chose the tribe of Judah, the mount Zion which he loved. (RV)

Jerusalem was built on Mount Zion as well as on Mount Ophel and Mount Moriah. God chose these mountains because they were not as high as the mountains surrounding them: he did not want his people to have a 'high place' as the other nations had. Some modern archeologists, such as Professor Mazar of the Hebrew University in Jerusalem, believe that at the beginning Mount Zion was another name for Mount Ophel and Mount Moriah, and that only in later times was it used for the southwest hill of the old city of Jerusalem, as it is today.

Secondly, the name Zion was used to represent the city of Jerusalem, and then the whole nation whose capital it was. Take, for example, 2 Samuel 5:7 –

> David captured the stronghold of Zion, that is the city of David. (NASB)

Or Psalm 48:1, 2 –

> Great is Jehovah, and greatly to be praised, in the city of our God, in his holy mountain. Beautiful in elevation, the joy of the whole earth, is mount Zion, on the sides of the north, the city of the great King. (ASV)

Or again, in Isaiah 60:14 –

> they shall call thee The city of the Lord, The Zion of the Holy One of Israel. (RV)

Thirdly, it is used of the Jewish people, of their longings and aspirations when in exile, for national liberation, sovereignty and fulfilment, and in particular of those movements which brought about their return to the land – as in Psalm 137:1-6 –

> By the rivers of Babylon, there we sat down, yea, we wept, when we remembered Zion. Upon the willows in the midst thereof we hanged up our harps. For there they that led us captive required of us songs, and they that wasted us required of us mirth, saying, Sing us one of the songs of Zion. How shall we sing the Lord's song in a strange land? If I forget thee, O Jerusalem, let my right hand forget her cunning. Let my tongue cleave to the roof of my mouth, if I remember thee not; if I prefer not Jerusalem above my chief joy. (RV)

Or Jeremiah 30:17 –

> ... and your wounds I will heal, says the Lord, because they have called you an outcast: 'It is Zion, for whom no one cares!' (RSV)

Or again, Jeremiah 50:4-5,

> "In those days and at that time," declares the Lord, "the sons of Israel will come, both they and the sons of Judah as well; they will go along weeping as they go, and it will be the Lord their God they will seek. They will ask for the way to Zion, turning their faces in its direction; they will come that they may join themselves to the Lord in an everlasting covenant that will not be forgotten." (NASB)

Fourthly, the name Zion is used to represent and express that eternal and spiritual reality which God has sought from the beginning. This is the most important meaning of all. Take, for example, Psalm 50:1-2,

> God, even God, the Lord, hath spoken, and called the earth from the rising of the sun unto the going down thereof. Out of Zion, the perfection of beauty, God hath shined forth. (RV).

I do not think that the Zion of this earth has at any time during its long history been the 'perfection of beauty'. It refers to that reality of which the earthly Zion and Jerusalem is but a symbol. We find this fourth use of the name Zion illustrated again in Isaiah 35:10 –

> And the ransomed of the Lord shall return, and come with singing unto Zion; and everlasting joy shall be upon their heads: they shall obtain gladness and joy, and sorrow and sighing shall flee away. (RV)

Or again, Hebrews 12:22 –

> But ye are come unto mount Zion, and unto the city of the living God, the heavenly Jerusalem, and to innumerable hosts of angels. (RV)

Compare this with Hebrews 13:14 –

> For we have not here an abiding city, but we seek after the city which is to come. (RV)

Those who are born again are in God's Zion: they belong to a divine and invincible movement for world liberation, in which the Spirit of God will take no rest, until the time for the restitution of all things has come to pass, and the 'knowledge of the glory of God covers the earth as the waters cover the sea'.

In this chapter I wish to consider more fully the third use of the name of Zion, and in doing so, raise a question which is in many minds: is there any basis in the Bible for believing that Zionism, that political movement for the national liberation and self-expression of the Jewish people, is of God? This is at the heart of the controversy which rages over Israel. Many would question whether a political movement, led by many self-confessed agnostics, could possibly be referred to in the word of God. I make no apology for asserting that it is. If the hand of God is behind the re-creation of the State of Israel, and if it is his prophetic word which has been and is being fulfilled, then surely the human means by which it has come to pass must also have been in the plan of God.

In Isaiah 66:7-8, we read:

> Before she travailed, she brought forth; before her pain came, she was delivered of a man child. Who hath heard such a thing? who hath seen such things? Shall a land be born in one day? shall a nation be brought forth at once? for as soon as Zion travailed, she brought forth her children. (RV)

To what does this refer? There is no doubt in my mind that it has reference to the 'Jerusalem that is above ... which is our mother' (Galatians 4:26). All those who have been born from above, redeemed by the blood of the slain Lamb, have become by his grace 'a holy nation, an elect race'.

Nevertheless this prophecy has a further and literal fulfilment. It speaks of *a land being born in one day* and *a nation being brought forth at once*. I believe that these words were fulfilled in the re-creation of the Jewish State on the 14th May, 1948. On that day the land of Israel was born, the nation of Israel was brought forth! I do not believe, as some do, that Isaiah is referring to the Jewish people being born again. There are other Scriptures which speak of that matter. This prophecy refers to the land and to nationhood.

Furthermore, it declares that 'as soon as Zion travailed she brought forth her sons'. There had been 1,900 years of Jewish exile, years of longing and of great anguish. Yet during those years the land was never regained, nor was national sovereignty ever restored. It was only in 1897 that Zionism came into being as a movement for national recovery and restoration. There followed the fifty most turbulent years of nearly two millennia of exile, witnessing the fiercest onslaught on Jewish existence ever known. Zionism never wavered, but through those years of crisis kept steadily moving towards the goal. It was an anguished travail, but it ended in birth. 'As soon as Zion travailed, she brought forth her sons.' On the 14th May, 1948, the miracle took place: that day the nation was re-created and its sovereignty restored.

Zionism was born out of two things: hope and hopelessness. In the long nineteen hundred years of exile, the scattered Jewish people never ceased to long for their lost homeland. In their imagination the land of Zion took on a new dimension. It was enshrined in their folklore. For them the fruit in Zion always tasted better, the wine more sweet; the sky was more blue, the rains more gentle. The imagery of their folklore was never the imagery of central Europe, or of Russia, or of the steppe lands of Siberia: it was the imagery of the land of Zion. It was the centre of all their aspirations and hopes for a better day. Although centuries passed away, Zion remained in the memory of the Jewish people lost and bitterly lamented.

Thousands of years earlier that longing and yearning hope had been movingly expressed in a psalm, written during the first bitter exile in Babylon:

> By the rivers of Babylon, there we sat down, yea, we wept, when we remembered Zion. Upon the willows in the midst thereof we hanged up our harps. For there they that led us captive required of us songs, and they that wasted us required of us mirth, saying, Sing us one of the songs of Zion. How shall we sing the Lord's song in a strange land? If I forget thee, O Jerusalem, let my right hand forget her cunning. Let my tongue cleave to the roof of my mouth, if I remember thee not; if I prefer not Jerusalem above my chief joy. (Psalm 137:1-6, RV.)

Some people may look upon this psalm as being merely an interesting relic of the past, the fossillized sorrow and yearning of God's people during the first exile in Babylon. If that is all that there is, one wonders what spiritual value and help it can have for us today. If we recognize within it the genuine travail of those who know and love God, a travail over the fulfilment and realization of his purpose, in days of spiritual apostasy, backsliding and decline, then the abiding values of the psalm can readily be seen.

However, there is a further way of understanding this psalm, for it crystallizes all the anguish, the sense of lost purpose and destiny, the aspiration and yearning of a people who have forfeited the heart and the meaning of their existence. It was out of such longing and anguish that Zionism was born. God kept alive an awareness in the soul of the Jewish people, which was to play a vital role in their survival. It was an awareness that although they were scattered into a million parts all over the world, they were yet one nation, and God would one day gather them back again to Zion. It was this refusal on the part of the Jewish people to forget Jerusalem, this refusal to let go of the dream of a Zion regained, that led finally to the birth of Zionism.

That deep, mysterious and painful consciousness of Zion within the Jewish soul caused it to be enshrined in the folklore, ceremony and liturgy of the exiled people. Every aspect of life, from birth to marriage, from marriage to death was lived within the shadow of Zion, within the shadow of its fearful loss and its eventual restoration. Prayers always ended with some plea concerning the return to Jerusalem and the land. Such a prayer is the *Amidah* ('standing') prayer recited three times daily, standing and facing Jerusalem. The prayer ends:

> Sound the great horn for our freedom; raise the ensign to gather our exiles, and gather us from the four corners of the earth ... and to Jerusalem, Thy city, return in mercy and dwell therein as Thou hast spoken; and rebuild it soon in our days as an everlasting building ...

The great festivals always ended with some expression of sorrow over that which had been lost and some expression of hope that it would some day be restored. Take, for example, the 'Amidah' prayer of the pilgrimage festivals, which contains these words:

> Bring our scattered ones among the nations near unto Thee and gather our dispersed from the ends of the earth. Lead us

with exultation unto Zion, Thy city, and unto Jerusalem, the place of Thy sanctuary, with everlasting joy.

Or the well-known words with which the Passover and the Day of Atonement end: 'Next year in Jerusalem.'

In order to remind the people of the loss of Zion, the rabbis created a number of regulations which were observed by the more religious throughout the years of the second exile. For instance, a bride was never to have any silver or gold ornament on her wedding gown; instrumental music was banned except on certain occasions; when a house was built, a small area near the entrance was to be left unfinished. In such ways the loss of Zion was engraved on both the communal and individual consciousness of the people. Whether it was the prayer book, or whether it was rabbinic literature, or Kabbalist mysticism, or Hassidic folk tales, Zion and the promised land remained the hub of yearning hope. Nor did it matter whether they were living in Russia, or Spain, North Africa, India or Europe, this longing for a lost Zion bound all Jews together. This consciousness of having lost the very heart of their being influenced everything. It produced a persistent investigation throughout those years into the causes, the significance and the purpose of the exile. It brought a stoop to their shoulders, a sob into the liturgy, a quaver into prayer, a mournful note into song. They looked upon the hatred and bigotry which they faced, the poverty and insecurity which dogged their steps, as part of God's judgement upon them, to be borne without resistance. They became, until the Hassidic era, like a people in mourning. In many senses this made the Jewish people singularly unattractive. They became like a home without a mother, like a violin with only one unbroken string, like a bird with damaged wings. It was as if the loss of Zion had robbed them of their manhood and turned a whole people into shadows.

Yet it was the hope of a restored Zion which kept them alive during the long years of their sorrow. No other people had survived such a consistent onslaught upon its existence. Whether they suffered as the 'Christ killers' or the 'well poisoners' of the dark ages, or as the parasitic middleman, the exploiter, the hated money-lender of the middle ages, or the 'root of all Europe's ills', the 'poison in European society' of the twentieth century, it made no essential difference: the hated problem was always the Jew.

The Crusaders are known to many Christians only for their chivalry, zeal and faith, and for their good and compassionate works. They have left, however, an indelible scar in the Jewish memory. From the Rhineland to the Holy Land, wherever the Crusaders came, they bathed the ground with Jewish blood. Women, children and babes in arms were butchered. In Jerusalem, they shut up the whole Jewish community in the great synagogue, the old and the young together, and burned them alive. All this was done 'in the name of Christ and in the sign of the cross'. The facts speak for themselves. In A.D. 1000 when the Crusaders arrived in the Holy land, there were 300,000 Jews living there. They had survived many centuries of Gentile domination, Roman, Byzantine, and Arab. With Crusader rule, however, a sad fact emerges. When Benjamin of Tudela, a Spanish Jew, visited the Holy Land in A.D. 1169, he found only some 1,000 Jewish families still alive. In less than two centuries of so-called Christian rule, the systematic and extensive policy of butchering the Jews had resulted in the destruction of the larger part of the Jewish community.

The period of the Inquisition (15th and 16th century) was no different. Most Christians remember the Inquisition for the many true believers who were tortured or burnt to death at the hands of demonized men – men who believed that what they were doing was for the good of the souls of their victims. What many Christians do not know is that hundreds of thousands of Jews died equally terrible deaths at the hands of the inquisitors – 'in the name of Christ and in the sign of the cross'. Whole Jewish communities, influential, aristocratic and famed for their learning, were destroyed. The great Spanish and Portuguese communities never recovered; others recovered only partially.

During the latter part of the last century and the beginning of this, the Jewish people suffered a renewal of organized persecution in what were called 'pogroms'. *Pogrom* is a Russian word meaning 'destruction' or 'devastation'. It was used to describe attacks on Jewish communities in Russia and the Ukraine, Poland, Rumania and some other parts of eastern Europe. There is little doubt that the authorities, especially in Russia, were behind these pogroms. They believed, cynically, that it would 'help them solve the Jewish problem'. They held the view that much of the revolutionary unrest was emanating from the unhappy Jewish masses and that harsh measures should therefore be taken against them.

The pogroms were sudden and violent attacks upon Jewish communities, often taking place at Christmas or Easter. In the early days of the pogroms, people were brutally beaten and property and possessions destroyed. Soon, however, came murder and carnage. I do not believe that truly born-again Christians were involved in these pogroms, but nevertheless they were done 'in the name of Christ and in the sign of the cross' and to the age-old cry of 'Christ-killers'.

At this point it is worth recording a fact which is often overlooked by Christendom, and which is to its shame, namely that Islam has not persecuted the Jews to the same degree and on the same scale as Christendom has. There has never been an Islamic equivalent of the Inquisition or the Holocaust, although in the last half century repeatedly-made Arab statements would suggest that had they been successful in any of the four wars of Israel's short history they would have repeated those horrors. On the other hand to state that before the advent of the State of Israel Islam did not persecute the Jews would be false. In its beginnings both Jews and Christians suffered greatly through Islam. Islam was often spread by the sword and not by the word, especially in Arabia and Persia. It was the Muslim invasion of Persia in the 7th century which caused large sections of Jewry to flee into Russia and eastern Europe, rather than be forcibly converted to Islam. There are a number of factual accounts of massacres of Jews in Islamic countries over the last millennium. And Christian minorities also suffered in the same way.

Nevertheless, the Islamic persecution of the Jew rarely reached the savagery of the 'Christian'. On the contrary, Islamic countries have often been the refuge for persecuted Jews fleeing from Christendom. Jews were able to attain some of the highest positions in the Arab world, often as physicians or advisors to Caliphs and Sultans, and played leading roles in trade and commerce. Jewish scholars were able to make major contributions to Jewish life and thought. Islamic persecution has tended to be more 'moral' than physical. Until the first world war it consisted of all kinds of especial restrictions, regulations and taxes, which made Jewish life in such countries miserable. Since then Islam has become the implacable antagonist of the Jewish people.

During these long years of persecution the hope of returning to the land of their fathers never died in the heart of the Jewish people. Indeed it is a strange fact that it burned most brightly during the severest persecution. This obsession with a lost statehood and a lost land only began to disappear with the nineteenth century, and then mainly in central and western Europe, though not among the poorer Jews of Russia and eastern Europe and the Orient. It was, on the other hand, a fashionable and liberal view, held by many middle and upper class Jews at the time, that racial and religious prejudices would ultimately vanish in an enlightened age. They believed that the hope of the Jewish people lay not in Jewish nationalism, nor in some literal return to Zion, but in their contribution to the life of the nations of which they were a part. They thought that the new age of enlightenment, with its motto of 'liberty, fraternity and equality' would destroy all discrimination against them and allow them to take their place in national life.

A new kind of Jew now began to appear – the assimilated Jew. To all infents and purposes these were nationals of the land in which they were born. Their ties with Judaism were loose and their view of it liberal and progressive. Their one aim was to serve the country of their birth, for they had no other Zion.

It was during this period that a certain German rabbi of Polish origin, Zvi Hirsch Kalischer (1795-1874), who led a sizable Ashkenazi congregation in East Prussia, scandalized the orthodox with his insistence that 'redemption' for the Jewish people would come in two stages. The first stage would be 'natural' redemption, consisting of a return to the promised land and the building up of the nation economically; the second stage would be supernatural. Another rabbi, Judah Alkalai (1798-1878), who led a Sephardic congregation in Semlin near Belgrade, held similar views. These two rabbis wrote a number of books and pamphlets, claiming support from Scripture and from Talmudic and traditional sources. Both were denounced in orthodox Jewish circles for 'heretical' teachings.

A man with a very different outlook, but deeply influenced by Rabbi Kalischer's writing, was Moses Hess (1812-1875). He was probably the first assimilated Jew to turn to Zionism. He had been born into an orthodox Jewish family in Bonn, Germany, and received an orthodox education. As a young man he became disillusioned with Judaism and became an 'idealistic' socialist. He believed that the Jews had accomplished their mission in history and should join others in the 'onward march of mankind'. Thus he considered himself first and foremost to be German. In those years, he influenced both Karl Marx and Engels. Then in 1857 he began to read the writings of Rabbi Kalischer and they led him to a thorough study of Jewish history. Five years later he wrote in his book *Rome and Jerusalem*:

> After twenty years of estrangement, I have returned to my people. Once again I am sharing in its festivals of joy and days of sorrow, in its hopes and memories ... a sentiment which I believed I had suppressed beyond recall is alive once again. It is the thought of my nationality, which is inseparably connected with my ancestral heritage, with the holy land and the eternal city ... for years this half-strangled emotion has been stirring in my breast and clamouring for expression, but I had not the strength to swerve from my own path, which seemed so far from the road of Judaism, to a new one which I could envisage only vaguely in the hazy distance.

Some forty years later, Theodor Herzl was to be enraptured by this book, although at the time it was written it had little influence.

These three men represent the two main streams of Jewish life in the 19th century from which the early Zionists were to spring. The two rabbis represent the traditional and orthodox stream, and Moses Hess the assimilated and agnostic stream.

These men lived at a time when Europe believed that nations were moving away from war into the realm of peace and unity, and replacing the prejudices of race, nationality and religion with universal brotherhood. They did not see the need of a reconstituted Jewish nation as a bastion of survival, as many were to recognize it later, but rather as a legitimate expression of Jewish nationalism and aspirations.

It was, however, the pogroms of Russia and eastern Europe, following a period of moderation and liberal reform under Czar Alexander II, and a renewal of anti-Semitism in Austria and France, which brought about a devastating disillusionment with the new age and created the conditions for the birth of Zionism. Lev Levanda (1835-88) was a Russian author and leading figure amidst the Russian Jewish intelligentsia and a powerful exponent of the Haskalah movement and assimilationism. In 1882, after some of these pogroms, he wrote in a Russian Jewish journal entitled *Daybreak*:

> When I think of what was done to us, how we were taught to love Russia and the Russian word, how we were lured into introducing the Russian language and everything Russian in our home ... and how we are now rejected and hounded ... my heart is filled with corroding despair from which there is no escape. [Howard M. Sachar, *A History of Israel* (1976), page 13.]

Another Russian Jew, Moshe Lilienblum (1843-1910), a distinguished humanist, critic and political journalist and another leader in the Haskalah movement, wrote at the same time, following a pogrom in which he had hidden for some days in a cellar: 'All the old ideals left me in a flash; there is no home for us in this or any Gentile land.' [Ibid., page 13.]

Leo Pinsker (1821-91), a distinguished doctor, a writer and leader in the Haskalah movement, summed up the mood of despair when he wrote in 1882:

> To the living, the modern Jew is a dead man, to the native-born, he is a stranger, to the long-settled, a vagabond, to the wealthy, a beggar, to the poor, a millionaire and exploiter, to the citizen, a man without country, to all classes, a hated competitor.

Pinsker, along with many other Jewish intellectuals at that time, began to write about the necessity for the Jewish people to become again a nation among the nations.

> The Jewish people has no fatherland of its own, no centre of gravity, no government of its own, no official representation .... There is something unnatural about a people without a territory, just as there is about a man without a shadow. [Ibid., page 15.]

He saw the Jews as a kind of phantom people, expressing all the characteristics of nationhood without having either national sovereignty or territory. As such they were irretrievably foreign and alien to all those around them and the hope of assimilation was impossible because the majority of Gentiles would not allow it.

It was as if Jewish intellectuals began to realize for the first time that anti-Semitism bore little relationship to education or progress. Leo Pinsker stated this lucidly:

> The prejudice of mankind against us rests upon anthropological and social principles, innate and ineradicable.' [Ibid., page 15.]

The only answer was a national home of their own, whether in Palestine or somewhere else; until they were a recognized people living on their own land with their own government, they would have neither safety nor respect.

Moshe Lilienblum, along with many others, believed that land was Palestine. In 1882 he wrote:

> This is the land in which our fathers have found rest since time immemorial, and, as they lived, so shall we live. Let us go now to the only land in which we will find relief for our souls that have been harassed by murderers for these thousands of years. Our beginnings will be small, but, in the end, we will flourish. [Ibid., page 14.]

Over the next twenty years many societies, study circles and clubs grew up. Although they had no central headquarters or organization, they were called 'Lovers of Zion', or in Hebrew, *Hovevei Zion.* It was as if the words of Jeremiah dawned upon them:

> ... they have called you an outcast: 'It is Zion, for whom no one cares!' (Jeremiah 30:17, RSV.)

While the Jewish people were without state or sovereignty, political unity or voice, they would always be at the mercy of any who preyed upon them; no one would fight for their rights or safeguard their interests, and they would never receive the respect accorded to a free and sovereign people. They were, and would continue to be, despised outcasts to be trodden underfoot by all and sundry. It was this consciousness that made Zionism inevitable. The set time for God to have mercy on Zion had arrived. All it awaited was the right man at the right time.

CHAPTER 7

I WILL MAKE THE OUTCASTS A STRONG NATION

The right man at the right time was Theodor Herzl. With his appearance upon the scene, the set time for the Lord to arise and have mercy upon Zion had finally arrived. The Lord had said:

> For I will restore health to you, and your wounds I will heal ... because they have called you an outcast: 'It is Zion, for whom no one cares! (Jeremiah 30:17, RSV).

The nations had treated the Jewish people as outcasts. Now the Lord declared that those whom the nations called 'an outcast' he would restore to health, and their long open wounds he would himself heal. Moreover he promised to work a miracle among the afflicted exiles: 'I will make the lame a remnant, and the outcasts a strong nation' (Micah 4:7, NASB).

It was with Theodor Herzl that Zionism as we know it came to birth. He was born in 1860, in Budapest, a citizen of the vast multi-lingual Austro-Hungarian empire. The son of a banking family, he was typical of thousands of middle-class Jewish families at the time: educated, sophisticated and assimilated. He read law at the University of Vienna, receiving his doctorate in 1884. He soon abandoned law and became a successful journalist and a not-so-successful playwright. He accepted and, indeed, fought for the then fashionable view that religious and racial prejudices would eventually disappear in an enlightened age. Although a citizen of the Hapsburg empire, a citizenship his parents had taught him to cherish, he was enamoured with German culture and ideals. For him Jewish fulfilment lay in Europe. At university debating societies he had argued that Jews should take their place in Austro-Hungarian society as equals with their 'Christian' brethren, even if it meant being christened or confirmed, in either the Catholic or the Lutheran church. At one point he even envisaged leading 'a great movement for the voluntary and honourable conversion of Jews to Christianity', taking place 'in the broad light of day at noon, on a Sunday in St. Stephen's Cathedral, with a solemn and festive procession accompanied by the pealing of bells'.

Increasingly, however, Herzl had to re-think his whole position. The renewal of anti-Semitism during the latter years of the 19th century and the discrimination against Jews at all levels of Hapsburg society began to disillusion him with the 'age of enlightenment'. It was not uncommon at that time for young Jewish graduates, finding so many doors closed to them through anti-Jewish discrimination, to commit suicide in despair. They included a number of Herzl's friends. The suicide of one of his closest friends, Heinrich Kana, had a profound effect upon him and caused him to begin to think deeply on the Jewish question.

It was, however, the trial in December 1894 of Alfred Dreyfus, a captain in the French army and a Jew, which was to bring Herzl to his destiny. Captain Dreyfus was convicted of treason and sentenced to life imprisonment on the infamous Devil's Island, in spite of his insistent pleas of innocence and the clear lack of any motive. The 'Dreyfus Affair', as it came to be called, rocked France and scandalized the rest of Europe. Years later, in 1906, Dreyfus was fully exonerated, reinstated and given the medal of the Legion of Honour. At the time of his trial, however, and in the immediately succeeding years, his case prompted a violent outpouring of anti-Semitism.

For Theodor Herzl it was the moment of truth. He was

in Paris covering the trial for one of Vienna's largest daily newspapers, *Neue Freie Presse*. Later he wrote:

> What made me into a Zionist was the Dreyfus Case ... At that time I was living in Paris as a newspaper correspondent and attended the proceedings of the military court until they were declared secret. I can still see the defendant coming into the hall in his dark artillery uniform trimmed with braid. I still hear him give his credentials: 'Alfred Dreyfus, Captain of artillery,' in his affected nasal voice. And also the howls of the mob in the street in front of the Ecole Militaire, where he was degraded, still ring unforgettably in my ears: 'Death! Death to the Jews! Death to Jews all because this one was a traitor? But was he really a traitor? At that time I had a private conversation with one of the military attaches ... The colonel did not know much more about the whole affair than had appeared in the paper; yet he believed in the guilt of Dreyfus, because to him it appeared impossible that seven officers should have been able to declare a comrade guilty without the most convincing proof. I, on the other hand, believed in his innocence, because I did not consider a Jewish officer capable of being a traitor to his country. Not that I regarded the Jews in general as better than other human beings. But under the particular circumstances in the case of Captain Dreyfus, who personally did not even make a favourable impression on me, the whole thing appeared unlikely to me. 'A Jew, who, as an officer on the General Staff, has a career of honour lying open before him, is incapable of committing such a crime," I said to the Colonel. In a lower stratum of society, I would deny such a possibility among Jews as little as among Christians. In Alfred Dreyfus' case, however, it was psychologically impossible. A wealthy man, who had chosen this career only through ambition, simply could not have committed the most dishonourable of all crimes. The Jews, as a result of their long having to do without civic honour, often have a pathological urge for honours, and in this regard a Jewish army officer is a Jew raised to the highest degree. My line of reasoning at that time was probably that of all our co-religionists since the beginning of the affair. Just because for all of us, the psychological impossibility was so clear from the very beginning, the Jews had foreshadowings on all sides as to the innocence of Dreyfus, even before the memorable campaign to establish the truth began ... But the Dreyfus case contains more than a miscarriage of justice: it contains the wish of the vast majority in France to damn one Jew and through him all Jews. 'Death to the Jews!' the crowd

> yelled when they ripped the Captain's stripes from his uniform. And since that time, 'Down with the Jews' has become a battle cry. Where? in France. In Republican, modern, civilized France, one hundred years after the Declaration of the Rights of Man .... Up to that time, most of us had believed that the solution of the Jewish question was to be expected from the gradual progress of mankind toward tolerance. But if an otherwise progressive, surely highly civilized people could come to such a pass, what was there to be expected from other people, who even today are not at the height at which the French have already been for a hundred years? [*My People*, pages 297-98.]

What had been slowly forming in Herzl's heart and mind over some years, now crystallized. For the first time he saw clearly that there was no other answer to the Jewish problem than the restoration of Jewish statehood. He wrote in his diaries in Paris in June 1895:

> Nobody has ever thought of looking for the promised land where it really is – and yet it lies so near – it is here; within ourselves .... Everyone will take over there, in himself, a piece of the promised land. This one, in his head; that one, in his hands; the third, in his savings. The promised land is where we shall take it.

He described it as

> the promised land, where we can have hooked noses, black or red beards, and bandy legs, without being despised for it. Where, at last, we can live as free men on our own soil; and where we can die tranquilly in our own homeland. Where we can expect the reward of honour for great deeds; where we shall live at peace with all the world, which we have freed through our own freedom, enriched by our wealth, and made greater by our greatness. So that the derisive cry of 'Jew' may become an honourable appellation, like German, Englishman, Frenchman – in short, like that of all civilized peoples. So that by means of our State we can educate our people for the tasks which still lie beyond our ken. For God would not have kept us alive so long, if there were not left for us a role to play in the history of mankind. [Lowenthal, page 46.]

The idea of a reconstituted Jewish nation on its own soil

dominated the last nine years of his life. At the beginning of his diaries he had written:

> I have been pounding away for some time at a work of tremendous magnitude. I do not know even now whether I will be able to carry it through. It bears the aspect of a mighty dream. For days and weeks it has saturated me to the limits of my consciousness; it goes with me everywhere, hovers behind my ordinary talk, peers at me over the shoulders of my funny little journalistic work, overwhelms and intoxicates me. What will come of it is still to early to say. However, I have had experience enough to tell me that even as a dream it is remarkable and should be written down – if not as a memorial for mankind, then for my own pleasure and meditation in years to come .... The title: *The Promised Land.*

So powerful was the vision that came to him that he wrote of it as 'possessing him walking, standing, lying down, in the street, at the table, at night time'. In June 1895 he wrote:

> During these days I have been more than once afraid that I was going mad. So wildly the streams of thought raced through my soul. A lifetime will not suffice to carry them out. But I am leaving behind me a legacy. To whom? To all men. I believe I shall be named among the great benefactors of mankind! Or is this belief the onset of megalomania?

Prophetically, he noted in his diaries: 'I believe that for me life has ceased and world history has begun.'

In 1895, seeking to persuade a well-known Jewish philanthropist, Baron Maurice de Hirsch, to support the case for a Jewish homeland, he submitted to him a twenty-two-page memorandum which contained the first written expression of his vision. He wrote:

> Throughout the 2,000 years of our dispersion, we have lacked unified political leadership. I consider this to be our greatest misfortune. It has done far more harm than all the persecutions. It has rotted and ruined us from within. There has been no one – even out of the selfish ambition to be our ruler

> – to train us in true manhood. On the contrary. We have been dragged into the shabbiest occupations and we have been locked up in ghettos, where side by side we have degenerated. And when the gates were opened, we were expected suddenly to have all the traits of a free people. If only we had unified political leadership ... we could initiate the solution of the Jewish problem.

Later he wrote the essay which was to have such tremendous influence upon the course of Jewish history. He entitled it *Der Judenstaat* or, as it has been translated, *The Jewish State.* It was published in Vienna in February 1896 and subtitled 'An attempt at a modern solution to the Jewish question'. In it he declared:

> We are a people – one people. We have honestly endeavoured everywhere to merge ourselves in the social life of surrounding communities and to preserve only the faith of our fathers. We are not permitted to do so. In vain are we loyal patriots, our loyalty in some places running to extremes; in vain do we make the same sacrifices of life and property as our fellow citizens; in vain do we strive to increase the fame of our native land in science and art, or its wealth by trade and commerce. In countries where we have lived for centuries we are still cried down as strangers, and often by those whose ancestors were not yet domiciled in the land where Jews had already had the experience of suffering .... In the world as it is now, and for an indefinite period will probably remain, might precedes right. It is useless, therefore, for us to be loyal patriots, as were the Huguenots, who were forced to emigrate. If we could only be left in peace ... but I think we shall not be left in peace. [Theodor Herzl, *The Jewish State*(trans. S. D'Avigdor 1972), page 15.]

Speaking of a restored sovereign Jewish State on its own soil, he wrote:

> The idea must radiate out until it reaches the last wretched nests of our people. They will awaken out of their dull brooding. Then a new meaning will come into the lives of all of us;

and he continued:

> therefore, I believe that a wondrous generation of Jews will spring into existence; the Maccabees will rise again ... and we shall at last live as free men on our own soil, and die peacefully in our own homes. [Ibid., page 79.]

On the 24th August 1897 a Zionist Congress was held in the Stadt Casino in Basel. It was the first official world-wide gathering of Jews since the beginning of the second exile in A.D.70. It was a resounding success, although bitterly assailed by Jew and non-Jew alike. In his inaugural address, Herzl began with prophetic words:

> We are here to lay the foundation stone of the house which is to shelter the Jewish Nation. [Sachar, page 45.]

Later in the Congress Max Nordau declared:

> It is a great sin to let a race, whose abilities even its worst enemies do not deny, degenerate in intellectual and physical misery ... the misery of the Jews cries out for help. The finding of that help will be the great task of this Congress. [Ibid., page 45.]

The Congress decided to establish a world-wide movement to be called the World Zionist Organization. Theodor Herzl was made its president; a Jewish flag was adopted, as also a Jewish anthem: *Hatikvah* (*The Hope*).

It had happened. The Lord had arisen and had had mercy upon Zion; for it was time to have pity upon her, yes, the set time had come (see Psalm 102:13). Within fifty years the miracle was to take place. They were to be years of unparalleled disturbance and unrest for the world, and years of bitterness and suffering for the Jewish people. Yet it was to be true that 'as soon as Zion travailed, she brought forth her sons' (Isaiah 66:8). It was at that time that Herzl recorded in his diary more prophetic words:

> If I were to sum up the Basel Congress in a few words – which I would not dare to make public – I would say, 'At Basel I

> founded the Jewish State.' If I said this aloud, it would be greeted with worldwide derision. In five years, perhaps, and certainly in fifty, everyone will see it. [Lowenthal, page 224.]

It was, in fact, almost exactly fifty years later, in November 1947, that the United Nations General Assembly made its historic decision to recognize the right of the Jewish people to have their own state.

There was to be in the remaining few years of the life of Theodor Herzl a great deal of conflict, labour and sorrow. He died on the 3rd July 1904, at the early age of forty-four. Shortly before his death, he pointed to the students guarding his room and prophesied to his doctor: 'They are marvellous, good people, my compatriots! You shall see, they shall enter the promised land one day!' To a Christian friend he said: 'Greet Palestine for me. I gave my heart's blood for my people.' He died worn out and broken-hearted. Some years before his death, he had written to a close friend that 'the basic feeling of life is grief, and joy comes only when, for a brief while, grief abates'. Certainly his words described his own life and experience. For nine years, one single idea had possessed him – a determination that, somehow, somewhere, sometime, the Jewish people should again become a nation. One man with one idea fired millions. Like Moses he led the people to the land but was not permitted to enter it, seeing it only from afar. At his funeral, six thousand people walked behind the coffin. Stefan Zweig has described the scene for us. Everything had been orderly and dignified until they arrived at the cemetery. Then, he wrote:

> Too many had suddenly stormed to his coffin, crying, sobbing, screaming, in a wild explosion of despair. It was almost a riot, a fury. All order was overturned through a sort of elemental ecstatic mourning, such as I have never seen before or since at a funeral. And it was this gigantic outpouring of grief from the depths of millions of souls that caused me to realize for the first time how much passion and hope this lone and lonesome man had borne into the world through the power of a single idea. [Sachar, page 63.]

In his will Herzl requested that his body should be buried next to his father's and remain there 'until the day when the Jewish people carry my remains to Palestine'. Forty-five years later his body was flown to Israel. On the 17th August 1949 it was re-interred on a hill-top in Jerusalem renamed 'Mount Herzl'.

God raised Theodor Herzl to do a specific work for the Jewish people. Shortly before he died Herzl told Reuben Brainin that when he was about twelve years of age, the King Messiah had appeared to him in a dream.

> He took me in his arms and carried me off on the wings of Heaven. On one of the iridescent clouds we met ... Moses. (His features resembled those of Michelangelo's statue. As a child I loved this marble portrait.) The Messiah called out to Moses, 'For this child I have prayed.' To me He said, 'Go and announce to the Jews that I shall soon come and perform great and wondrous deeds for My people and for all mankind.' I have kept this dream to myself, and did not dare tell anyone. [Amos Elon, *Herzl*, page 16.]

If there were many Jews who were fired by Herzl's vision, there were also as many who opposed it. In their eyes it was a dangerous notion, playing into the hands of their enemies. Stefan Zweig has described the general reaction to the publication of *Der Judenstaat:*

> I can still remember the general astonishment and annoyance of the middle class Jewish elements of Vienna. 'What has happened,' they said angrily, 'to this otherwise intelligent, witty and cultured writer? What foolishness is this that he has thought up and writes about? Why should we go to Palestine? Our language is German, not Hebrew, and beautiful Austria is our homeland. Are we not well off under the good Emperor Franz Josef? Do we not make an adequate living, and is our position not secure? ... Why does he who speaks as a Jew and who wishes to help Judaism place arguments in the hands of our worst enemies and attempt to separate us, when every day brings us more closely and intimately into the German world?

Editorials of German Jewish newspapers went further and

described the Zionist Congress as treason to the German fatherland and a danger to Judaism. Herzl went everywhere in Europe and Russia pleading with the leaders of Jewry to listen to him, but they would not. At the worst he was derided as a vulgar rabble-raiser and at the best treated as a Jewish Jules Verne. German Jews, deeply concerned about the supposed danger to which he was exposing them, said: 'We are more German than the Germans!' It was no different in France, for they appeared to have the same spirit as that of earlier French Jewish Leaders who had told Napoleon, 'Paris is our Jerusalem.'

The deeply religious and orthodox were no less outraged by Herzl's Zionism. To them his writings and speeches amounted to heresy, for they appeared to contradict their teaching of the Scriptures and their conceptions concerning the Messiah's coming. In 1897 the executive committee of the Association of German Rabbis declared:

> 1. The efforts of so-called Zionists to found a Jewish National State in Palestine contradict the messianic promises of Judaism as contained in Holy Writ and in later Jewish sources.
> 2. Judaism obligates its adherents to serve with devotion the Fatherland to which they belong and to further its national interests with all their heart and with all their strength. [Sachar, page 44.]

History has revealed who was right in this controversy. Nazism did not regard the love of these assimilated Jews for German culture, language and ideals, or the loyalty of these orthodox Jews to the German fatherland, as grounds for sparing them from liquidation. Herzl had subtitled *Der Judenstaat* 'An attempt at a modern solution to the Jewish Question', but it was Adolf Hitler's 'Final Solution of the Jewish Question' which provided the dynamic for the last stage in the restoration of Zion. For when in the most horrific circumstances six million Jewish men, women and children had died – for no other reason than that they were Jews – and with no regard for their loyalty and love for the lands of their birth, the remnants of European Jewry realized that Theodor Herzl was right. There was no future for Jews without a Jewish State. The Scripture says: 'the wrath of man shall praise Thee' (Psalm 76:10, NASB), and God overruled the wickedness and bestiality of demonized Nazis to bring about the fulfilment of his prophetic word.

Jeremiah prophesied:

> Hear the word of the Lord, O ye nations, and declare it in the isles afar off; and say, He that scattered Israel will gather him, and keep him, as a shepherd doth his flock. For the Lord hath ransomed Jacob, and redeemed him from the hand of him that was stronger than he. And they shall come and sing in the height of Zion ... for I will turn their mourning into joy. Thus saith the Lord: A voice is heard in Ramah, lamentation, and bitter weeping, Rachel weeping for her children; she refuseth to be comforted for her children, because they are not. Thus saith the Lord: Refrain thy voice from weeping, and thine eyes from tears: for ... they shall come again from the land of the enemy. And there is hope for thy latter end, saith the Lord: and thy children shall come again to their own border. (Jeremiah 31:10-12, 13, 15-17, RV).

The famous rabbi Isaac Luria, known to most Jews as the Ari, the Kabbalist leader in the 16th century, once said to his disciple Abraham Berukim, 'Go up to Jerusalem and pray before the Western Wall and you will be found worthy to see the Divine Presence.' The disciple went to the Wall and uttered fervent prayers and supplications. After a while he saw a shape on the wall, the shape of a woman dressed in black. Shocked, he fell on his face and into a deep sleep. In a dream he saw the Divine Presence, who said, 'Be comforted, My son Abraham, for there is hope for thy future ... and thy children shall return to their own border.'

Whether the story is historical or legendary, it expresses a truth based on Jeremiah's prophecy: in the end the Jewish people would come back to their own borders and 'sing in the height of Zion'. Their long night of mourning and sorrow would be over. It has come to pass. In spite of every attempt to assimilate them or to eradicate them, in spite of their children 'who are not', they have come back from the land of the enemy to their own country.

Zionism is a strange mixture of agnosticism and faith. So many Zionists have not been orthodox in their religious outlook. Indeed, in their view of the Scriptures most would be termed liberal. Some, in fact, were atheists, and many agnostics. They present to us a paradox, for in some strange way, they have felt compelled to engrave on the foundation stones or in the entrance halls, or on plaques in the central squares of rebuilt cities, the ancient prophetic Scriptures which have been so obviously fulfilled. It is this deep spiritual awareness and consciousness within the Jewish people, often masked by agnosticism, that will one day ignite into dynamic faith. It will be the sovereign work of God himself.

Even the official emblem of the State of Israel, the seven branched lampstand (the Menorah), with the two olive branches, one on either side, illustrates this point. It was taken from Zechariah 4. There is a Jewish tradition that when Zechariah saw the lampstand alight, he saw in the flame of each of the seven lamps one Hebrew word of Zechariah 4:6 'Not by might, nor by power, but by my spirit'. In Hebrew this sentence consists of seven words. The re-establishment of the State of Israel was not by human might or power. The only adequate answer seems to be that it was the work of the Holy Spirit.

Furthermore, it is significant that so many of the early Zionists spoke of something infinitely greater than themselves or their work leading them; of being aware of an irresistible destiny in what they did; of being introduced into a mind and a power not their own. They speak of the way Zionism came to them as something like 'the heavens opening', of it 'filling them utterly', of their being swept along by some huge tide of destiny. It seems to me that it was the hand of God which was upon them, although they did not know it.

On the 10th November 1975 the United Nations General Assembly resolved by a two-thirds majority that Zionism was a form of racism and racial discrimination. Israel was a 'racist regime in occupied Palestine'. It is incomprehensible how every other movement for national liberation can be recognized and even applauded, except the Jewish. Zionism enshrines the national aspirations of the Jewish people. It is the expression of the long Jewish struggle for national liberation and dignity. As such it is wholly legitimate and worthy of the recognition and respect of all honourable nations and people. There are genuine problems which have to be solved, but to deny a people 4,000 years old what is allowed to so many others seems a classic example of discrimination.

Moreover, we must ask ourselves what alternative the Jewish people has to the State of Israel. The bloodied centuries have proved that there is no safety for the Jew where there is no sovereign Jewish State. The Gentile nations, the so-called 'Christian' nations foremost among them, have made it starkly clear. By their treatment of the Jew over long years, culminating in the horrors of this century, they have themselves provided the justification for the Jewish State. They branded the Jew as the 'parasitic middleman', the 'money-lender', the 'exploiter of wealth', yet they made the Jew such, by taking away, for instance, his rights to farm land, or to belong to craftsmen's guilds, or to enter the professions, allowing him only to handle money. They complained of his 'unhealthy clannishness' and yet they herded him into unhygienic ghettos, refusing to allow him to live where he wished. They accused him of his poverty and at the same time of his wealth, of his intelligence and shrewdness and at the same time of his superstitious practices. They hounded him, repressed him, beat him, used him and robbed him, and, when he became a shadow of himself, a sad figure with haunted eyes, they hated him the more. They have ensured that there was no alternative to the Jewish State, and when at length it came to pass, they described it as 'racism and racial discrimination'.

When we take into account the fact that the Jewish people has been scattered to the ends of the earth and have survived the long history of violent persecution, the bigoted antagonism towards them, the many repressive limitations placed upon their life, and the ferocious attempts to liquidate them, culminating in the holocaust of 1939-45, we can only recognize that there is more to the re-creation of the State of Israel than flesh and blood. It is not simply the result of a nationalist movement called Zionism, nor the fruit of political agitation. The hand of God is behind it.

Furthermore, the history of Israel since the regaining of sovereignty and statehood on the 14th May 1948 provides more evidence for this. In four wars, faced with colossal problems, this little nation has triumphed. Again and again the world has held its breath, believing that each war would spell the end of Israel, but it has not. Instead, it has proved a further stage in the 'building up of Zion'. God has made the outcasts a strong nation.

The apostle Paul, inspired by the Spirit, wrote:

> I would not, brethren, have you ignorant of this mystery, lest ye be wise in your own conceits, that a hardening in part hath befallen Israel, until the fulness of the Gentiles be come in; and so all Israel shall be saved: even as it is written, There shall come out of Zion the Deliverer; he shall turn away ungodliness from Jacob: And this is my covenant unto them, when I shall take away their sins. (Romans 11:25-27, RV.)

The apostle was quoting Isaiah 59:20, which in our Old Testament reads:

> And a redeemer shall come to Zion, and unto them that turn from transgression in Jacob, saith the Lord. (RV)

(Paul was in fact quoting the Septuagint version, the

Greek translation of the Old Testament, commonly used by the early church. Hence the difference in wording.) It is true that the Redeemer did come to Zion and did come to those among the Jewish people who turned from transgression. The Septuagint quotation which Paul uses in this passage points to the restoration of the Jewish people: 'There shall come *out of Zion* the Deliverer.' It is as if it suggests that the person and work of the Lord Jesus encompasses the complete history of the Jewish people in this age – not only the coming of the Messiah and the saving of a godly Jewish remnant at the beginning of the age, but also the final ingathering of Jewish people at its end. So shall all Israel be saved.

The Lord said through Jeremiah:

> For I will restore health to you, and your wounds I will heal ... because they have called you an outcast: 'It is Zion, for whom no one cares!' (Jeremiah 30:17, RSV).

This prophecy the Lord has fulfilled, and will fulfil on every level, spiritual and earthly. Since 'no one' cared for the Jewish people, God himself has restored health to them, and is healing them of their wounds; he has made the outcasts a strong nation, and will continue to do so. He is their Guardian and Protector, and finally will reveal himself as their Everlasting Redeemer.

CHAPTER 8

THE BATTLE FOR ISRAEL WON

The presence of Israel on the contemporary world scene is a miracle of no mean order. Their survival as a people, their return to the promised land, the rebirth of Hebrew and the re-creation and triumph of the new and tiny Jewish State, surrounded as it is by rabid hostility, is evidence enough. But when we add to all that the prophetic word of God uttered thousands of years ago by men inspired through the Holy Spirit, we enter a new dimension in our understanding. Through this one small nation, the living God is speaking to the nations of the world. He has made every aspect of Israel's story unique, so that the message is clear and cannot easily be explained away.

Seventy years ago Palestine was a province in the great Ottoman empire, an empire which had lasted for some 400 years. There seemed little likelihood of its disappearing, still less of its permitting a Jewish State to be set up within its borders. The Balfour Declaration of 1917 would have been considered an impossibility. Even thirty-five years ago there was no Israel and no Jewish State. Indeed, the news of the mass destruction of European Jewry was only then beginning to filter through to the free world and the mammoth proportions of that disaster were being only dimly recognized. It was enough, however, to make any serious or realistic thought of a renewed Jewish State on their own ancestral soil appear an absurdity.

Today no one doubts the existence of Israel. She stands firmly at the heart of world politics and debate. She may be a small nation, with no more than 3,500,000 people in a territory less than the size of Portugal or the state of Indiana in the USA, but her significance and importance are out of all proportion to her size.

I have often thought that if the Welsh people had been exiled from Wales and dispersed among the nations of the earth; if Welsh had ceased to be the spoken language of home and hearth for 2,000 years, being used only as the sacred language of worship and hymn-singing in the chapel; and then if after 2,000 years they had been brought back to their original land, their sovereignty restored and their statehood renewed; if reborn Welsh had become again the spoken language of the whole nation; and, most remarkably of all, if God had prophesied in Welsh thousands of years before that they would be exiled but would finally return home again; then the whole world would surely marvel at the Welsh and consider their renewed statehood miraculous. Yet this is precisely what has happened to the Jewish people.

The history of this nation is the story of conflict. From the day their history began, some 4,000 years ago, they have had to fight for their survival, and it has always been the battle of the few against the many. The story of David and Goliath is the story of Jewish history from its beginnings until today. Yitzak Rabin, the former Israeli Prime Minister, commenting on the great Entebbe rescue, said:

> No other people in history has been so compelled by circumstances to secure its own self-protection – from the time that Moses rescued his fellow-Jews from the Egyptian whip to the time when the Israel Defence Forces rescued their fellow Jews from Entebbe.

All the great powers of the ancient world – Egypt, Assyria, Babylon, Greece, Rome – all have sought to swallow up Israel, to subject her people to themselves, to their own religion and culture; either to assimilate them or to destroy them. The Psalmist accurately describes the main thrust and purpose of this opposition and antagonism:

> Behold, Thine enemies make an uproar; and those who hate Thee have exalted themselves. They make shrewd plans

> against Thy people, and conspire together against Thy treasured ones. They have said, "Come, and let us wipe them out as a nation; that the name of Israel be remembered no more". For they have conspired together with one mind; against thee do they make a covenant. (Psalm 83:2-5, NASB.)

It was as if the powers of darkness, dimly recognizing the purpose of God, were bent on the destruction of this people.

Nor did the attempt to destroy them cease with their fall in A.D. 70. In the long years of their dispersion, the battle to assimilate or to eradicate them continued. For 1900 years the battle has raged, and the Jewish people have fought constantly for their survival. At times it must have seemed to them a hopeless fight; that the powerful forces arrayed against them must win. Those forces, energized by spiritual beings, have not won the battle for the simple reason that God was in it. Even the British empire, at first the initiator and protector of a 'Jewish homeland' in Palestine, and then finally the great antagonist of it, wearily gave up the fight in 1947, and began its wane. The purpose of God was to be neither frustrated nor hindered, and in 1948 Israel became a fact of modern history.

I do not need to point out that the conflict has not ended with the regaining of their sovereignty in their own land. It has continued bitterly for the last thirty years, and it is not likely to cease until the Messiah comes. Indeed, all the final battles of world history as predicted in the Bible are related to this nation and its land. Such are the battles prophesied by Zechariah:

> It shall come to pass in that day, that I will make Jerusalem a burdensome stone for all the peoples; all that burden themselves with it shall be sore wounded; and all the nations of the earth shall be gathered together against it .... And it shall come to pass in that day, that I will seek to destroy all the nations that come against Jerusalem. (Zechariah 12:3, 9, RV.)

Such also are the Gog and Magog war prophesied in Ezekiel 38 – 39, and the great final battle of Armageddon in Revelation 16:13-16. If anything, as the end of the age approaches, the struggle will become more intense, more fierce, and more universal.

It is therefore important for us to recognize that God is behind these battles over Israel. Note carefully Zechariah 12:2, 3, 9–

> *I will make* Jerusalem a cup of reeling unto all the peoples round about ... *I will make* Jerusalem a burdensome stone for all the peoples ... in that day ... *I will seek to destroy* all the nations that come against Jerusalem. (RV)

And again in Zechariah 14:2–

> For *I will gather* all nations against Jerusalem to battle. (RV)

In Ezekiel 39:2, speaking about the armies of Gog of the land of Magog, the Lord says:

> *I will turn thee about*, and *will lead thee on*, and *will cause thee to come up* from the uttermost parts of the north; and *I will bring thee* upon the mountains of Israel. (RV)

All this is of the highest significance. It reveals that the Lord is using Israel to demonstrate that he governs all history according to his own purpose and end, determining the rise and fall of empires, the course of nations, and the duration of political systems and ideologies. Israel is no political accident but evidence to the nations that God is true, that his word is accurate, reliable and relevant. The Lord intends to vindicate himself, his authority and his word, in a manner which leaves the nations of the world without excuse. He will use Israel as the means to draw them out and confound them and, finally, to shatter them. In this small land the nations will come up against something invincible, indestructible and immovable. Their vast military might will not be able to save them, nor their huge superiority in numbers. They will all break themselves upon her.

In Ezekiel 38:16, 23, God says:

> It will come about in the last days that I shall bring you against My land, *in order that the nations may know Me when I shall be sanctified through you before their eyes, O Gog*.... And I shall magnify Myself, sanctify Myself, and make Myself known in the sight of many nations; and they will know that I am the Lord. (NASB)

Then the Lord explains how he will use the history, survival and triumph of the Jewish people to reveal himself to the nations:

> And I shall set My glory among the nations; and all the nations will see My judgement which I have executed, and My hand which I have laid on them. And the house of Israel will know that I am the Lord their God from that day onward. And the nations will know that the house of Israel went into exile for their iniquity because they acted treacherously against Me, and I hid My face from them; so I gave them into the hand of their adversaries, and all of them fell by the sword .... Therefore thus says the Lord God, "Now I shall restore the fortunes of Jacob, and have mercy on the whole house of Israel; and I shall be jealous for My holy name .... When I bring them back from the peoples and gather them from the lands of their enemies, then I shall be sanctified through them in the sight of the many nations. Then they will know that I am the Lord their God because I made them go into exile among the nations, and then gathered them again to their own land; and I will leave none of them there any longer. And I will not hide My face from them any longer, for I shall have poured out My Spirit on the house of Israel," declares the Lord God. (Ezekiel 39:21-23, 25, 27-29, NASB.)

The Lord scattered his people into all the earth, as a sign of what happens when they reject the Prince of Peace and transgress the law of God. The whole world has known the story. Then, because 'the gifts and the calling of God are irrevocable', he gathers them back in the sight of all the nations. He draws them back in unbelief, spiritually blind to the Messiah, fulfilling his word:

> I will bring the blind by a way that they know not; in paths that they know not will I lead them: I will make darkness light before them, and crooked places straight. These things will I do, and I will not forsake them. (Isaiah 42:16, RV).

They have indeed come back, and planted again the vineyards on the arid hills, and turned malarial swamp-lands into fields and orchards and gardens; they have rebuilt the ruined ancient cities, and have triumphed in spite of war and all the odds arrayed against them. Through this physical fulfilment of his word, God is demonstrating to the nations that there is a living God and that his word is truth, and that, in the end, light will gloriously overcome the darkness. It is precisely this truth that the Psalmist expresses: 'Thou shalt arise, and have mercy upon Zion: for it is time to have pity upon her, yea, the set time is come .... *So the nations shall fear the name of the Lord, and all the kings of the earth thy glory.* (Psalm 102:13, 15 RV).

Another ancient prophecy has its literal fulfilment in the story of modern Israel:

> But Zion said, "The Lord has forsaken me, and the Lord has forgotten me." "Can a woman forget her nursing child, and have no compassion on the son of her womb? Even these may forget, but I will not forget you." ... "Your builders hurry; your destroyers and devastators will depart from you." ... "For your waste and desolate places, and your destroyed land – surely now you will be too cramped for the inhabitants, and those who swallowed you will be far away. The children of whom you were bereaved will yet say in your ears, 'The place is too cramped for me; make room for me that I may live here.' Then you will say in your heart, 'Who has begotten these for me, since I have been bereaved of my children, and am barren, an exile and a wanderer? And who has reared these? Behold, I was left alone; from where did these come?'"
>
> Thus says the Lord God, "Behold, I will lift up My hand to the nations, and set up My standard to the peoples; and they will bring your sons in their bosom, and your daughters will be carried on their shoulders." ... "Can the prey be taken from the mighty man, or the captives of a tyrant be rescued?"

> Surely, thus says the Lord, "Even the captives of the mighty man will be taken away, and the prey of the tyrant will be rescued; for I will contend with the one who contends with you, and I will save your sons." (From Isaiah 49:14-25 NASB.)

Nevertheless, it will not only be through the physical survival and triumph of Israel in the wars forced upon her by hostile forces that the Lord will demonstrate his power. The spiritual blindness of the Jewish people will be turned into clear and radiant sight. God will use the national mourning predicted in Zechariah 12:10-14 as a further means of speaking to the nations. That mourning over the way in which the Lord Jesus was crucified will be turned into spiritual awakening and salvation, sublime in its consequences. It will be for the redeemed 'life from the dead' and for the nations the last opportunity to turn in repentance to God and to his Messiah, Jesus.

The threat to Israel, however, is not only from without and it would be well to draw attention to this fact. The enemy of God has worked, and is working ceaselessly to destroy her from within. By creating and exploiting faction and dissension, by using the national tendency to hold and express strong opinion, and by working through unrighteousness and immorality, the powers of darkness are seeking to achieve what they have been unable to achieve by war and terrorism.

Anyone acquainted with modern Israel knows that the nation is not made up of saints, that miracles are not worked in every Israeli household, and that Israeli attitudes and actions are not unfailingly right. There is a seamy side to Israeli life, and for those who deeply love Israel that is a cause for genuine concern and grief. It would be stupid to claim that every action of successive Israeli governments has expressed the mind of God, and been right, just and pure. Every Israeli government is human and as subject to error as any other human government. If we judged Israeli society and life by the word of God, there is much within it that we could only describe as sinful. Relatively speaking there is the same kind of racketeering, immorality and selfishness as found in any other nation. In the last few years there has been a concerted attempt by the Israeli authorities to deal with the 'Mafia' type underground rackets and the tentacles of corruption in national life. The evil is there, although it may be checked at present. Even if we were to apply to Israel only the burden of Micah 6:8 the need for repentance is clear:

> He hath shewed thee, O man, what is good; and what doth the Lord require of thee, but to do justly, and to love mercy, and to walk humbly with thy God? (RV)

The Israelis are not totally unaware of this need, for a frequent complaint is that contemporary life does not match the idealism and vision of the early founding fathers, nor does the national character match that envisaged by the early Zionists.

Israel as a nation is unique, yet she is very much like other nations when it comes to a propensity for sin, and for things which mar and spoil life. The divine call to repentance is, therefore, paramount, and the love of God is cornering the Jewish people step by step. There will be no escape from their salvation and destiny, which will be preceded by divinely granted repentance.

Romans 11:26 states that 'there shall come out of Zion the deliverer; he shall turn away ungodliness from Jacob' (RV). This is the Septuagint translation of Isaiah 59:20: 'A redeemer shall come to Zion, and unto them that turn from transgression in Jacob' (RV). The Redeemer and Deliverer who 'turns away ungodliness in Jacob' does it in, and through, those who, by his grace alone, 'turn from transgression in Jacob'. The preceding and oft-quoted statement, 'so all Israel shall be saved', must be read and understood in this light. Those who constitute 'all Israel' are those who have 'turned from transgression in Jacob' and have been saved through the finished work of the

Messiah. 'All Israel' does not mean that every Jew will automatically be saved, any more than the phrase 'the fullness of the Gentiles' (Romans 11:25) means that every Gentile will automatically be saved. All those whom God saves, who turn from transgression in Jacob to him through the Messiah Jesus, constitute the true Israel of God. This 'turning to him' is surely that which is predicted in Zechariah 12:10-14, and will be a repentance and a godly sorrow which will lead to salvation. Thus God will use not only the hostile nations and forces surrounding Israel, but he will also use her inner need and disillusionment with herself, to lead her to his salvation.

Furthermore, the future of this nation is unique. Peoples have come and gone, empires have risen and fallen, but the nation of Israel goes on. Of the future of many nations and peoples we have no specific prophetic word, except that finally they will all come under the judgement of God. But of Israel it is said by the Lord:

> In the last days it shall come to pass, that the mountain of the house of the Lord shall be established in the top of the mountains, and it shall be exalted above the hills; and people shall flow unto it. And many nations shall come, and say, Come, and let us go up to the mountain of the Lord, and to the house of the God of Jacob; and he will teach us of his ways, and we will walk in his paths: for the law shall go forth of Zion, and the word of the Lord from Jerusalem. And he shall judge among many people, and rebuke strong nations afar off; and they shall beat their swords into plowshares, and their spears into pruninghooks: nation shall not lift up a sword against nation, neither shall they learn war any more. But they shall sit every man under his vine and under his fig tree; and none shall make them afraid: for the mouth of the Lord of hosts hath spoken it. (Micah 4:1-4, AV.)

That will be like a day of radiant sunshine after a dark and seemingly endless night, like a day of clear shining after the tempestuous rain of sorrow and tribulation. The former things of mourning, crying and pain will have passed away for ever, and death will be no more. The purpose of God for Zion, for his elect and redeemed people, will have finally been realized, and the whole Israel of God will have been saved.

The uniqueness of Israel as a nation is summed up in the words of the Lord in Jeremiah 31:35-37 –

> Thus saith the Lord, which giveth the sun for a light by day, and the ordinances of the moon and of the stars for a light by night, which stirreth up the sea, that the waves thereof roar; the Lord of hosts is his name: If these ordinances depart from before me, saith the Lord, then the seed of Israel also shall *cease from being a nation* before me for ever. Thus saith the Lord: If heaven above can be measured, and the foundations of the earth searched out beneath, then will I also cast off all the seed of Israel for all that they have done, saith the Lord. (RV)

It is right to take these words as being fulfilled in that spiritual Israel and Zion which is the church of God: however, they also have their literal fulfilment in the Jewish people. The 'seed of Israel' has never ceased from being a nation, because of the faithfulness of God himself. There is no other explanation. It is a further illustration of the total reliability and accuracy of even the most seemingly obscure passages of prophetic Scripture in relation to Israel and her place in the purpose of God. In the words of King David:

> For thy word's sake, and according to thine own heart, hast thou wrought all this greatness, to make thy servant know it. Wherefore thou art great, O Lord God: for there is none like thee, neither is there any God beside thee, according to all that we have heard with our ears. And what one nation in the earth is like thy people, even like Israel ...? (2 Samuel 7:21-23, RV.)

PART III

THE UNIQUENESS OF THE CITY

This is Jerusalem; I have set her in the centre of the nations, with countries round about her.

Ezekiel 5:5 (RSV)

CHAPTER 1

THIS IS JERUSALEM

Some cities have an outward beauty, plastic and cosmetic. It is real but superficial and consists of those tangible things which make an immediate impact upon our senses. Jerusalem's beauty is not of that order. It is true that she has her own physical beauty. That kind of beauty can be seen, for instance, in her setting; located amongst mountains, she presents a breathtaking view. It can be seen at sunset when the colour of her stone glows with ethereal light, or when the first rays of the rising sun transform her stones into the proverbial 'Golden City'. It can also be seen in her ancient buildings, lanes and souks which breathe the atmosphere of an historic past.

Yet Jerusalem's essential beauty does not consist of these things. There are other cities which far exceed Jerusalem in that kind of beauty, cities which are more elegant and sophisticated, more commercially attractive and wealth-inducing, more grand in their planning concepts and design. Paris with its elegance and sophistication, Rome with its history and ingrained atmosphere of religion, New York with its incredible air of excitement and business, cannot be compared with Jerusalem. London may be a world centre of finance and power, with a sense of enduring solidity, but it cannot be compared with Jerusalem. Jerusalem is unique amongst the cities of the world, for her beauty is the beauty of a spiritual ideal, a thought out of the mind of God, crystallized in stone and history.

Jerusalem today is one of the oldest continuously inhabited cities in the world, built on four thousand years of history. At some places within her walls the bed-rock lies ninety feet below the present surface, and today's buildings and lanes rest on the destruction of the past. Layer upon layer of history lie beneath her, reaching back into the mists of antiquity. On every level one finds the evidence of her long story – Jebusite, Jewish, Roman, Byzantine, Arab, Crusader, Turkish. Even above the surface, it is there for those who have eyes to see – great Herodian blocks of stone, Byzantine arches, Hellenic pillars, Arab motifs, Crusader vaults, Jebusite stones, Turkish walls.

Jerusalem is first mentioned in the Bible in Genesis 14:18, where she is called 'Salem', which means 'Peace':

> Melchizedek king of Salem brought forth bread and wine: and he was priest of God Most High. (RV)

This would have been about the 19th century B.C. She is also mentioned in Egyptian execration texts of the 19th-18th century B.C. From the way she is mentioned in certain Scriptures, such as Joshua 15:63 or Judges 1:21, we know that in the 14th century B.C. she was a Jebusite city. We find confirmation for this in the Tel el Amarna letters of that period. She was still a Jebusite city when King David captured her in the 10th century B.C. (2 Samuel 5:6-9). David made her the capital of a united Israel, and from that day she became the spiritual centre of the children of Israel and of the Jewish people. It was David who became the inspiration under God for the building of the Temple on Mount Moriah in Jerusalem, though it was Solomon, his son, who translated the vision into practical reality and built it there. From that time Jerusalem was not only the political capital but the focal point of a spiritual and eternal reality.

Jerusalem has known more devastation than most other cities, both from wars and from earthquakes. In the 2,565 years between 587 B.C. and A.D. 1978 she was conquered more than twenty times. Yet today Jerusalem still stands more or less where she has ever stood. Her centre has moved a little northwards, but her present boundaries include the entire area of the ancient city at every phase of her history.

The city of Jerusalem is unique because of the way she was selected to be the capital of the nation. Most capital cities of the world have become capitals because of their situation. They are on important trade-routes or major cross-roads, possess large natural harbours, or are beside navigable rivers. They have been chosen because they are commercially viable and attractive centres, naturally drawing trade to themselves and providing a good venue for business. Jerusalem never had any of these natural advantages. She was not situated on any major cross-roads, or indeed on any important trade-routes. The major highways and trade-routes of antiquity ran either to her east or to her west. To her east, the King's Highway linked Arabia with Damascus; to her west, the Way of the Sea connected Egypt with Damascus, Mesopotamia and Asia Minor.

Jerusalem had no natural harbour; she was situated neither on the coast, nor on any river, navigable or otherwise. Indeed Jerusalem had no major water supply other than the Gihon Spring, and that was originally outside the city walls. It was King Hezekiah who recognized the serious threat which this represented to Jerusalem's security and survival, and took action which has amazed engineers ever since. He had a tunnel 1,777 feet long hewn out of the solid rock which brought the waters of Gihon within the city, to the Pool of Siloam (2 Kings 20:20). This matter of its water supply must surely make Jerusalem unique. One may well ask whether there has ever been another capital city with so precarious a water supply as Jerusalem had!

Jerusalem became the capital of the nation because God chose her. In Deuteronomy 12:5,13-14, God had said:

> But unto the place which the Lord your God shall choose out of all your tribes to put his name there, even unto his

> habitation shall ye seek, and thither thou shalt come .... Take heed to thyself that thou offer not thy burnt offerings in every place that thou seest: but in the place which the Lord shall choose in one of thy tribes, there thou shalt offer thy burnt offerings, and there thou shalt do all that I command thee. (RV)

This place which the Lord chose was Jerusalem. As the Psalmist says:

> The Lord hath chosen Zion; he hath desired it for his habitation. This is my resting place for ever: here will I dwell; for I have desired it. (Psalm 132:13-14, RV.)

Jerusalem is therefore unique among the cities of the world. She was not chosen for natural advantages, for she had none; she was chosen for spiritual reasons alone.

The divine choice of Jerusalem not only makes her a unique city, but has also made her the focal point of enduring and violent conflict. For she was not chosen by God merely to be the physical capital of an earthly nation, but to embody and represent a spiritual ideal. She has not, therefore, been merely the bone of contention between nations, the flashpoint of clashing national and religious interests. Behind all the fighting, devastation and sorrow lie spiritual forces bent on destroying even the earthly symbol of God's eternal purpose and calling.

The history of Jerusalem has been the history of battles. Her story is the story of triumph and achievement, of suffering and sorrow. It is a chronicle of great saintliness and of deep sinfulness; of enduring loyalty and of dark treachery; of triumphant faith and devastating defeat. Her history is aptly summed up in an ancient Jewish saying: 'Ten measures of suffering were sent by God upon the world, and nine of them fell upon Jerusalem.' The story of Jerusalem is the evidence that the narrow way of God is fraught with suffering and tribulation. She is a microcosm of every believer's life, an illustration of the truth that we enter the kingdom of God through much tribulation; she is a cameo in which we see depicted the great affliction and battle involved in the building up of that spiritual Zion which is the church. The list of the nations and peoples who have fought for Jerusalem is almost endless: Assyrians, Egyptians, Babylonians, Greeks, Romans, Byzantines, Persians, Arabs, Crusaders, Tartars, Mamelukes, Turks, Britons, Jordanians.

Nor is the story finished. The word of God predicts that there will be many more battles over Jerusalem. In Zechariah 12:2-3 the Lord says:

> Behold, I will make Jerusalem a cup of reeling unto all the peoples round about, and upon Judah also shall it be in the siege against Jerusalem. And it shall come to pass in that day, that I will make Jerusalem a burdensome stone for all the peoples; all that burden themselves with it shall be sore wounded; and all the nations of the earth shall be gathered together against it; (RV)

and in verse 9 he says:

> It shall come to pass in that day, that I will seek to destroy all the nations that come against Jerusalem; (RV)

and again, in Zechariah 14:2 –

> I will gather all nations against Jerusalem to battle. (RV)

Zechariah's words are relevant to this generation: 'A cup of reeling unto all the peoples round about', that is, a drugged cup impairing normal faculties; and 'a burdensome stone for all the peoples', that is, a heavy stone rupturing those who lift it. It is precisely what she has become and is becoming. Everyone who meddles and interferes with Jerusalem's destiny will be 'sore wounded'. It does not matter whether it is the great superpowers, the United Nations, or any particular nation, all will come to grief if they 'burden themselves' with Jerusalem.

Zechariah 12:6 is also remarkable. In the prediction of future battles over Jerusalem, the Lord says:

> ... and Jerusalem shall yet again dwell in her own place, even in Jerusalem. (RV)

In Monsignor Knox's translation, it reads:

> Jerusalem shall stand, when all is over, where Jerusalem stood.

It is a fact that, in spite of all the conflict and its many destructions, Jerusalem stands today where Jerusalem has ever stood through the years. Nineveh and Ur and Babylon have come and gone, Thebes and Raamses have come and gone, but Jerusalem remains. One day Washington will fall, as will Moscow, Peking and London. All the great cities of the world will pass away, except Jerusalem.

This Jerusalem is age-abiding, if not eternal. Even in the last great battle, we are told that when the city is taken, and half her population taken into captivity,

> then shall the Lord go forth, and fight against those nations, as when he fought in the day of battle. And his feet shall stand in that day upon the mount of Olives, which is before Jerusalem on the east. (Zechariah 14:3-4, RV.)

If nothing else makes Jerusalem unique, this does. She will be the first city of the world to receive the Messiah, for God has stated that his blessed and pierced feet will stand again within her walls. The Lord Jesus loved Jerusalem deeply. It was not only the material city, but what she represented and embodied of his Father's purpose and design. He referred to her as 'Jerusalem ... the city of the great King' (Matthew 5:35). She was his city, the earthly city as well as the heavenly Jerusalem. A week before his death, as he came over the brow of the Mount of Olives from Bethany and saw the whole city lying before him, he wept over her:

> If you had known in this day, even you, the things which make for peace! But now they have been hidden from your eyes. For the days shall come upon you when your enemies will throw up a bank before you, and surround you, and hem you in on every side, and will level you to the ground and your children within you, and they will not leave in you one stone upon another, because you did not recognize the time of your visitation. (Luke 19:42-44, NASB.)

We hear the heartbreak in his voice when, a few days later, after one of the most solemn denunciations he had ever uttered, he said:

> O Jerusalem, Jerusalem, who kills the prophets and stones those who are sent to her! How often I wanted to gather your children together, the way a hen gathers her chicks under her wings, and you were unwilling. (Matthew 23:37, NASB.)

This was the city in which Jesus was crucified and buried; the city in which he arose from the dead and from which he ascended to his Father, there to reign for ever. And it is to this city that he will return with glory and great power. Then the prophecy of Isaiah will be fulfilled:

> And it shall come to pass in the latter days, that the mountain of the Lord's house shall be established in the top of the mountains, and shall be exalted above the hills; and all nations shall flow unto it. And many peoples shall go and say, Come ye, and let us go up to the mountain of the Lord, to the house of the God of Jacob; and he will teach us of his ways, and we will walk in his paths: for out of Zion shall go forth the law, and the word of the Lord from Jerusalem. And he shall judge between the nations, and shall reprove many peoples: and they shall beat their swords into plowshares, and their spears into pruninghooks: nation shall not lift up sword against nation, neither shall they learn war any more. (Isaiah 2:2-4, RV.)

Then, and only then, will the long travail of Jerusalem be over, and God's purpose concerning her be fulfilled.

There is no other city in the world to be compared with Jerusalem. She began as the choice of God; she has been preserved through his grace; and she will end in his glory. Jerusalem is unique.

CHAPTER 2

IF I FORGET THEE, O JERUSALEM

Through the centuries Jerusalem has drawn to herself people of greatly diverse race, nationality and religion. She has had a mysterious and magnetic attraction for them. Her attraction for the Babylonian, the Egyptian, the Persian, the Greek or the Hellenist, and the pagan Roman, was for the most part as a prize of war, or as a subject for colonization. For them she was either another city to be added to an empire, or another city to be subjected to their own culture and religion. For Christian Byzantine and Crusader, for Muslim Arab and Turk, the attraction of Jerusalem was religious. For the true Christian, she was the city where the Lord Jesus died and rose again, and to which he would return; she was the city of the great King. As such she had a compelling attraction. For large sections of Christendom, however, Jerusalem, although held as sacred, was not the *first* city. For the Roman Catholic Church, Rome was *the* city in Christendom; while for the Orthodox Church, Byzantium, later called Constantinople, took precedence. For Islam, Jerusalem was only third in order of sacredness: Mecca came first, and then Medina. Nevertheless, for all of these Jerusalem occupied, and continues to occupy an especial place in their esteem and love.

For the Jew, however, Jerusalem is unique; there is no other city! No matter what sacred association other places have held in Jewish history, Jerusalem occupies a dimension which no other city can share. For the Jew there has never been an alternative to Jerusalem, nor can there be. In his eyes, she remains supreme.

From the time of King David onwards, Jerusalem has

been the national and spiritual centre of the Jewish people. In the 3,000 years since King David's day there has been an unbroken link between the Jewish people and Jerusalem. If at times the link was not physical, it was certainly always spiritual. For even during the periods of exile the Jewish people have never forgotten Jerusalem. Indeed, during those times she has been even more alive in their consciousness and thinking.

Even during the long centuries of the second exile, there have been relatively few years in which Jews have not lived in Jerusalem. The periods when all Jews were officially expelled from Jerusalem were from 587 to 537 B.C. and again in A.D. 135 when Hadrian drove all Jews out of the city and sought to destroy every connection with the Jewish people, renaming the city 'Aelia Capitolina' and forbidding any circumcised person to enter the city. These conditions lasted until the beginning of the Byzantine era, when in A.D. 362 the Roman emperor Julian 'the Apostate' permitted Jews to return to the city. The presence of a Jewish community in Jerusalem was, however, short-lived, and they were again expelled until 438 when the empress Eudocia allowed them back. In 629 the Jews were once more expelled, but returned with the Arab conquest nine years later. In 1099 the Crusaders captured the city and massacred the whole Jewish community, men, women and children, leaving virtually no Jews in the city for almost two centuries.

The last attempt to expel the Jews from Jerusalem was in 1948. In fact, the Jordanian authorities said that Jews who wished to remain in the Old Jewish Quarter of the city could do so, but it became quite clear, by the way the Arabs systematically destroyed the whole Jewish Quarter, that it would be impossible for any Jew to stay. The whole community of some 1200 people left, and for nineteen years there were no Jews in the Old City of Jerusalem, though the new western city remained in Israeli hands. For nineteen years, however, no Jew was permitted to go to the Western Wall, or to visit either the ancient synagogues of the Jewish Quarter or the Jewish tombs on the Mount of Olives. During those years, fifty-eight synagogues, some of them of great antiquity, were destroyed or desecrated. Some of those that were not destroyed were used as stables, hen coops and even toilets. Of the 50,000 tombstones on the Mount of Olives, 38,000 were torn up or broken. All this ended in 1967 with the lightning victory of the Israeli defence forces and the re-unification of Jerusalem.

The evidence for the continued connection with Jerusalem during the long years of the second exile is impressive. In AD 333, the Pilgrim of Bordeaux wrote:

> At the side of the Sanctuary, there is a pierced stone. Jews visit there once a year, pour oil over it, lament and weep over it, and tear their garments in token of mourning. Then they return home.

Although Jews were not allowed even to enter the city for most of these years, they were given permission to visit the city once a year on the 9th Av, the anniversary of its destruction in both 587 B.C. and A.D. 70. It was to this occasion that Jerome referred when he wrote in 392:

> On the anniversary of the day when the city fell and was destroyed by the Romans, there are crowds who mourn, old women and old men dressed in tatters and rags, and from the top of the Mount of Olives this throng laments over the destruction of its Sanctuary. Still their eyes flow with tears, still their hands tremble and their hair is dishevelled, but already the guard demands his pay for their right to weep.

There is a story told of Napoleon that he passed a crowded synagogue on the 9th Av and, arrested by the noise of obvious weeping and sorrow, he asked what it meant. He was told that they were weeping in the synagogue for their country and their sanctuary which had been destroyed some 1800 years before. Napoleon, deeply moved, observed that 'a people which weeps and mourns for the loss of its homeland 1800 years ago and does not forget –

such a people will never be destroyed. Such a people can rest assured that its homeland will be returned to it.'

In A.D. 640 the Caliph Omar allowed seventy families to live near the Western Wall. In 691, the Caliph Abd el Malik, who built the Dome of the Rock on the site of the Temple, gave Jewish families hereditary rights to be caretakers of the Temple mount.

In 981 Salman, son of Yeruham, a Karaite sage, wrote:

> For 500 years, Jews could not enter Jerusalem without risking their lives .... However, when the Ishmaelite Kingdom [the Arabs] was founded, they were permitted to settle in the city ... but later the Ishmaelites wanted to expel them altogether. [Quoted in Charif and Raz (ed.), *Jerusalem : The Eternal Bond*, page 72.]

In 1165 Rabbi Benjamin of Tudela referred to the wretched condition of the impoverished Jewish community in Jerusalem:

> There is a dyeing plant in Jerusalem which the Jews rent ... they live at the edge of the city, below the House of David ... in caves or hidden hovels and fast every day of their life. [Ibid., page 72.]

In 1267, Nahmanides, one of the greatest Jewish sages, wrote to his son:

> What shall I say of this land? ... The more holy the place the greater the desolation. Jerusalem is the most desolate of all .... There are about 2,000 inhabitants, including about 300 Christians, refugees who escaped the sword of the Sultan; but there are no Jews, for, after the arrival of the Tartars, the Jews fled, and some were killed by the sword. There are now only two brothers, dyers, who buy their dyes from the government. At their place, a quorum of worshippers meets on the Sabbath, and we encouraged them, and found a ruined house, built on pillars, with a beautiful dome, and made it into a synagogue .... People regularly come to Jerusalem, men and women from Damascus and from Aleppo and from all parts of the country, to see the Temple and weep over it. And may

He who deemed us worthy to see Jerusalem in her ruins, grant us to see her rebuilt and restored, and the honour of the Divine Presence returned.

In 1420 Rabbi Simeon Duran reported:

The people of Jerusalem filled the synagogue in Jerusalem all the year round.

In 1491 Martin Kabatnik, a Catholic monk, wrote:

There are but few Christians but there are many Jews. A Jew whose house collapses is not permitted to build a new one in its place, but must again buy the plot from its owner at a high price. Christians and Jews go about Jerusalem dressed as would beggars in our country. They are not permitted to wear good coats. But, in spite of all the troubles and the oppression that they suffer at the hand of the non-Jews, the Jews refuse to leave the place. [Charif and Raz, page 81.]

In 1610 George Sandys, an English traveller, wrote of his visit to Jerusalem:

Here be also some Jews, yet inherit they no part of the land, but in their own country do live as aliens. A people scattered throughout the whole world, and hated by those amongst whom they live; yet suffered as a necessary mischief ... many of them have I seen abused, some of them beaten, yet never saw I a Jew with an angry countenance.

In 1751 Friedrich Hasselkvist, a Swedish doctor and botanist, wrote:

The populace of Jerusalem includes about 20,000 Jews. Most of them are paupers and have no source of livelihood. [Charif and Raz, page 84.]

In 1824 Rabbi David Hillel wrote:

Jerusalem has more than 3,000 Jewish families – native-born and those who have come from all parts of the world. [Ibid, page 85.]

This refusal to forget Jerusalem was aptly summed up by W. H. Bartlett in 1844:

> Here then among the ruins of Zion still lingers a remnant of the chosen people – but how changed their circumstances! Instead of the mighty man, and the man of war, the judge and the prophet, and the prudent and the ancient, the captain of fifty, and the honourable man, and the counsellor, and the cunning artificer, and the eloquent orator, we see a depressed body, chiefly of exiles, crouching under general dislike and persecution; yet with inflexible tenacity clinging to the spot which recalls their past greatness, and inspires visionary hopes of future domination. [W.H. Bartlett, *Walks About Jerusalem*, page 188.]

It is striking that when Jerusalem has been in Jewish hands, it has usually tended to prosper, but under foreign rule it has shrunk and decayed. Before its destruction in A.D. 70, Jerusalem had a total population of 200,000. During the emperor Hadrian's rule it became a provincial town. During the Byzantine period (324-614) it had a population of 80,000. After the Arab conquest in 638, it fell to 30,000, and in Crusader times (1099-1291) as low as 3,000. During the Mameluke period (1250-1517) it rose to 30,000 and then dropped to 10,000. During the Ottoman rule (1517-1917) it ranged between 10,000 and 60,000.

It is often forgotten that from 1840 onwards, the Jews constituted the largest of the three communities living in Jerusalem – Muslim, Christian and Jewish. In fact in 1844 they numbered just under half of the population – 7,120 out of 15,510. Commenting on this fact Dr John Kitto wrote in 1847, 'Although we are much in the habit of regarding Jerusalem as a Moslem city, the Moslems do not actually constitute more than one third of the entire population.' In 1876 the Jews numbered 12,000; twenty years later the figure was 28,000. In 1905 they numbered 40,000 out of a population of 60,000; in 1912 45,000 out of 80,000; in 1976 260,000 out of 356,000.

If however, the physical link between the Jewish people and Jerusalem during the last 3,000 years has had its interruptions, the spiritual link has never been broken. It is poignantly expressed in a Psalm written during the first exile:

> By the rivers of Babylon,
> There we sat down and wept,
> When we remembered Zion. . . .
> How can we sing the Lord's song
> In a foreign land?
> If I forget you, O Jerusalem,
> May my right hand forget her skill.
> May my tongue cleave to the roof of my mouth,
> If I do not remember you,
> If I do not exalt Jerusalem
> Above my chief joy.
> (Psalm 137:1, 4-6, NASB.)

These words express the aspiration and feeling of God's people at all times of exile. The more bitter their persecution, the more rejected they were as Jews, the greater the darkness that lay upon them, so the more profound became the yearning for Jerusalem. Jerusalem lived in their hearts as it had never lived in their hearts before, in the long years of Jewish history. It haunted their thoughts, and became the focal point of all their dreams and aspirations. Three times a day they stood, facing towards Jerusalem, and prayed for the day when she would be rebuilt. Jews recited Psalm 137 before every meal on weekdays, and on sabbaths and holy days recited Psalm 126:

> When the Lord turned again the captivity of Zion, we were like unto them that dream. Then was our mouth filled with laughter ... turn again our captivity, O Lord. (RV)

In all festivals and holy days, Jerusalem figured at their heart. It was this vision of a restored Zion, of a rebuilt Jerusalem, which sustained the Jewish people through the long years of their sorrow and suffering. Some cities draw people like a magnet. It may be for religious reasons, such as Rome or Mecca or, in days passed, Lhasa; or because of their beauty, architecture, or culture, like Athens, Prague, Florence or Peking. For the Jew there is but one city, Jerusalem.

Judge Nash wrote in 1844 that 'every attempt to colonize the Jews in other countries has failed – their eye has steadily rested on their beloved Jerusalem'. In 1892, Elhanan Levinski, a Russian Jewish writer, expressed this enduring attachment to Jerusalem when he wrote:

> The land of Israel without Jerusalem is like a body without a soul. In the very name "Jerusalem" there lies concealed something powerful, unknown and mysterious that draws the Jewish heart. [Charif and Raz, page 80.]

Judah haLevi, born in Spain in 1075, and the greatest Jewish poet of the Middle Ages, declared: 'My heart is in the East, and I am in the uttermost West.' In his *Ode to Zion*, composed for the Fast on the 9th Av, when the Jewish people mourn the double anniversary of the destruction of Jerusalem and the Temple by Nebuchadnezzar in 587 B.C. and by Titus in A.D. 70, he wrote:

> Oh, who will lead me on
> To seek the spots where, in far distant years,
> The angels in their glory dawned upon
> Thy messengers and seers!
>
> Oh, who will give me wings
> That I may fly away,
> And there, at rest from all my wanderings,
> The ruins of my heart among thy ruins lay?
>
> I'll bend my face unto thy soil, and hold
> Thy stones as special gold.

He expressed this longing of the Jewish heart for Jerusalem even more beautifully in the words:

> And who shall grant me, on the wings of eagles,
> To rise and seek thee through the years,
> Until I mingle with thy dust beloved
> The waters of my tears?

I seek thee, though thy King be no more in thee,
Though where the balm hath been of old –
Thy Gilead's balm – be poisonous adders lurking,
Wingèd scorpions manifold.

Shall I not to thy very stones be tender?
Shall I not kiss them verily?
Shall not thine earth upon my lips taste sweeter
Than honey unto me?

Legend has it that as he came near to Jerusalem, and knelt in its dust in prayer and worship, an Arab horseman, leaving by one of the city gates, trampled him to death. As he lay dying, the story goes, he recited this poem.

No city in the world has ever meant more to a particular people than Jerusalem has meant to the Jews. Its destruction in A.D. 70 became an anguish of soul which never left them in nearly 2,000 years of exile. Its loss was deeply mourned through those years as if it had taken place only the day before, and its restoration was longed for with consuming emotion, amounting at times to an almost pathological yearning. It was this which led Hanmer Dupuis to write in 1856:

> Jerusalem is the centre around which the Jew builds in airy dreams the mansions of his future greatness. Thither he returns from Spain, Portugal, Germany, Barbary, etc. after all his toilings and all his struggles up the steps of life, to walk the streets of his own happy Zion. [Hanmer L. Dupuis, *The Holy Places* (2 vols).]

Rabbi Samuel ben Samson described the emotion of first seeing the city:

> We arrived at Jerusalem by the western end of the city, rending our garments on beholding it, as it has been ordained that we should do. It was a moment of tenderest emotion, and we wept bitterly, Rabbi Jonathan, the great priest of Lunel, and I.

To many who are not Jews the attraction of Jerusalem is inexplicable. Many are greatly disappointed with its religious commercialism and exploitation, its dirt and dust, its 'baksheesh' atmosphere. Colonel C.R. Conder's description of the city (in *The Latin Kingdom of Jerusalem*, 1897) more nearly expresses their feelings:

> Jerusalem is a very ugly city. It is badly built of mean stone houses poised on the slope of the watershed and seems in instant danger of sliding into the Kedron valley;

or Mark Twain's description in *Innocents Abroad* (1869):

> Rags, wretchedness, poverty and dirt ... Jerusalem is mournful, and dreary and lifeless. I would not desire to live here.

W.H.Bartlett (in *Walks about the City and Environs of Jerusalem*, 1842) said:

> If the traveller can forget that he is treading on the grave of a people from whom his religion has sprung, on the dust of her kings, prophets and holy men, there is certainly no city in the world that he will sooner wish to leave than Jerusalem. Nothing can be more void of interest than her gloomy, half ruinous streets and poverty-stricken bazaars ....

Yet the city described in such terms by Colonel Conder, Mark Twain and W.H. Bartlett is the same city which has so deeply moved others. The explanation is to be found in the words of Elhanan Levinski: 'In the very name "Jerusalem" there lies concealed something powerful, unknown and mysterious which draws the Jewish heart.' All saw the same ruins, the same desolation, the same soil and dust; for some, that was all they saw; for others, the very ruins, the very stones, the very dust held an invincible attraction, because they expressed not only the glory and the sorrow of the past but the certain hope of a glorious future.

The prophet Zechariah prophesied:

> Then the word of the Lord of hosts came saying, "Thus says the Lord of hosts, 'I am exceedingly jealous for Zion, yes, with great wrath I am jealous for her.' Thus says the Lord, 'I will return to Zion and will dwell in the midst of Jerusalem. Then Jerusalem will be called the City of Truth, and the mountain of the Lord of hosts will be called the Holy Mountain.' Thus says the Lord of hosts, 'Old men and old women will again sit in the streets of Jerusalem, each man with his staff in his hand because of age. And the streets of the city will be filled with boys and girls playing in its streets.' Thus says the Lord of hosts, 'If it is too difficult in the sight of the remnant of this people in those days, will it also be too difficult in My sight?' declares the Lord of hosts. Thus says the Lord of hosts, 'Behold, I am going to save My people from the land of the east and from the land of the west; and I will bring them back, and they will live in the midst of Jerusalem, and they will be My people and I will be their God in truth and righteousness.'" (Zechariah 8:1-8, NASB.)

In spite of the fact that for almost a century the Jews had constituted the majority of the population in Jerusalem, it seemed in 1948 as if the Old City of Jerusalem was lost for ever to the Jewish people. Many of the most revered synagogues and *yeshivot* in Judaism were out of their reach. The greatest grief of all, however, was the loss of the Western Wall.

The Western Wall, called by Christians the 'Wailing Wall', is the most revered and treasured place in Judaism. It is the last remaining part of the ancient retaining wall of the second Temple. One cannot fail to be moved by the Western Wall. It seems to represent the history, the sorrow and the aspiration of the Jewish people crystallized in stone. It is as if that wall, scarred with age and with battle, embodies the triumph and the tragedy of the Jewish nation. For this reason many legends have surrounded it.

One legend relates that, when the Temple was being built, the work was divided up among the different sections of the population and the building of this part of the wall was given to the poor. When many years later, the enemy destroyed the Temple, angels spread their wings over this portion of the wall and declared 'this wall, the work of the poor, shall never be destroyed."

Another legend relates that, at midnight on the 9th Av, the anniversary of the destruction of the Temple, a white dove hovers over the wall, moaning mournfully because of its destruction. It is the Spirit of God. Yet another legend relates that on that same night the wall also weeps, joining the people in their mourning over the destruction of the Temple and of the City.

It is true that there are many doves which nest in the crevices of the wall, and some of them are white. It is also true that when there is a night with a heavy dew, condensation can run down the face of the stone. What these legends reveal, however, is the way the Western Wall has become for the Jewish people the symbol of a lost glory and the hope of final redemption. When access to it was denied, during the nineteen years of Jordanian rule, it seemed the cruellest blow of all.

The Lord Jesus had said:

> And they shall fall by the edge of the sword, and shall be led captive into all the nations: and Jerusalem shall be trodden down of the Gentiles, until the times of the Gentiles be fulfilled (Luke 21:24, RV)

In June 1967, in a lightning move by the Israeli Defence Forces, the Jordanian Army was thrown back and Jerusalem was re-united. In a sudden, spontaneous outburst, it seemed as if the whole population of Western Jerusalem poured into the Old City, making for the Western Wall. Some weeks later, speaking at a ceremony at the Hebrew University in Jerusalem, Yitzak Rabin, former Prime Minister of Israel, said:

> The entire nation was exalted and many wept when they heard of the capture of the Old City. Our Sabra youth, and most certainly our soldiers, do not tend to be sentimental and they shrink from any public show of feeling, but the strain of battle, the anxiety which preceded it, and the sense of salvation and of direct confrontation with Jewish history

> itself, cracked the shell of hardness and shyness and released well-springs of emotion and stirrings of the spirit. The paratroopers who conquered the Western Wall, leaned on its stones and wept.

It was for only a few months in the year A.D. 134-135, during the revolt of Bar Kokhba, that Jerusalem was under Jewish control. It is true that when the Persians overthrew the Byzantine rulers in 614 they allowed the Jews to govern the city for three years. It was, however, a form of home rule covering only the city. From the destruction of Jerusalem in A.D. 70, it had never really come under a sovereign Jewish government, and was certainly never the capital of a Jewish State. Jerusalem has been the capital of the nation occupying the land only at those times when the Jewish nation has been sovereign, with the one exception of the Crusader kingdom of 1099-1187. From 1000 to 587 B.C. it was capital of the kingdom; from 515 B.C. to A.D. 70 it was capital of the Jewish State; and from 1948, when Western Jerusalem was declared to be the capital of Israel. At all other times in her long history, Jerusalem was not the capital city but part of empires ruled from distant capitals.

On the 7th June 1967 the miracle happened and the ancient city was re-united with the western city to become the capital of Israel. That day Moshe Dayan, then Minister of Defence, said: 'We earnestly stretch out our hands to our Arab brethren in peace, but we have returned to Jerusalem never to part from her again.' The words of the Lord Jesus were fulfilled: the times of the Gentiles' treading down of Jerusalem were over. Henceforth Jerusalem awaits the final chapter of her long and troubled history.

CHAPTER 3

A TALE OF TWO CITIES

In the Bible two cities are frequently mentioned from the moment they first appear in the divine record. They are Jerusalem and Babylon. Throughout the Bible they are seen in contradistinction to each other. This is not a coincidence, for the Holy Spirit has taken the two cities to symbolize two diametrically opposed principles, one the eternal and the heavenly, and the other the transient and the earthly. One represents man in all his sin and weakness, saved by the grace of God, and brought back to God's original purpose, God becoming his life and all. The other represents fallen man, hopelessly and helplessly self-centred, even in his noblest aspirations and ideals, in bondage to the corrupting influence of his self-seeking. Furthermore, the biblical history of these two cities reveals the antipathy between them: it is the flesh warring against the Spirit, and the Spirit against the flesh. These two principles of life cannot co-exist.

The story of the two cities runs from Genesis, right through the Bible, until it reaches its climax in the final chapters of the last book, Revelation. There we see the issue put starkly: Babylon, in all its worldly pomp and show, destroyed, and Jerusalem 'coming down out of heaven, having the glory of God'. We could well entitle the Bible, 'A tale of two cities'.

Genesis 11 tells how fallen men sought to build a city. It is clear from the record that this was far more than an attempt to build a new town. They said:

> Come, let us build us a city, and a tower, whose top may reach unto heaven, and let us make us a name; lest we be scattered abroad upon the face of the whole earth. (Genesis 11:4, ASV, RV.)

That this was much more than an innocent attempt to build a new city can be seen from the fact that the Lord himself was grieved and cut the work short. This city became known as 'Babel', and was the beginning of Babylon. Throughout the Old Testament the name for Babylon in Hebrew is always 'Babel'. This is obscured by our English translations, which apart from Genesis, use the Greek name 'Babylon'. Genesis 12 tells how God called Abram (later Abraham) out of one of the neighbouring cities of Babel, the city of Ur in Chaldaea:

> Get thee out of thy country, and from thy kindred, and from thy father's house, unto the land that I will shew thee. (Genesis 12:1, RV.)

Stephen described this event in the New Testament:

> The God of glory appeared unto our father Abraham, when he was in Mesopotamia, before he dwelt in Haran, and said unto him, Get thee out of thy land, and from thy kindred, and come into the land which I shall shew thee. (Acts 7:2-3, RV.)

The writer to the Hebrews explains the reason:

> By faith Abraham, when he was called, obeyed to go out unto a place which he was to receive for an inheritance; and he went out, not knowing whither he went ... *for he looked for the city which hath the foundations, whose builder and maker is God.* (Hebrews 11:8, 10, RV.)

Abraham was the inhabitant of no mean city. He was not, as he is so often represented, some wandering and ignorant nomadic shepherd; he was a man of culture and sophistication, belonging to one of the aristocratic families of Ur, a city with a very high level of civilization. It was while Abraham was living in such a city that the God of glory appeared to him, and in that revelation, Abraham saw the city of God. *He saw the city of God in the person of the God of glory.* How he saw the Lord, or what he saw, we do not know, but from that moment he was spoiled for anything less. From then on he 'looked for the city which has the foundations'. He forsook the splendour of his native city, with its high standards of education and culture, and never returned to it. Abraham had 'seen through it'; for him it was now meaningless and futile. He saw that it had no true foundations: that it was built on the sands of human genius, human resourcefulness and human ability, and that it must, therefore, pass away. Apprehended by the God of glory, he sought 'the city which has the foundations, whose builder and maker is God'. The city which he sought was the heavenly Jerusalem, of which the earthly Jerusalem is but the symbol. It is noteworthy that although Abraham visited Jerusalem, he never lived in it. His life had become centred in the eternal.

From that point onwards in the Bible, there are only two cities to which men can belong: Babylon or Jerusalem. At first, this is not clearly set out, but as the biblical story unfolds, the choice becomes clearer, until finally the issue of all human history is revealed in the Bible's closing chapters. At the time when Revelation was written, the earthly city of Babylon no longer existed. Yet it figures largely in those chapters. It represents, of course, the fallen world. The cities of the world, whether the cities of that day such as Rome, Athens, or Alexandria, or those of our own time, express the glory, philosophy and power of that fallen world. They are all 'Babylon'. It is the sum of human genius and human glory. We also see New Jerusalem – not coming out of the earth, for it is not created by man, nor even built on the earth – but coming down out of heaven, having the glory of God. It was the 'God of glory' who had appeared to Abraham and in whom Abraham had seen that city. He had seen it in its relation to the glory of God.

Babylon symbolizes the ingenuity, abilities and aspirations of fallen man. Babylon is his creation. Within it is beautiful music, the language of his soul; magnificent architecture, which Goethe called 'frozen music'; and meaningful literature, expressing both the sorrowful realities of his fallen existence and the hope for something better. We also find profound ideals and philosophy, intense commercial acumen and shrewdness, and much religion. All this is not to be discounted. It appears to be a success story until seen in the light of the eternal. Then it all turns to ashes before our gaze.

The words of the builders of Babel reveal the heart of the matter:

> Let us build us a city, and a tower, whose top may reach unto heaven, and let us make us a name. (Genesis 11:4.)

Within these words are found all the aspirations, noble and base, which we discover in the human city. They sum up the ambition which has driven man to glorify himself, the restless desire for self-expression and self-fulfilment, the dynamic lying behind success – commercial, artistic and cultural alike. We do great injustice to this truth if, as Christians, we discount everything that proceeds from fallen man as base and ignoble. The aspirations and longings of fallen humanity are often noble, high and good, and there is much in human philosophy which is commendable; yet it all forms a city without foundations. Architectural foundations are normally deeply hidden. Yet they are vital to any structure which is to last. Babylon appears to have great and solid foundations: in fact, she is built on sand. She is built upon the top-soil of human resourcefulness and not upon the bed-rock of divine grace and salvation.

The words of Genesis 11:4, 'Let us build us ... a tower, whose top may reach unto heaven,' reveal the whole story of fallen man. They can be taken as both motto and epitaph of human history. From the beginning man has sought to bridge the gulf between earth and heaven and regain paradise lost; to create a utopia upon the earth and bring in the Golden Age of equality, justice and peace for all men. This has characterized much of the human story. It has been the guiding force and dynamic of great historic personalities, as well as the basis of ancient human philosophies and ideologies. Yet, in the end, all has been turned into ashes.

Even in modern times many efforts have been made to bring in the Golden Age. The old League of Nations and the present United Nations have been attempts to bring in a utopian new age. Great ideologies that hold powerful sway over men's minds in our day – such as Marxism – aim, in their purest form, to produce a human paradise on earth. All these attempts of fallen man, though in some cases noble and good, have failed and will fail. They fail because they represent a 'city without foundations'. The foundation of God's truth, righteousness and salvation is missing. These attempts to create a new society either leave out the living God, or use his name and his work as a façade to disguise self-aggrandizement and glory. Much religion, whatever its name, falls within this latter category, and Babylon is a city of religion. Whether it is artistically ornate or whether it is simple, it is a form of godliness without the power of God.

They called their city in those days: *Bab il*, probably from the old Assyrian *Bab illi*, which means 'Gate of God'. They understood their attempt to create a city as the divine gateway into a paradise on earth. God called it not *Bab il*, but *Babel*, which in Hebrew means 'confusion'. They had sought to build something which would bring heaven down to earth and earth up to heaven; something to span the gulf between man and heaven, and realize the golden ideal.

Human history is the record of how fallen mankind has continued to follow the same pathway. We see it expressed in the cities of the world, whether ancient or modern. Rome, Paris, Washington, London, Moscow, Peking – all are the expression of man's wealth and genius, man's ambition and power. These cities are the flower and fruit of fallen man, manifesting what is good and noble as well as what is evil and ugly. They represent building without proper foundations: Babylon.

This explains why whatever man sets out to do inevitably ends, partly or wholly, in defeat. He begins with high ideals of equality and justice and freedom, and ends with bondage, injustice and inequality. For this reason God calls Babylon 'confusion'. It is his verdict on human history. It fittingly describes the human story, the millennia of human endeavour and aspiration, and the woeful failure of every human attempt to realize its ideals.

Babylon, at its zenith, was one of the greatest cities of all time. Its hanging gardens and fine avenues, its great commercial centres and banking houses, its famous iron gates, its palaces and temples, its canals which brought sea-faring ships up from the Persian Gulf, made Babylon justly famed. By comparison Jerusalem appears like some insignificant hill-country town. Jerusalem has no fine boulevards, no canals to bring ships up from the sea, no laid-out gardens, no magnificent, triumphal, processional routes. Yet it is not what is seen but what is unseen which counts in the end. Whereas God's verdict on Babylon is that she has no foundations and is 'confusion', he describes Jerusalem as 'the city which hath the foundations'. Jerusalem has none of the natural advantages of Babylon, yet the Lord selected it as the capital for his people, and chose it without any of the normal advantages man associates with a capital city. He wanted to make it clear that this was no ordinary capital, but one that represented his heart's desire for man. From the very beginning God's desire was to dwell with men and to set his throne in the midst of them. That is the significance of Jerusalem.

The Lord said of Jerusalem:

> This is my resting place for ever: here will I dwell; for I have desired it. (Psalm 132:14, RV.)

and again,

> At that time they shall call Jerusalem the throne of the Lord ... (Jeremiah 3:17, RV.)

and again,

> Great is Jehovah, and greatly to be praised,
> In the city of our God, in his holy mountain.
> Beautiful in elevation, the joy of the whole earth,
> Is Mount Zion, on the sides of the north,
> The city of the great King.
> God hath made himself known in her palaces
> for a refuge ... God will establish it for ever.
> (Psalm 48:1-3, 8, ASV.)

The city of God is *the* issue behind the whole history of mankind; she lies at the heart of the human story.

Some Christians believe that 'redemption' is the issue of human history. I cannot agree. Without doubt redemption and salvation are fundamental matters. *But they are God's means to his end, and not the end itself.* God's plan of salvation was designed by him to bring us back to his original purpose for mankind. The means are obviously essential and vital, but are not greater than the end. God's purpose is that man, saved and joined to him in the Messiah Jesus, should become his eternal dwelling-place and home. This is clearly stated in Ephesians 2:21-22:

> in whom the whole building, being fitted together is growing into a holy temple in the Lord; in whom you also are being built together into a dwelling of God in the Spirit. (NASB)

This 'dwelling of God' is looked at in many different ways in Scripture. It is variously called the 'temple of God', the 'house of God', the 'body of the Lord Jesus the Messiah', the 'bride' or 'wife of the Lamb', the 'city of God'. The last two terms figure in Revelation 21:

> I saw the holy city, new Jerusalem, coming down out of heaven from God, made ready as a bride adorned for her husband. And I heard a great voice out of the throne saying, Behold, the tabernacle of God is with men, and he shall dwell

> with them, and they shall be his peoples, and God himself shall be with them, and be their God. (Revelation 21:2-3, RV.)

and again:

> Come hither, I will shew thee the bride, the wife of the Lamb. And he carried me away in the Spirit to a mountain great and high, and shewed me the holy city Jerusalem, coming down out of heaven from God, having the glory of God. (Revelation 21:9-11, RV.)

This city is called, on the one hand, the 'bride, the wife of the Lamb', and on the other hand, the 'holy city, new Jerusalem', a combination of two quite different ideas which are not normally associated. The bride represents the most intimate union known to man; the most direct, loving relationship, in which two people share one name, one life, one home and one future. A city, however, represents a centre of administration and government. Thus we have two vital matters. We have the desire of God to bring us into an eternal union with himself, in which we become partakers of eternal life, and at the same time, his desire that we should reign with him from his throne and, by his training and discipline, be qualified to govern with him and administer his will.

If Babylon is the product of man from beginning to end, the sum of man's glory, Jerusalem is totally concerned with God. She begins with God, with God's election and choice. She continues by the grace of God: her life, her survival and preservation, her development – all are of God. Time and again God has allowed this city to face total destruction. Then, when all was most dark and impossible, God has stepped in and delivered her. This has been the history of Jerusalem, whether the earthly or the spiritual city. Jerusalem also ends with God. She is brought at last to the glory of God, and becomes the eternal home of God, the place of his throne.

If Babylon is the symbol of man, Jerusalem is the symbol of God. Jerusalem represents the rule of heaven, as opposed to man's rebellion against divine authority; she represents the eternal as opposed to the transient and the corruptible. She represents the spirit as opposed to the flesh; the way of God as opposed to the way of this world. This is why even the Jerusalem of this earth has stood like a rock throughout the ages. Babylon, with all its pomp, its world-wide empire, its great system of government, its high-sounding philosophy and strength of human will and character, finally passes away. Jerusalem, however, abides for ever. From one standpoint, the Jerusalem of this earth is the same as any other city. For example Revelation 11:8 describes her as

> the great city which spiritually is called Sodom and Egypt, where also our Lord was crucified (RV);

and Galatians 4:25:

> Now this Hagar is Mount Sinai in Arabia, and corresponds to the present Jerusalem, for she is in slavery with her children. (NASB)

The writer of the letter to the Hebrews says:

> For we have not here an abiding city .... (Hebrews 13:14, RV)

Nevertheless, the earthly Jerusalem is still the symbol of the eternal. Augustine referred to her as 'that shadow of a city, Jerusalem'. As such she is unique and we cannot and must not devalue her. She will never pass away until the New Jerusalem takes her place. The Psalmist declares:

> God is our refuge and strength, a very present help in trouble. Therefore will we not fear, though the earth do change, and though the mountains be moved in the heart of the seas; though the waters thereof roar and be troubled, though the mountains shake with the swelling thereof.
>
> There is a river, the streams whereof make glad the city of

> God, the holy place of the tabernacles of the Most High. God is in the midst of her; she shall not be moved: God shall help her, and that right early. The nations raged, the kingdoms were moved: he uttered his voice, the earth melted. The Lord of hosts is with us; the God of Jacob is our refuge. (Psalm 46:1-7, RV.)

In the midst of all the struggle the city of God stands firm. It makes no difference on what level the conflict rages: whether it is the spiritual conflict which has raged through the ages over the purpose of God and its realization, or whether it is the earthly battles which have raged over the earthly city of Jerusalem. In the midst of all the shaking, all the change, the city of God stands firm. God is in her and therefore she will not be moved. Because God is in her she will finally triumph. In fact, in order that this may be so, God has made a special provision for her. It is a provision unseen by human eyes, but which enables her to endure and finally to triumph and inherit. It is the 'river, the streams whereof make glad the city of God'. In the great battle between the kingdom of heaven and the powers of darkness, the 'spirit that worketh in the sons of disobedience', God has made a provision of divine life and power that will enable us to overcome. If this is true of the spiritual, it is also true of the earthly. For God will not suffer Jerusalem to be moved until his purpose is fulfilled. Sometimes there is a dark night of trial and affliction to be endured, when all seems lost from the human viewpoint, but 'at the dawn of the morning' God helps her and delivers her (Psalm 46:5, RV margin).

The fact that in Jerusalem God is everything, is beautifully expressed in Psalm 87:

> His foundation is in the holy mountains. The Lord loveth the gates of Zion more than all the dwellings of Jacob. Glorious things are spoken of thee, O city of God. I will make mention of Rahab and Babylon as among them that know me: behold Philistia, and Tyre, with Ethiopia; this one was born there. Yea, of Zion it shall be said, This one and that one was born in her; and the Most High himself shall establish her. The

> Lord shall count, when he writeth up the peoples, this one was born there. They that sing as well as they that dance shall say, All my fountains are in thee. (RV)

When God counts up the nations, he says of certain ones not that they were born in Babylon or Philistia, in Tyre or Egypt or Ethiopia; they were born in Zion. They belong not to this world, but to God and his kingdom; not to Babylon, to the city of this world, but to the 'city of God', to the 'city which hath the foundations'.

The Psalmist declared: 'His foundation is in the holy mountains. The Lord loveth the gates of Zion' and 'Glorious things are spoken of thee, O city of God', and 'of Zion it shall be said, This one and that one was born in her'. Three matters are vitally related: true foundations, things of glory, and a new birth. The glory of God can never be given to anything which does not have the foundations of God. It was because man sinned that he fell short of the glory of God (Romans 3:23). But we who have been born again from above have been born in Zion: as we read in Galatians 4:26-28:

> But the Jerusalem that is above is free, which is our mother. For it is written, Rejoice, thou barren that bearest not; break forth and cry, thou that travailest not: for more are the children of the desolate than of her which hath the husband. Now we, brethren, as Isaac was, are children of promise. (RV)

And if the 'Jerusalem that is above is our mother', then we have been called by the 'God of all grace ... unto his eternal glory in Christ' (I Peter 5:10, RV). We need to see that this glory to which we have been called relates to our being a part of his bride, and a part of his city.

The writer of the letter to the Hebrews says:

> But ye are come unto Mount Zion, and unto the city of the living God, the heavenly Jerusalem. (Hebrews 12:22, RV.)

A little later he adds:

> For we have not here an abiding city, but we seek after the city which is to come. (Hebrews 13:14, RV.)

On the one hand, we are born in Jerusalem, and on the other hand, we are coming to it, by the grace of God and his overcoming power. This was the city for which Abraham sought (Hebrews 11:10), and not only Abraham but also the rest of his family.

> But now they desire a better country, that is, a heavenly: wherefore God is not ashamed of them, to be called their God: for he hath prepared for them a city. (Hebrews 11:16, RV.)

Nor does this concern only Abraham's immediate family. Joseph, Moses, Joshua, Rahab, Gideon, Barak, David, Samuel and others are mentioned in this chapter. They too belong to this city:

> Wherefore God ... hath prepared for them a city .... These all, having had witness borne to them through their faith, received not the promise, God having provided some better thing concerning *us*, that *apart from us they should not be made perfect.* (Hebrews 11:16, 39-40, RV.)

In other words, all who are redeemed by God are, in some wonderful way, bound up with this 'Jerusalem which is above'.

This explains why the twelve gates of New Jerusalem have the names of the twelve tribes of the children of Israel engraved upon them, and the twelve foundations of the wall of the city have the names of the twelve apostles of the Lamb on them (Revelation 21:12, 14). We have represented in this city an elect people drawn from both the Old and the New Covenant. The twenty-four elders, who are mentioned a number of times in Revelation, may be symbolic of the twelve patriarchs of the Old Covenant and the twelve apostles of the New. Certainly this city is the calling of all true believers, the 'goal' of which the apostle Paul spoke when he said:

> I press on toward the goal unto the prize of the high calling of God in Christ Jesus. (Philippians 3:14, RV.)

Whatever questions remain, one thing is clear: in the last chapters of the Bible, Babylon finally comes under the judgement of God and is destroyed (Revelation 16:1 – 19:21). Some Christians find it hard to understand the reaction of the great multitude in heaven to the judgement of Babylon as it is recorded in Revelation 19:1-8. The great 'Hallelujah' chorus, which ascends to God at its destruction, does not seem in their eyes to be very 'Christian'! There is so much about the human city which appeals to us, and we fail to see that it has no foundation. In fact, for many of us, the practical problem is that we still have 'one foot in it'. The Lord Jesus said: 'Where thy treasure is, there will thy heart be also' (Matthew 6:21, RV) and some of our 'treasure' still lies in Babylon. For this reason, some find it hard to believe that *all* of Babylon will be destroyed. We can understand the evil and ugly things in it being destroyed, but feel that the better things in it, such as its music, literature and architecture, should be preserved. Yet all that which does not originate in God will be destroyed, however beautiful or fine it may seem to be.

Sometimes, as Christians, we forget that it was God who planted in man the creative genius which has produced so much; that, in fact, it is a pale reflection of his own creative nature. This basic energy to create or invent stems from the fact that man was made 'in the image of God, after his likeness'. The Lord is not against creativeness as such, in whatever realm it may be found, nor against the many ways in which man expresses genius. In truth, when all those 'first things' have passed away, when that whole realm which belongs to fallen human history has been terminated, then a new age will begin with the most glorious potentialities and possibilities. John declares this in Revelation 21:3-5 –

> I heard a great voice out of the throne saying, Behold, the tabernacle of God is with men, and he shall dwell with them ... and death shall be no more; neither shall there be mourning, nor crying, nor pain, any more: the first things are passed away. And he that sitteth on the throne said, Behold, I make all things new. (RV)

Man in union with God will blossom into all that for which he was originally created. With the Lord as both centre and circumference of his life, the creative genius in him will only then come into its own. The fact is that fallen mankind, the human city, even at its best and most noble, has no foundations. Only Jerusalem has eternal foundations.

Isaiah records a remarkable prophecy concerning Babylon's final judgement:

> And Babylon, the glory of kingdoms, the beauty of the Chaldeans' pride, shall be as when God overthrew Sodom and Gomorrah. It shall never be inhabited, neither shall it be dwelt in from generation to generation: neither shall the Arabian pitch tent there; neither shall shepherds make their flocks to lie down there. But wild beasts of the desert shall lie there; and their houses shall be full of doleful creatures. (Isaiah 13:19-21, RV.)

This was fulfilled concerning the physical Babylon exactly as the Lord had prophesied.

Even more remarkable is Isaiah 14:12 –

> How art thou fallen from heaven, O day star, son of the morning! how art thou cut down to the ground, which didst lay low the nations! (RV)

This is generally understood to be a prophecy concerning Satan. If that is so, we have come to the heart of the matter. Babylon is energized by Satan himself; the poison of the serpent is in the blood-stream of unsaved mankind, and human history provides the evidence. The problem for man goes far deeper than a few unfortunate weaknesses. The cure required is fundamental. Man does not need a 'facial uplift' consisting of various cosmetic changes; he needs a new heart and a new spirit.

It is therefore not a question of separating the good and noble from that which is evil and base. It is no more possible for this to be done than it is to separate good food from contaminated, once poison has been introduced into it. The whole meal has to be destroyed and another provided. Sin has made eternal foundations an impossibility. With the noblest ideals and aspirations, fallen man is trapped within his own unsaved nature. It is precisely this that the Messiah, the Lord Jesus, came tc deal with. He came as the Lamb of God to take away the sin of the world and to save all those who would put their trust in God through him. Furthermore, by his finished work, man may not only be delivered from sin but be born anew, receiving a new heart and a new spirit. It was of this that the prophet Ezekiel spoke:

> A new heart also will I give you, and a new spirit will I put within you: and I will take away the stony heart out of your flesh, and I will give you an heart of flesh. And I will put my spirit within you, and cause you to walk in my statutes, and ye shall keep my judgements, and do them. (Ezekiel 36:26-27, RV.)

The great joy of the innumerable multitude in heaven is, however, not merely over the destruction of Babylon, but even more over the fact that Jerusalem comes down out of heaven, having the glory of God. God and truth have finally won. A new age and a new man with a new and glorious destiny have begun.

The Jerusalem of this earth represents and symbolizes this spiritual ideal and reality. For this reason the Lord said:

> This is Jerusalem; I have set her at the center of the nations, with lands around her. (Ezekiel 5:5, NASB.)

God has made her an object lesson to the nations of the world throughout history and to the end of the age. That simple but profound fact makes her unique among the capital cities of the world. That is why she has never disappeared from human history, and will never disappear, until the Messiah stands again within her streets, and she herself fades away before the radiant glory of the Jerusalem which is eternal.

PART IV

THE UNIQUENESS OF THE MESSIAH

For unto us a child is born, unto us a son is given; and the government shall be upon his shoulder: and his name shall be called Wonderful, Counsellor, Mighty God, Everlasting Father, Prince of Peace. Of the increase of his government and of peace there shall be no end, upon the throne of David, and upon his kingdom, to establish it, and to uphold it with judgement and with righteousness from henceforth even for ever.

Isaiah 9:6-7 (RV)

CHAPTER 1

I BELIEVE WITH PERFECT FAITH THAT THE MESSIAH WILL COME

As King David lay dying, he uttered a prophecy as significant and as beautiful as any he had ever spoken:

> The Spirit of the Lord spake by me, and his word was upon my tongue. The God of Israel said, the Rock of Israel spake to me: One that ruleth over men righteously, that ruleth in the fear of God, he shall be as the light of the morning, when the sun riseth, a morning without clouds; when the tender grass springeth out of the earth, through clear shining after rain. Verily my house is not so with God; yet he hath made with me an everlasting covenant, ordered in all things, and sure: for it is all my salvation, and all my desire, although he maketh it not to grow. (2 Samuel 23:2-5, RV.)

Whether or not these words contain a reference to the Messiah, one thing is clear: David knew that the Lord had made with him an eternal covenant which was 'ordered in all things and sure', and recognized that all his salvation and desire were centred in that covenant. In fact, the Lord had sworn to David, saying:

> Moreover the Lord telleth thee that the Lord will make thee an house. When thy days be fulfilled, and thou shalt sleep with thy fathers, I will set up thy seed after thee, that shall proceed out of thy bowels, and I will establish his kingdom. He shall build a house for my name, and I will establish the throne of his kingdom for ever.... And thine house and thy kingdom shall be made sure for ever before thee: thy throne shall be established for ever. (2 Samuel 7:11-13, 16, RV.)

David referred to this when he said:

> Therefore I will give thanks unto thee, O Lord, among the nations, and will sing praises unto thy name. Great deliverance giveth he to his king; and showeth lovingkindness to his anointed, to David and to his seed, for evermore. (Psalm 18:49-50, RV.)

In a Psalm of much later date, the Psalmist takes up this theme again:

> Then thou spakest in vision to thy saints, and saidst, I have laid help upon one that is mighty; I have exalted one chosen out of the people. I have found David my servant; with my holy oil have I anointed him.... My covenant will I not break, nor alter the thing that is gone out of my lips. Once have I sworn by my holiness; I will not lie unto David; his seed shall endure for ever, and his throne as the sun before me. It shall be established for ever as the moon, and as the faithful witness in the sky. (Psalm 89:19-20, 34-37, RV.)

In the phrases 'to his anointed' and 'with my holy oil have I anointed him' (Psalms 18:50; 89:20), the Hebrew word used is a derivative of the word for 'Messiah'. 'Messiah' comes from the Hebrew *Mashiach* which means 'anointed one'. The Greek form *Christos*, from which comes our English word 'Christ', has the same meaning.

Gradually, as David's successors on the throne first brought disillusionment and then disappeared altogether from history, it was recognized that the Lord had promised a messianic king, a Saviour-King, who would be not only of David's line but a 'greater David'. Isaiah expressed it in these words:

> There shall come forth a shoot out of the stock of Jesse, and a branch out of his roots shall bear fruit: and the Spirit of the Lord shall rest upon him.... And it shall come to pass in that day, that the root of Jesse, which standeth for an ensign of the peoples, unto him shall the nations seek; and his resting place shall be glorious. (Isaiah 11:1-2, 10, RV.)

By New Testament times the concept was clear. It was an expectation of an anointed Saviour-King, the Messiah, who would break the yoke of the oppressor, deliver his people, and restore the kingdom for ever.

The concept of a Messiah is unique to Judaism and Christianity. It is not necessary to say much about Christianity, since as its very name implies, it is essentially messianic. If the anglicized Hebrew form, 'Messiah', had been used instead of the anglicized Greek, 'Christ', it would have been called 'Messianity'! Every born again Christian is a messianic believer; each is 'Christ's one', 'Messiah's one', saved by the work of the Messiah Jesus, reconciled to God through him, and awaiting his return.

For Judaism, however, the Messiah has not yet come. 'I believe with perfect faith that the Messiah will come, and though he tarry I will wait daily for his appearance.' Thus runs the 12th Article of Faith composed by Maimonides, the great Jewish scholar of the 12th century A.D. The belief in the coming of a personal Messiah had become an integral part of the Jewish outlook by the time of King Herod the Great. Without qualification the Talmud states that 'all the prophets have prophesied concerning the days of the Messiah' (Berakoth Sanhedrin 34b). The Targums are intensely messianic, and they refer to the Messiah in at least seventy-two passages of the Old Testament. Almost every authoritative Jewish commentator has taught that the Old Testament predicted the coming of a personal Messiah. Even Maimonides, who reacted strongly against pseudo-Messiahs and the unhealthy extremism they engendered, as well as against the traditional Christian interpretation of Old Testament prophecies, believed in the coming of a Messiah. Kabbalism, the movement of Jewish mysticism which began in the 12th century A.D., and which was to influence Jewish life for centuries, was also fundamentally messianic, especially in the book of Zohar, the product of Spanish Kabbalism in the 13th century. Only in the last few centuries has the traditional view been widely forsaken, as has been the case in nominal Christian circles, and a belief in a 'messianic age', a golden age of human prosperity and peace, been substituted.

The promise of a Messiah goes back to the very first chapters of the Bible, and unfolds in more and more detail the further we read on. If the messianic concept in itself is unique, the progressive prophecy concerning his coming, his person, his work and his glory is also unique. The scope of the present book does not allow an exhaustive treatment of the subject, important as it is, but let us consider certain major prophecies as examples of it.

The Lord said to the serpent in Genesis 3:15 –

> I will put enmity between you and the woman, and between your seed and her seed; he shall bruise your head, and you shall bruise his heel. (RSV)

Both Christians and Jews take this verse as the watershed of all messianic prophecy. The Jerusalem Targum (about 4th century A.D.) paraphrases this verse with explicit reference to the Messiah. One of the most famous rabbis, Rabbi David Kimchi (1160-1235), popularly known as Radak, commented on this verse 'As thou wentest forth for the salvation of thy people by the hand of the Messiah, the son of David, who shall wound Satan, the head, the king and prince of the house of the wicked ....' The promise of the Messiah in Genesis 3:15 is as yet veiled but, nonetheless, it is sure. It is the promise that the tempter and destroyer of mankind will finally be overcome by the seed of the woman.

In Genesis 49:9-11, we read:

> Judah is a lion's whelp; from the prey, my son, you have gone up. He couches, he lies down as a lion, and as a lion, who dares rouse him up? The sceptre shall not depart from Judah, nor the ruler's staff from between his feet, until Shiloh comes, and to him shall be the obedience of the peoples. He

> ties his foal to the vine, and his doneky's colt to the choice vine; he washes his garments in wine, and his robes in the blood of grapes. (NASB)

This prophecy contains the first clearly defined promise of the Messiah. He will come from the tribe of Judah; he will be the Lion of Judah (cf. Revelation 5:5). We are also told that 'the sceptre shall not depart from Judah, nor the ruler's staff from between his feet, until Shiloh comes.' This is better rendered 'nor the ruler's staff from between his feet, until he comes to whom it belongs' (RSV).

This is the promise that the Messiah will come not only from the tribe of Judah but from its royal house, the house of David, and that he will be the divinely anointed King to whom the obedience of the peoples will be. In ancient Jewish sources nearly every phrase is treated messianically. For instance, 'the lion's whelp' is taken as a reference to the Messiah no less than five times in Yalkut 160, while the phrase 'until Shiloh comes' is explained in the Jerusalem Targum as 'until the time that King Messiah shall come who shall arise from Judah'. Rashi (Rabbi Shlomo Izaaki, 1040-1105) said: '"until Shiloh come", that is King Messiah, whose is the kingdom.' The Midrash Bereshit Rabbah links Genesis 49:10 with Isaiah 11:10 –

> And it shall come to pass in that day, that the root of Jesse, which standeth for an ensign of the peoples, unto him shall the nations seek; and his resting place shall be glorious; (RV)

and Genesis 49:11 with Zechariah 9:9 –

> Rejoice greatly, O daughter of Zion; shout, O daughter of Jerusalem: behold thy king cometh unto thee; he is just, and having salvation; lowly, and riding upon an ass, even upon a colt the foal of an ass. (RV)

The coming of a divinely anointed deliverer is predicted even more clearly in Numbers 24:16-19 –

> The oracle of him who hears the words of God, and knows the knowledge of the Most High, who sees the vision of the Almighty, falling down, yet having his eyes uncovered. I see him, but not now; I behold him, but not near; a star shall come forth from Jacob, and a sceptre shall rise from Israel, and shall crush through the forehead of Moab, and tear down all the sons of Sheth. And Edom shall be a possession, Seir, its enemies, also shall be a possession; while Israel performs valiantly. One from Jacob shall have dominion, and shall destroy the remnant from the city. (NASB)

In the first place, this is a prophecy concerning King David; he was the one who, in fact, 'crushed through the forehead of Moab' and 'possessed Edom' (see Psalm 108). However, the prophecy also contains the promise of David's son, the One who would be born of his line, and who would finally deliver the people of God from all their enemies. According to both the Targum Onkelos and the Jerusalem Targum these verses refer to the Messiah.

Deuteronomy 18:15, 18-19 contains a further prophecy:

> The Lord thy God will raise up unto thee a prophet from the midst of thee, of thy brethren, like unto me; unto him ye shall hearken .... The Lord said unto me . . . I will raise them up a prophet from among their brethren, like unto thee; and I will put my words in his mouth; and he shall speak unto them all that I shall command him. And it shall come to pass, that whosoever will not hearken unto my words which he shall speak in my name, I will require it of him. (RV)

The Messiah is to be a prophet, like Moses, speaking the Word of God. As Moses brought the people out of Egypt, founded the nation, and was the vehicle through which God revealed his mind, so there would come One who would redeem a people out of bondage, create a spiritual and eternal nation, and reveal the mind of God. Rabbi Levi Ben Gershon (A.D. 1288-1344) commenting on this verse said: 'Moses by the miracles which he wrought drew but a single nation to the worship of God, but the Messiah will draw all nations to the worship of God.' Rabbi Shalom

(15th century A.D.) said: 'The King Messiah shall be exalted above Abraham, be high above Moses.'

In sum, these prophecies teach that the Messiah would be born of woman and that as the seed of the woman, he would crush the serpent's head and would overcome all that has corrupted and destroyed mankind; that he would come from the tribe of Judah, and from the royal house of David; that he would be a prophet like Moses, marking a new beginning. This is expressed in a prophecy contained in Isaiah 11:1-10, which is messianically interpreted in many Jewish writings:

> And there shall come forth a shoot out of the stock of Jesse, and a branch out of his roots shall bear fruit. And the Spirit of Jehovah shall rest upon him, the spirit of wisdom and understanding, the spirit of counsel and might, the spirit of knowledge and of the fear of Jehovah. And his delight shall be in the fear of Jehovah; and he shall not judge after the sight of his eyes, neither decide after the hearing of his ears; but with righteousness shall he judge the poor, and decide with equity for the meek of the earth; and he shall smite the earth with the rod of his mouth; and with the breath of his lips shall he slay the wicked. And righteousness shall be the girdle of his waist, and faithfulness the girdle of his loins.
>
> And the wolf shall dwell with the lamb, and the leopard shall lie down with the kid; and the calf and the young lion and the fatling together; and a little child shall lead them. And the cow and the bear shall feed; their young ones shall lie down together; and the lion shall eat straw like the ox. And the sucking child shall play on the hole of the asp, and the weaned child shall put his hand on the adder's den. They shall not hurt nor destroy in all my holy mountain; for the earth shall be full of the knowledge of Jehovah, as the waters cover the sea.
>
> And it shall come to pass in that day, that the root of Jesse, that standeth for an ensign of the peoples, unto him shall the nations seek; and his resting-place shall be glorious. (ASV)

The coming of the Messiah, however, is even more explicitly predicted. We have the details of the place of his birth, the nature of his birth, his character, ministry and work, and his sufferings and the glory that would follow. In Micah 5:1-5 it is prophesied:

> ... they shall smite the judge of Israel with a rod upon the cheek. But thou, Bethlehem Ephratah, though thou be little among the thousands of Judah, yet out of thee shall he come forth unto me that is to be ruler in Israel; whose goings forth have been from of old, from everlasting. Therefore will he give them up, until the time that she which travaileth hath brought forth: then the remnant of his brethren shall return unto the children of Israel. And he shall stand and feed in the strength of the Lord, in the majesty of the name of the Lord his God; and they shall abide: for now shall he be great unto the ends of the earth. And this man shall be the peace .... (AV)

The Messiah's birthplace was to be Bethlehem, in Judah. He would be born of woman, and born to be king. We are also told that his 'goings forth have been from of old, from everlasting', or 'from the days of eternity' (AV margin; NASB). These mysterious words are the first indication that the One who is to come is not an ordinary human being. He has had a pre-birth existence. Furthermore, we are told 'this man shall be the peace', or better, as in NASB, 'This One will be our peace'. It does not mean only that he will bring peace in place of war, but that he will himself be our peace. In the days of the second Temple, this prophecy was considered to be messianic (see Matthew 2:4-6). The Jerusalem Targum says: 'Out of thee, Bethlehem, shall Messiah go forth before me to exercise dominion over Israel.'

In Isaiah 7:13-14 we read:

> Hear ye now, O house of David; is it a small thing for you to weary men, that ye will weary my God also? Therefore the Lord himself shall give you a sign; behold, a virgin shall conceive, and bear a son, and shall call his name Immanuel. (RV)

There has been much discussion over this verse, as to whether the Hebrew should be translated 'virgin' or 'maiden', 'young woman' or 'girl'. The liberal critical view of this verse is that it referred to the son of a contemporary young woman and not a virgin, who would be named 'Immanuel', signifying nothing more than that

God would be providentially with the nation. The Hebrew word is translated 'virgin' in the AV, RV, ASV, NASB and New International Version, and 'young woman' in the RSV, New English Bible and Good News Bible. Apart from the fact that the word is never used in the Old Testament for a married woman, one wonders what the sign was meant to convey if it referred only to a young woman conceiving and bearing a son. That is quite normal and commonplace. In fact, it would be more of a sign if it were an *old* woman who was to conceive and bear a son. What then constituted the divinely given sign? Surely it was that the young woman who conceived and bore a son would be a *virgin*, and the One to whom she gave birth would be 'Immanuel', 'God with us'. Furthermore, if the meaning of that was simply that God was behind the nation, blessing it, supporting it, guarding it, what would be unusual? From the beginning, the people of God had known the blessing and deliverance of the Lord. There must be a deeper significance in the name 'Immanuel' than this, and the fact that there is no record of anyone born at that time being called Immanuel only emphasizes it the more. The significance is surely this, that although the house of David, represented at that time by the reign of the evil king Ahaz, had failed, and would fail in spite of the reigns of the good kings Hezekiah and Josiah, nevertheless God's promise to David would be fulfilled: the messianic King would come, and his birth would be the breaking into human history of God himself. He would be *Immanu-El*, God with us.

This is borne out clearly by the prophecy in Isaiah 9, where we discover a prediction of One who would be born of the royal line of David, who would be truly human, and who would take the throne and the kingdom and reign over it for ever. So verses 6-7:

> For unto us a *child is born*, unto us *a son is given*; and the *government shall be upon his shoulder* and of the increase of his government and of peace there shall be no end, *upon the*

> *throne of David, and upon his kingdom*, to establish it, and to uphold it with judgement and with righteousness from henceforth even for ever. (RV)

The life of this one would have much to do with the north of the country, with Galilee, with that area traversed by the great highway, the Way of the Sea, and would give to it a new glory – verse 1:

> In the former time *he brought into contempt the land of Zebulun* and the *land of Naphtali*, but in *the latter time hath he made it glorious, by the way of the sea*, beyond Jordan, *Galilee* of the nations. (RV)

Furthermore, the ministry of this promised Messiah would be as light dispelling darkness, bondage, and death – verse 2:

> The people that walked in darkness have *seen a great light*: they that dwelt in the land of the shadow of death, *upon them hath the light shined*. (RV)

Now all of this could speak of a normal human birth and a normal human being, albeit of royal blood, until we come to the heart of the prophecy in verse 6:

> and his name shall be called Wonderful Counsellor, Mighty God, Everlasting Father, Prince of Peace.

With these titles we are face to face with the divine mystery of the Messiah's person. In Isaiah 28:29 we have a similar phrase:

> This also cometh forth from the Lord of hosts, which is wonderful in counsel, and excellent in wisdom. (RV)

'Wonderful Counsellor' *could* be a human title, but it is described here as an attribute of God himself. The Hebrew word translated 'wonderful' signifies something extraordinary or miraculous, a phenomenon that lies beyond human understanding. The next two titles, however, leave us in no doubt – 'Mighty God, Everlasting Father'. How can a child born to us, a son given to us, be the Mighty God, the Everlasting Father? In Isaiah 10:21 we have the same phrase:

> A remnant shall return, even the remnant of Jacob, unto the mighty God. (RV)

Rabbi Abraham ben Ezra (1093-1167) said of this prophecy:

> There are some interpreters who say that 'Wonderful ... Everlasting Father' are names of God, and only 'Prince of Peace' is the name of the child. But according to my view the interpretation is right which says all are names of the child.

Thus we are confronted with the essential mystery of the person of the Messiah. This one born to us as a child, as a human being, is the Mighty God, the Everlasting Father. He is 'Immanuel', God with us. It is not fanciful to note the mystery of his person expressed in the words 'unto us *a child* is *born*, unto us a *son* is *given*'; the child is born to us, but the son is given to us. The Messiah is not only a human being, he is 'the only begotten Son, who is in the bosom of the Father': he is God the Son, the heart of God revealed. He is also the 'Prince of Peace', not only making peace with God for us, but becoming our peace. With this promised Messiah, the reign of God begins and will go on for ever (Isaiah 9:7): 'Of the increase of his government and of peace there shall be no end' (RV).

The Lord Jesus was born of woman, of the tribe of Judah, and of the royal house of David. He was born in Bethlehem and lived for nearly thirty years in Nazareth in Galilee, a few miles north-west of the Via Maris, the Way of the Sea, and for the last three years of his life in Capernaum, on the north-west shore of the lake of Galilee, situated a little to the east of the Via Maris. He was born of a virgin; in all the records of his birth and life we come face to face with the mystery of his person. He is 'Immanuel', God with us. The apostle John put it simply but profoundly:

> In the beginning was the Word, and the Word was with God, and the Word was God. The same was in the beginning with God. All things were made by him; and without him was not anything made that hath been made. In him was life; and the life was the light of men .... And the Word became flesh, and dwelt among us (and we beheld his glory, glory as of the only begotten from the Father), full of grace and truth. (John 1:1-4, 14, RV.)

This was he 'whose goings forth have been from of old, from everlasting', whose name is Wonderful Counsellor, Mighty God, Everlasting Father, Prince of Peace.

Furthermore, it was not only his person and birth which were predicted, but his ministry:

> The spirit of the Lord God is upon me; because the Lord hath anointed me to preach good tidings unto the meek; he hath sent me to bind up the brokenhearted, to proclaim liberty to the captives, and the opening of the prison to them that are bound; to proclaim the acceptable year of the Lord, and the day of vengeance of our God; to comfort all that mourn; to appoint unto them that mourn in Zion, to give unto them a garland for ashes, the oil of joy for mourning, the garment of praise for the spirit of heaviness; that they might be called trees of righteousness, the planting of the Lord, that he might be glorified. (Isaiah 61:1-3, RV.)

The four gospels reveal how these words were fulfilled in the public ministry of the Lord Jesus. He indeed was the Messiah, the One anointed by the Lord to preach the gospel, the good tidings, to the meek. He was the prophet like Moses whom God had promised to raise up, who spoke in a manner never before known; the great light for those who walked in darkness. He was the one anointed by God to bring hope and salvation, the opening of the prison to the social outcast and misfit. By him the deaf heard, the dumb spoke, the blind saw, the lame walked, the leper was cleansed, the dead lived, and, above all, the sinner was saved. Truly he was the 'Wonderful Counsellor', the one whose whole ministry was filled with marvellous and extraordinary miracles, with phenomena beyond human conception. His gospel turned the world upside down, and has continued to do so wherever it has been preached in power.

The triumphal entry of the Messiah into Jerusalem is also predicted:

> Rejoice greatly, O daughter of Zion; shout, O daughter of Jerusalem: behold, thy king cometh unto thee: he is just, and having salvation; lowly, and riding upon an ass, even upon a colt the foal of an ass. ... and he shall speak peace unto the nations: and his dominion shall be from sea to sea, and from the River to the ends of the earth. (Zechariah 9:9-10, RV.)

The Messiah would come neither as a conquering warlord, nor as some proud potentate, but as the Prince of Peace. The horse was often associated with military power and pride in the ancient east, but the ass was associated with peace and humble, routine civil life.

The Midrash Bereshit Rabbah applies Zechariah's prophecy to the Messiah and links it with the words of Genesis 49:11 –

> binding his foal unto the vine, and his ass's colt unto the choice vine; he hath washed his garments in wine, and his vesture in the blood of grapes. (RV)

Matthew 21:1-11 and Luke 19:29-40 tell how, to popular acclaim, the Lord Jesus rode into Jerusalem as the messianic King on a colt, the foal of an ass, which his disciples had found and untied. (Was it tied up to a vine?) This took place one week before he was crucified, when, as it were, he 'washed his garments in wine and his vesture in the blood of grapes'. The treading out of the grapes is used in Scripture as a picture of judgement, and it was the judgement of our sins which he bore.

The rabbis had noted early on an apparent discrepancy in the prophecies concerning the actual coming of the Messiah. They observed that this prediction in Zechariah of the coming of the Messiah in a lowly manner does not correspond with Daniel 7:13-14. The Talmud records that:

> Rabbi Alexandri said: Rabbi Joshua opposed two verses: It is written, 'and behold, one like the son of man cometh with the clouds of heaven,' while elsewhere it is prophesied he comes 'lowly, and riding upon an ass'. If they are meritorious, he will come with the clouds of heaven; if not, lowly, and riding upon an ass. (Sanhedrin 98a)

If there were many who found God, and began to understand the word of God more deeply than ever before, who were touched by the love and compassion of God, and freed by the truth of God, there were also many for whom the Lord Jesus, his person, his words and his works, were a 'stone of stumbling' and a 'rock of offence' – an obstacle over which they tripped, and a rock upon which they fell and were broken, as is described by Isaiah:

> The Lord of hosts, him shall ye sanctify; and let him be your fear, and let him be your dread. And he shall be for a sanctuary; but for a stone of stumbling and for a rock of offence to both the houses of Israel, for a gin and for a snare to the inhabitants of Jerusalem. And many shall stumble thereon, and fall, and be broken, and be snared, and be taken. Bind thou up the testimony, seal the law among my disciples. And I will wait for the Lord, that hideth his face from the house of Jacob, and I will look for him. Behold, I and the children whom the Lord hath given me are for signs and for wonders in Israel from the Lord of hosts, which dwelleth in Mount Zion. (Isaiah 8:13-18, RV.)

When Jesus was circumcised in the Temple on the eighth day after his birth, that godly Jew Simeon said to his mother:

> Behold, this child is set for the falling and rising of many in Israel; and for a sign which is spoken against; yea and a sword shall pierce through thine own soul; that thoughts out of many hearts may be revealed. (Luke 2:34-35, RV.)

The prophecies of both Isaiah and Simeon were to be fulfilled in the minutest detail. Many indeed were to fall because of him, and many were to rise because of him. There has never been any neutral ground when it comes to the person and work of the Lord Jesus. Throughout history, he has been either the narrow way by which men find God, or the rock over which men trip and fall. To those who have believed, and are saved, he is the Power of God and the Wisdom of God, but to those who do not believe, and are perishing, he is a 'stumbling block' and 'foolishness'. He becomes a trap into which men fall through unbelief, a snare which, once sprung, cannot be forced open by human energy.

CHAPTER 2

IN THE SCROLL OF THE BOOK IT IS WRITTEN OF ME

Thus far we have not reached the heart of the messianic promise, although we have considered a number of messianic prophecies. Its heart is the divine promise of a redeemer. It is the promise of one who would save his people *from their sins* as well as realize the divine purpose for the nation:

> A redeemer shall come to Zion, and unto them that turn from transgression in Jacob, saith the Lord .... Arise, shine; for thy light is come, and the glory of the Lord is risen upon thee. For, behold, darkness shall cover the earth, and gross darkness the peoples: but the Lord shall arise upon thee, and his glory shall be seen upon thee. (Isaiah 59:20 – 60:2, RV.)

This 'redemption' was popularly understood in Jewish circles, then as now, to be a physical and national deliverance, rather than a salvation from the power and consequence of sin. Yet the divine promise of a Messiah was not only that he should be a glorious king, emancipating his people from all foreign occupation and limitation, setting up the eternal kingdom of God and causing the rule of God to extend to the ends of the earth; it was also the promise of one who would, by the sacrifice of himself, deal with sin, the root problem of human history and experience.

So far the prophecies we have considered have spoken about the kingdom and glory of the Messiah. It is true, however, that those prophecies which deal with the supreme work for which he came dwell much upon his sufferings. Rabbinic circles early recognized two lines of messianic prophecy in the Old Testament, one predicting the Messiah's triumph and glory, and the other his humiliation and suffering. It resulted in the concept of two Messiahs. One was the Messiah, Son of Joseph, who would suffer and die in conflict with the enemies of God and of Israel, and the other was the Messiah, Son of David, who would reign in glory and power, having defeated those enemies, reconciled the people to God, and restored the universe to him.

To the Christian the two lines of prophecy concerning the person, the coming and the work of the Messiah relate to one person, not two, and that is Jesus. It is a far more simple and satisfying answer to see all these messianic prophecies fulfilled in one person who would come twice. It is even more convincing when we begin to see how the first coming of the Lord Jesus, when he suffered, died, arose, and ascended, and his second coming in glory, perfectly fulfil all the requirements of the two lines of messianic prophecies.

The most remarkable of all the messianic psalms is Psalm 22. It is a point worthy of deep consideration that here we have a description of Calvary that exceeds anything in the gospels. The gospels reverentially say little about what people saw of the sufferings of the One upon the cross. In the psalm it is through the eyes of the One crucified that the details are given. How can this incredible fact be explained? It not only fits the accounts in the gospels, it is also a testimony given by the Sufferer years before the event took place. It is interesting that in the Yalkut at least two of these verses are referred to the Messiah, and particularly to the Messiah, Son of Joseph. 'My God, my God, why hast thou forsaken me?' Those opening words of the psalm were repeated by the Lord Jesus at the darkest and most awesome point of his sufferings, when he bore away the sin of the world. We shall never fully comprehend what happened when the Sinless One was made sin on our behalf, and the judgement of our sin fell upon him. At that moment, when he was alienated from the Father for the first and only time, and when this cry was wrung from his anguished heart, even the universe was affected, for the sun was darkened for three hours. For those who have been saved by his finished work on the cross, the unbearable agony of his soul that was expressed so poignantly in these words betokens the mystery of their salvation.

Verses 6-8 exactly describe the jeering crowd around the cross, their gesticulations and remarks:

> I am a worm, and no man; a reproach of men, and despised of the people. All they that see me laugh me to scorn: they shoot out the lip, they shake the head, saying, Commit thyself unto the Lord; let him deliver him; let him deliver him, seeing he delighteth in him. (RV)

In verses 12, 13 and 16 we have a vivid description, through the eyes of the crucified One, of the exulting hatred of those who had engineered his crucifixion, and apparently triumphed over him at last.

> Many bulls have compassed me; strong bulls of Bashan have beset me round. They gape upon me with their mouth, as a ravening and a roaring lion ... For dogs have compassed me: a company of evil-doers have inclosed me. (ASV)

Like angry bulls they did encircle him, like hungry and ravening lions with mouths open in anticipation of their prey. Those evil-doers were like a pack of wild dogs circling around their victim.

Or consider verses 14-15:

> I am poured out like water, and all my bones are out of joint: my heart is like wax; it is melted within me. My strength is dried up like a potsherd; and my tongue cleaveth to my jaws; and thou hast brought me into the dust of death. (ASV)

This precisely describes the sufferings of crucifixion, the dehydration of the victim, the weight of the body pulling the bones out of joint. Verses 16 and 18 accurately detail what happened to the Lord Jesus when he was crucified. They did pierce his hands and his feet, his bones were not broken but when he died were all intact, and they did divide his garments among them, casting lots upon his clothing. The vividness and originality of this whole account is well summed up in the one sentence: 'They look and stare upon me.'

It is a most striking fact that the one who suffered so deeply and who was brought by God 'into the dust of death' (verse 15) is the same one who triumphantly declares

> ... thou hast answered me. I will declare thy name unto my brethren: in the midst of the assembly will I praise thee. (Verses 21-22, ASV.)

He is also the one that all the ends of the earth shall remember when they turn to the Lord (verse 27); the one of whom they shall come and shall *declare his righteousness* unto a people that shall be born, that *he hath done it* (verse 31, RV). The suffering one, the Messiah, whose hands and feet have been pierced, has become 'Lord of all', the glorious 'King of kings and Lord of lords'.

One wonders when and how the psalmist had such an experience? If, as the title suggests, it was a psalm composed by David, we do not know of any experience, as recorded in his life story in the Bible, which would correspond to this description. But whether we accept his authorship or the assertion (now largely discredited) that it dates from the second century B.C., Psalm 22 is a remarkable prophecy fulfilled in detail when the Lord Jesus died, as told through the eyes and the heart of the One who was crucified. For this there can be only one valid explanation: the Spirit of Messiah was in the writer of this Psalm testifying beforehand to the sufferings of Messiah and the glories which would follow. (See 1 Peter 1:10-11.)

If Psalm 22 gives us a precise description of what happened at Calvary, the prophecy recorded in Isaiah 52:13 – 53:12 gives us the most remarkable interpretation of the significance of that death, an interpretation unrivalled even in the New Testament.

This passage is explained messianically in many Jewish sources, in the Talmud, the Jerusalem Targum, the Yalkut, the book of Zohar, and also by a number of famous rabbis. It is summed up by the famous Rabbi Alsheikh (1508-1600): 'Our rabbis with one voice accept and affirm the opinion that the prophet is speaking of the King Messiah and we shall ourselves also adhere to the same view.' It later became fashionable to interpret 'the Servant' in these prophecies as referring to Israel, a view I find untenable.

In this prophecy of Isaiah we are told that the Messiah would suffer greatly:

> Like as many were astonished at thee (his visage was so marred more than any man, and his form more than the sons of men) (52:14, ASV);

or:

> He was despised, and rejected of men; a man of sorrows, and acquainted with grief: and as one from whom men hide their face he was despised; and we esteemed him not (53:3, ASV);

or again:

> He was oppressed ... by oppression ... he was taken away (53:7-8, ASV).

We are also told that this suffering would not be because of sin or guilt on his part; he would be guiltless and without sin:

> although he had done no violence, neither was any deceit in his mouth ... my righteous servant (53:9, 11, ASV).

The Messiah would offer no resistance to his arrest and execution; he would remain silent before his accusers:

> He was oppressed, yet when he was afflicted he opened not his mouth; as a lamb that is led to the slaughter, and as a sheep that before its shearers is dumb, so he opened not his mouth (53:7, ASV).

He would die with criminals, and in some way be associated with a rich man in his death:

> they made his grave with the wicked, and with a rich man in his death ... and he was numbered with the transgressors (53:9, 12, RSV).

Now all this has had a remarkable fulfilment in the sufferings and death of the Lord Jesus. He was without sin and guiltless. Not a single substantiated charge against him worthy of death has come down to us from history, nor the record of any sin. All bore witness to his unblemished character and purity. He was despised, misunderstood, and misinterpreted by many, and especially by the influential and powerful leaders of the day. His trials, both ecclesiastical and civil, were a farce, and during them he offered no resistance and made no defence, but remained silent before all his accusers; he died with two criminals, while a wealthy member of the Sanhedrin, Joseph of Arimathea, gave his new grave for his burial.

If, however, all of that speaks of a real degree of suffering, it cannot be compared with the significance of the death of the Messiah. There is a profound meaning for ever beyond the finite mind of man in the words:

> Surely he hath borne our griefs, and carried our sorrows: yet we did esteem him stricken, smitten of God, and afflicted. But he was wounded for our transgressions, he was bruised for our iniquities: the chastisement of our peace was upon him; and with his stripes we are healed. All we like sheep have gone astray; we have turned every one to his own way; and the Lord hath laid on him the iniquity of us all. (53:4-6, RV.)

Here is the heart of the Messiah's work, the redemption of fallen man. This is further emphasized in the words 'and he shall bear their iniquities' (53:11, RV) and 'he poured out his soul unto death ... yet he bare the sin of many, and made intercession for the transgressors' (53:12, RV). Like the Passover lamb, the Messiah would be slain for us that we might be saved and delivered; he would die for our sins that we might be redeemed.

Commenting on these verses, Rabbi Elijah de Vidas (16th century A.D.) said:

> The meaning of 'He was wounded for our transgressions, bruised for our iniquities' is, that since the Messiah bears our iniquities, which produce the effect of His being bruised, it follows that whoso will not admit that the Messiah thus suffers for our iniquities must endure and suffer for them himself.

In the book of Zohar we read:

> It is written 'He was wounded for our transgressions', etc. The Messiah ... summons every sickness, every pain and every chastisement of Israel; they all come and rest upon Him. And were it not that He had thus lightened them off Israel and taken them upon Himself, there had been no man able to bear Israel's chastisements for the transgression of the law; and this is that which is written: 'Surely our sickness He hath carried'.

This work of the Messiah was divinely foreordained. It would not be an accident or a 'mistake used by God'. We are told plainly, although it is a mystery:

> *Yet it pleased the Lord to bruise him; he hath put him to grief*: when thou shalt make his soul an offering for sin, he shall see his seed, he shall prolong his days, and *the pleasure of the Lord shall prosper in his hand.* (53:10, RV.)

In Luchot Habberit (242a) it is said: 'He (the Messiah) will give Himself and His life over unto death, and His blood will atone for His people.'

It was this mysterious being 'stricken' by God (53:4) which caused the title 'Leprous' to be given to the Messiah in the Talmud (Sanhedrin 98b). The Hebrew word translated 'stricken' in this verse, is translated 'plague' in Leviticus 13:13. It means a stroke or a blow; or infliction of evil or plague (especially as a divine judgement); or spot, or mark (as of leprosy). There could have been no clearer intimation of that truth concerning the work of the Messiah which the apostle Paul stated so plainly in Galatians 3:13-14,

> Messiah redeemed us from the curse of the law, having become a curse for us; for it is written, Cursed is every one that hangeth on a tree: that upon the Gentiles might come the blessing of Abraham in Messiah Jesus. (RV, reading *Messiah* for *Christ*.)

Again in 2 Corinthians 5:21,

> Him who knew no sin, he [God] made to be sin on our behalf; that we might become the righteousness of God in him. (RV)

If the work of the Messiah is explained and interpreted, so also is its consequence. We read in Isaiah 53:11,

> By the knowledge of himself shall my righteous servant justify many; and he shall bear their iniquities. (ASV)

Here we come to the meaning of the name 'Jesus'. 'Jesus' is from the Greek form of the Hebrew *Yeshua*, or 'Joshua', as we know it in the Old Testament. That name means 'the Lord is salvation'. The angel of the Lord told Joseph in a dream:

> Thou shalt call his name Jesus, for it is he that shall save his people from their sins. (Matthew 1:21, RV.)

Speaking of the Messiah, the prophet Jeremiah said:

> Behold, the days come, saith the Lord, that I will raise unto David a righteous Branch, and he shall reign as King and deal wisely, and shall execute judgement and justice in the land. In his days Judah shall be saved, and Israel shall dwell safely:

> and this is his name whereby he shall be called, The Lord is our Righteousness. (Jeremiah 23:5-6, RV.)

The 'Branch' is recognized by both Jewish and Christian sources to be a messianic title. This then is an amazing prophecy, for it predicts that the Messiah, the Branch, will be called 'The Lord is our righteousness' or 'The Lord our righteousness'. In the Targum Jonathan this is applied to the Messiah, as in many other Jewish sources. In the Midrash Mishle it is said: 'Rab Huna counted amongst the seven names of the Messiah also: "Jehovah Zidkenu", the Lord, our righteousness.' Rabbi Joseph Albo (15th century A.D.) said: 'The Scripture calleth the name of the Messiah "Jehovah Zidkenu", because He is the mediator through whom we shall obtain the righteousness of the Lord.' If the Messiah is only man, how can he be 'our righteousness'? If, however, the Messiah is the Son of God, God incarnate, and was made to be sin on our behalf that we might become the righteousness of God in him, we can understand this prophecy. Thus the Messiah 'by the knowledge of himself' will 'justify many' because 'he bore their iniquities'. Many have experienced the fulfilment of this in the person and work of the Lord Jesus.

In Zechariah 6:12-13 it is written:

> Thus speaketh the Lord of hosts, saying, Behold the man whose name is the Branch; and he shall grow up out of his place, and he shall build the temple of the Lord: even he shall build the temple of the Lord; and he shall bear the glory, and shall sit and rule upon his throne; and he shall be a priest upon his throne: and the counsel of peace shall be between them both. (RV)

For born-again believers these two prophecies are highly instructive. The first speaks of the Messiah's work in salvation, and the second of his work in building God's spiritual house, his eternal dwelling-place.

The glory that would follow the Messiah's sufferings is predicted in Psalm 2, recognized as a messianic psalm by both Jewish and Christian sources:

> Yet I have set my king upon my holy hill of Zion. I will tell of the decree: the Lord said unto me, Thou art my son; this day have I begotten thee. Ask of me, and I will give thee the nations for thine inheritance, and the uttermost parts of the earth for thy possession. (Verses 6-8, RV.)

No matter what withstands the purpose of God concerning his Messiah, it will all fail and be broken. God's purpose will be fulfilled in every detail. The nations will become his inheritance and the uttermost parts of the earth his possession. Furthermore the references to the Son have never been adequately explained in Jewish sources: 'Thou art my son' (verse 7); 'Kiss the son, lest he be angry, and ye perish in the way, for his wrath will soon be kindled. Blessed are all they that take refuge in him' (verse 12, ASV). The Messiah of verse 6 is the Son of verses 7 and 12. How is it possible to take refuge in a human being? The inference is plain: the Messiah is the Son of God. He is 'Immanuel', God with us. And who could this Son be if he is not the Lord Jesus?

The triumph of the rejected and executed Messiah occurs in other prophecies. Consider, for example, Psalm 118:

> The right hand of the Lord is exalted: the right hand of the Lord doeth valiantly. I shall not die, but live, and declare the works of the Lord .... The stone which the builders rejected is become the head of the corner. This is the Lord's doing; it is marvellous in our eyes. This is the day which the Lord hath made; we will rejoice and be glad in it. (Verses 16-17, 22-24, RV.)

It was predicted that the Messiah would be rejected by the 'builders', but that he would nevertheless become the key to the whole building. We discover this also in Psalm 110:

> The Lord saith unto my lord, Sit thou at my right hand, until I make thine enemies thy footstool. The Lord shall send the rod of thy strength out of Zion: rule thou in the midst of thine enemies. (Verses 1-2. RV.)

In spite of all the opposition and rebellion, the Messiah would reign from the right hand of God. As Isaiah had prophesied:

> He shall be exalted and lifted up, and shall be very high. (Isaiah 52:13, RV.)

These significant messianic psalms have been gloriously fulfilled in the person of the Lord Jesus. His rejection and crucifixion, far from being his end, formed his path to eternal glory and honour. His words, his work and, above all, his salvation have come to the ends of the earth, bringing countless thousands to God and influencing even the course of nations. In the Midrash Rabbah it is said:

> In future God will let the Messiah sit at his right hand, as it is written, 'The Lord saith unto my lord, sit thou at my right hand.'

God has exalted the Lord Jesus to his own right hand, there to reign until his enemies become the stool for his feet.

This glorious triumph of the Messiah will one day be publicly manifested and the whole world will see his glory. Daniel prophesies this:

> I saw in the night visions, and, behold, there came with the clouds of heaven one like unto a son of man, and he came even to the ancient of days, and they brought him near before him. And there was given him dominion, and glory, and a kingdom, that all the peoples, nations, and languages should serve him: his dominion is an everlasting dominion, which shall not pass away, and his kingdom that which shall not be destroyed. (Daniel 7:13-14, RV.)

Zechariah spoke of the Messiah's return to Jerusalem, to the Mount of Olives:

> 'Then shall the Lord go forth, and fight against those nations, as when he fought in the day of battle. And his feet shall stand in that day upon the mount of Olives, which is before Jerusalem on the east .... (Zechariah 14:3-4, RV.)

That will be the day when peace will come at last to this sad and war-torn world, for the Messiah will reign to the ends of the earth, and righteousness and mercy, not diplomacy and compromise, will be the basis of all government and all decision-making. The Lord Jesus referred to these prophecies in his trial before the high priest:

> ... the high priest asked him ... Art thou the Christ [the Messiah], the Son of the Blessed? And Jesus said, I am: and ye shall see the Son of man sitting at the right hand of power, and coming with the clouds of heaven. (Mark 14:61-62, RV.)

Speaking earlier to his disciples about the signs of the end, he had said:

> Then shall appear the sign of the Son of man in heaven: and then shall all the tribes of the earth mourn, and they shall see the Son of man coming on the clouds of heaven with power and great glory. (Matthew 24:30, RV.)

The two angels also referred to this when they asked the wondering disciples at the ascension of the Lord Jesus from the Mount of Olives:

> Men of Galilee, why do you stand looking into the sky? This Jesus, who has been taken up from you into heaven, will come in just the same way as you have watched Him go into heaven. (Acts 1:11, NASB.)

How can we explain these prophecies which have been so significantly fulfilled in not only the person and coming of the Lord Jesus, but also in his death and resurrection? If it is all coincidence, it must surely be among the most incredible series of coincidences in history! In Psalm 40 it is written:

> Then I said, "Behold, I come; in the scroll of the book it is written of me; I delight to do Thy will, O my God; Thy law is within my heart." (Verses 7-8, NASB.)

These words are messianic. After his resurrection the Lord Jesus said to his disciples,

> These are My words which I spoke to you while I was still with you, that all things which are written about Me in the Law of Moses and the Prophets and the Psalms must be fulfilled. (Luke 24:44, NASB.)

In these last two chapters I have quoted a number of messianic prophecies from the law of Moses, the prophets, and the psalms, and shown how they have been fulfilled in the Lord Jesus. On this theme there could be no end of writing. It is this wealth of prophecy and prediction which makes the Messiah unique. Of no one else in the history of mankind has there been so much said and written before he was even born.

Zechariah prophesied:

> They shall look unto me whom they have pierced: and they shall mourn for him, as one mourneth for his only son, and shall be in bitterness for him, as one that is in bitterness for his firstborn. (Zechariah 12:10, RV.)

In the Talmud (Sukkah 52a) this prophecy is applied to the Messiah, the son of Joseph:

> It is well according to him who explains that the cause is the slaying of the Messiah, the son of Joseph, since that well agrees with the Scripture verse: 'And they shall look unto Me whom they have pierced, and shall mourn for him ....'

Rashi said:

> Our Rabbis interpreted it as referring to Messiah ben Joseph.

Rabbi Moses Alsheikh (1508-1600) said:

> 'They shall look unto me', for they shall lift up their eyes unto me in perfect repentance, when they see him whom they have pierced, that is Messiah, the son of Joseph; for our Rabbis of

> blessed memory have said that he will take upon himself all the guilt of Israel, and shall then be slain in the war to make atonement in such manner that it shall be accounted as if Israel had pierced him, for on account of their sin he has died; and, therefore, in order that it may be reckoned to them as a perfect atonement, they will repent and look to the blessed One, saying that there is none beside him to forgive those that mourn on account of him who died for their sin: this is the meaning of 'they shall look unto me'.

It would seem to me to be an extraordinary coincidence if this did not refer to the Lord Jesus. For of all those who have been 'pierced' in Jewish history, he is the most outstanding, and his crucifixion has had the most tremendous influence on the course of Jewish history, whether it has been recognized or not. If this is so, according to Zechariah there will come a day when Jewish people will recognize him as the Messiah and turn to him in deep repentance and faith.

Then will the cry of the crucified Messiah be heeded with the most glorious consequences:

> Is it nothing to you, all ye that pass by? Behold, and see if there be any sorrow like unto my sorrow, which is done unto me, wherewith the Lord hath afflicted me in the day of his fierce anger. (Lamentations 1:12, RV.)

These words referred to the day of Jerusalem's destruction by Nebuchadnezzar and were written, according to ancient tradition, in the cave at the foot of 'Gordon's Calvary' in Jerusalem. Nevertheless they are also surely messianic, foreshadowing the suffering Messiah in the day when they will be heeded by 'all who turn from transgression and ungodliness in Jacob'. Then they will behold in the face of the one who was 'esteemed stricken, smitten of God, and afflicted' the light of the knowledge of the glory of God.

CHAPTER 3

THE KING OF THE JEWS

'Where is he that is born King of the Jews?' enquired the wise men, after their long journey from the East. They had seen his star, and it had been of such significance and singularity that they had set out in quest of him. There must have been something striking about these men, for their arrival soon set Jerusalem talking! Before long the news reached the ears of King Herod the Great, and he summoned the chief priests and the scribes to tell him where the Messiah should be born.

Evidently there was no doubt in King Herod's mind that this talk of a 'King of the Jews' referred to the messianic Saviour-King who was expected by such a large number of people at that time. The chief priests and scribes replied that according to Micah 5:2 the Messianic King would be born in Bethlehem of Judah. Herod intuitively felt that his position as King was threatened by the possibility of the advent of the Messiah, and took the matter seriously enough to make very careful enquiry concerning the observations and findings of the wise men. We know from history that Herod suffered from paranoia and anything which he thought threatened his throne immediately provoked him. He wanted to know the exact time that the star first appeared, and then he commanded the wise men to inform him when they had found the babe. When they failed to return he issued orders for the execution of every male child under two years of age in the Bethlehem region (Matthew 2:16-18). Herod was sufficiently disturbed to believe that this was indeed the Messiah, and therefore took drastic action.

Jesus was born King of the Jews in the most humble

surroundings. His mother Mary was of the royal seed of David, as indeed was his earthly 'father', Joseph. We have two genealogies which trace the line of Jesus; they differ from one another after King David, only Zerubbabel and Shealtiel being the same in both pedigrees. The first, in Matthew 1:1-16, is apparently the genealogy of Joseph, while the second, in Luke 3:23-38 is apparently Mary's. Many Christian scholars question this and propose that the Matthew pedigree is the legal descent, i.e. those who were heir to the throne at any given time; and that the Luke pedigree is the natural descent, i.e. the particular and actual genealogy. It is noteworthy that in the Talmud (Sanhedrin 43a) it is stated, '... Jesus, who was of royal descent'. It is highly significant that in spite of their antagonism towards Jesus, the chief priests and scribes never once challenged the claim of Jesus to be of the royal house of David. Until the fall of Jerusalem in A.D. 70, the registries containing genealogies were intact and could easily have been consulted. Since the Jewish Establishment of the day so earnestly desired to discredit Jesus in the eyes of the people, this would have been the most simple and effective way to achieve that end. The fact that they never once tried to use this weapon to disprove his claim is eloquent and powerful testimony to its truth.

There is the ring of authenticity about the gospel narratives relating to the birth of the Lord Jesus. When Mary's cousin met her, we are told that 'the babe leaped' in Elizabeth's womb, and filled with the Holy Spirit she exclaimed with a glad cry:

> Blessed art thou among women, and blessed is the fruit of thy womb. (Luke 1:42, RV.)

Or, as The Living Bible puts it:

> You are favoured by God above all other women, and your child is destined for God's mightiest praise. What an honour this is, that the *mother of my Lord* should visit me!

And Mary responded:

> Oh, how I praise the Lord. How I rejoice in God my Saviour! For he took notice of his lowly servant girl, and now generation after generation forever shall call me blest of God. For he, the mighty Holy One, has done great things to me. (Luke 1:46-49, The Living Bible.)

Eight days after Elizabeth's baby John was born, on the occasion of his circumcision (Berit Milah), her husband Zacharias, a priest, was suddenly filled with the Holy Spirit and prophesied:

> Praise the Lord, the God of Israel, for he has come to visit his people and has redeemed them. He is sending us a Mighty Saviour from the royal line of his servant David, just as he promised through his holy prophets long ago — someone to save us from our enemies, from all who hate us.
>
> He has been merciful to our ancestors, yes, to Abraham himself, by remembering his sacred promise to him, and by granting us the privilege of serving God fearlessly, freed from our enemies, and by making us holy and acceptable, ready to stand in his presence forever.
>
> And you, my little son, shall be called the prophet of the glorious God, for you will prepare the way for the Messiah. You will tell his people how to find salvation through forgiveness of their sins. All this will be because the mercy of our God is very tender, and heaven's dawn is about to break upon us, to give light to those who sit in darkness and death's shadow, and to guide us to the path of peace. (Luke 1:68-79, The Living Bible.)

From the manner in which Zacharias spoke of the birth of his own son and of the coming birth of Jesus, there can be no doubt that he too believed that Jesus was the Messiah.

There were others who thought the same. When Mary and Joseph brought the infant Jesus into the Temple for circumcision, they were met by the godly Simeon. The Holy Spirit had revealed to him that he would not die until he had seen the Messiah. He took Jesus into his arms, and blessed God with the words:

> Lord ... now I can die content! For I have seen him as you promised me I would. I have seen the Saviour you have given to the world. He is the Light that will shine upon the nations, and he will be the glory of your people Israel! (Luke 2:29-32, The Living Bible.)

And to Mary his mother he said:

> Behold, this Child is appointed for the fall and rise of many in Israel; and for a sign to be opposed — and a sword will pierce even your own soul — to the end that thoughts from many hearts may be revealed. (Luke 2:34-35, NASB.)

There was also an old prophetess, Anna, evidently well known in the Temple for her life of prayer, who recognized the babe as the messianic Saviour-King, and 'spoke of him to all those who were looking for the redemption of Jerusalem' (Luke 2:38-39).

If Jesus was born King of the Jews, he also died King of the Jews. In the end, when the accusations brought against him failed, the Jewish leaders brought a new charge to the Roman Governor, Pontius Pilate. They said:

> We found this man perverting our nation, and forbidding to give tribute to Caesar, and saying that he himself is Messiah a king [*or* the messianic King]. (Luke 23:2, RV reading *Messiah* for *Christ.*)

This disturbed Pilate, and he asked Jesus whether he really was King of the Jews. The answer of Jesus is most revealing. He said to Pilate, 'Do you feel this yourself, or is it that others have told you?' (See John 18:34.) Pilate replied: 'I am not Jewish. I do not understand the intricacies and complexities of your sacred Scriptures and of your traditions. Your own nation and leaders have brought you to me. Tell me what you have done.'

Jesus then answered: 'My kingdom is not of this world. If my kingdom were of this world, then would my servants fight.' Pilate again said to him: 'Are you a king then?'

Jesus said: 'Leave it as you say, because to this end have I been born and to this end have I come into the world, that I should bear witness to the truth. Everyone that is of the truth hears my voice.' He was saying in effect, 'Those who believe in truth and belong to the kingdom of God and of light will recognize whether I am King of the Jews or not.' It was then that Pilate said, 'what is truth?' (See John 18:33-40.)

Pilate was clearly impressed. Twice he pronounced the official verdict, 'Not guilty'. When, however, the rabble grew in size and noise, he became afraid that serious rioting might result. Finally, when the Jewish leaders ominously declared, 'If you release this man, you are not a friend of Caesar's – everyone that makes himself a king is guilty of rebellion against Caesar,' Pilate compromised and, washing his hands of the whole affair, sentenced Jesus to death by crucifixion (John 19:1-16).

Thus Pilate abdicated all responsibility! He knew what was right, but he had to choose in the end between self and Jesus, and he chose self. He had made an effort to save him, but he could not pay the price when faced with the stark alternatives. Either he appeased the Jewish establishment and the mob they had inspired (evil and wicked as he knew them to be) by crucifying the Messiah, or he deliberately released an innocent man and faced a riot, with all the damage that that could do to his career. It was political expediency at the expense of righteousness. When the veiled threat was made concerning his loyalty to Caesar, Pilate solemnly washed his hands, had Jesus flogged, and signed the death sentence. Flogging which preceded crucifixion often proved fatal in itself. The whip used was made of leather thongs tipped with sharp pieces of metal and bone. It inflicted severe injuries. Pilate probably thought that the pitiable sight of Jesus, badly flogged, his claim to be King and Messiah held up to derision and contempt, would have excited compassion and caused the crowd to relent. But even this failed. Through sheer self-protection Pilate was forced to sentence the Messiah to death.

So imperial Rome in the person of Pilate tried the Lord Jesus and sentenced him to death. We could have expected no other outcome. Furthermore, we see an extraordinary alliance of two mutually hostile and suspicious worlds, the Gentile and the Jewish, combining together to destroy the messianic King. There is perhaps no clearer picture of the essential difference between the Messiah and this world than here. For when this world knows what is right, but is faced with the stark choice of either self-interest or God, it will always seek to destroy God and choose self. We might well wonder then how it is possible to trust such a nature and character, or to put confidence in that kind of man or society, even in its noblest form, which can wash its hands and commit murder. Yet we have here a picture, a cameo of human history; a key to the endless breakdown of human society, be it primitive or sophisticated. It is as if we are looking through a window into the very character and nature of fallen man, and of the society he has produced. We see the hopelessness of man and society and their inevitable breakdown, even when representing and giving lip service to the highest ideals and ethics.

Thank God, in the Messiah we see something wholly different. In the garden of Gethsemane he also faced the choice of self or God; of self-sacrifice or self-interest. He chose God; he deliberately chose to lay down his life for the nation and for the world. In him we see another kind of man, the kind of man God longs for, the kind of character God himself has, and the kind of service which flows out of a heart of love.

He stands there condemned, a lonely figure. Mocked, beaten, disfigured, bloodied, humiliated, he endures all in silence, the silence of a measureless love. He endures that he might save us; that he might provide us with the way out of this kind of man and society, out of this kind of nature, out of this 'rat race', into another kingdom, the kingdom of God. At no point does the Lord Jesus reveal his inherent worthiness to be king more than here. As we see him face all that man finds most fearful and terrible – pain, suffering, derision, loneliness, evil, death, the unknown – we see a dignity, a majesty, a kingliness beyond compare and without equal. It shines through all. Lacerated and bleeding, spittle on his face, a butt for coarse jokes, jeered at and despised, his human strength giving way under the physical weight of his cross, nailed through hands and feet to a great stake, all hell let loose in a few hours of satanic fury and darkness – through it all shines an authority, a dignity, a majesty this world does not know. Even when, forsaken by God for the first and only time, this universe heard that most terrible, most awesome, and most agonized cry – so that even the sun hid its face – his inherent kingliness is still apparent.

Jesus reveals a concept of kingship and leadership which is different from the concept held by this world. It is not a matter of the right genealogy, or of outward pomp and show, or of autocratic power and might; nor, on a more spiritual level, even a matter of the divine right to be king by predestination. It is true that Jesus was the messianic King long promised; he was divinely chosen and predestined; he was born of the royal seed. Nevertheless his kingship is based on more than that. He reveals the kind of character that can do no other than reign, an authority and dignity that is not dependent on office, title or position, but springs spontaneously from spiritual strength and uprightness. His kingship is based on love and truth, on righteousness, justice and mercy, on holiness and compassion. Its foundation is sacrificial service and incorruptible character. Through thirty-three years of earthly life, lived in average circumstances and conditions, he proved inherently worthy of God's throne and kingdom. This God attested when he transfigured him in glory. And nowhere did the Lord Jesus more clearly reveal his worthiness to be king than in his humiliation, suffering and death, divested of all that normally makes for the 'mystique' of royalty. We have a King who bears nailmarks in his hands and feet for ever, the eternal emblem of his undying love for us. Here is no king concerned about his own future, reputation or glory, but One who can lay aside his glory, and die for those who are totally unworthy that he might bring them into God's Kingdom.

Rome had no idea of the immense issues involved in the trial of this 'Jewish Messiah'. Unbeknown to her, her day of judgement had dawned. Rome might mouth her high ideals, preach her noble ethics, and define her just laws; but her real character was to be seen in Pilate. Rome might wash her hands a thousand times, it made no difference! The trial of the Messiah exposed her for what she was. In trying him, she put herself on trial and was judged. In signing his death sentence, she signed her own. In the end it is proud, imperial Rome which crumbles into the dust, and it is the King of the Jews, Jesus, standing that day in the praetorium, rejected and despised, who ascends the throne of God and of the universe to reign for ever.

CHAPTER 4

BEHOLD, YOUR KING!

Was Pilate being cynical or genuine when he said to the Jewish leaders, 'Behold, your King'? Was he being genuine when the mob howled for Jesus' blood and he asked, 'Shall I crucify your King?' Did Pilate recognize something in Jesus that was authentic and true?

This was undoubtedly so with many who came into touch with the Lord Jesus during his ministry. Pilate was surely not playing with Jesus, but making a last appeal to the conscience of the Jewish establishment. Of course, he had no need to make such an appeal, for he was Governor and as such his word was final. In fact, he was meant to ensure that the law was properly administered. His guilt is, therefore, as great as any who had a part in the crucifixion of the Lord Jesus, if not greater than all. It seems clear from the superscription that he ordered to be written, that he was impressed by Jesus. This superscription normally contained the charge upon which the criminal had been found guilty. It was either carried before him on his way to execution or hung around his neck, finally being nailed above his head. The one Pilate wrote for Jesus read, in Hebrew, Latin, and Greek: 'Jesus of Nazareth, the King of the Jews.' The Jewish leaders were scandalized, and vehemently protested to the Governor. They asked for the wording to be changed to 'Jesus of Nazareth, who said that he was King of the Jews'. But Pilate answered them in those immortal words: 'What I have written, I have written.' And Jesus died King of the Jews, as he was born King of the Jews.

One who recognized him as the messianic King during his public ministry was Nathanael, who declared: 'Thou art the Son of God; thou art King of Israel' (John 1:49, RV); another disciple, Peter, confessed: 'Thou art the Messiah, the Son of the Living God' (Matthew 16:16); and blind Bartimaeus had cried out, 'Jesus, thou Son of David, have mercy on me,' and was healed (Mark 10:47). It is significant that, at one point, the people of Galilee were so moved that they would have come and taken him by force and made him king, unless he had withdrawn himself from them (John 6:15).

A week before he died he made a triumphal entry into Jerusalem, which appears to have called forth a spontaneous expression of the common people's feeling for Jesus. It seems that they readily recognized his messianic claims, and were prepared publicly to express their sentiments. In John 12:12-16, we read:

> On the morrow a great multitude that had come to the feast, when they heard that Jesus was coming to Jerusalem, took the branches of the palm trees, and went forth to meet him, and cried out, Hosanna: Blessed is he that cometh in the name of the Lord, even the King of Israel. And Jesus, having found a young ass, sat thereon; as it is written, Fear not, daughter of Zion: behold, thy King cometh, sitting on an ass's colt. These things understood not his disciples at the first: but when Jesus was glorified, then remembered they that these things were written of him, and that they had done these things unto him. (RV)

If his disciples did not understand the full meaning and significance of that event, the Pharisees and the establishment most certainly did. They said,

> We've lost. Look — the whole world has gone after him! (John 12:19, The Living Bible.)

It seems that among ordinary people there was a widespread recognition that Jesus was the messianic King, of the royal house of David, and that his kingship was not just a matter of pedigree, but was authenticated by the signs and miracles he performed, by the way in which he spoke, and above all, by his inward and spiritual character. It is an interesting fact that during his trial and in his degradation at the hands of the Roman soldiers it was the claim that he was King of the Jews that was bandied about. Even when he was crucified, the chief priests called out to him:

> Let the Messiah, the King of Israel, now come down from the cross, that we may see and believe. (Mark 15:32, RV reading *Messiah* for *Christ*.)

What other explanation is there for the person of Jesus, than that he was what he claimed to be – not only Messiah, but King? Putting aside for one moment the signs and miracles, can we believe that his words are the words of a self-deluded actor? No one ever spoke as he did. A careful consideration of his words must surely lead to the conclusion that they are genuine. And after the words, miracles and signs, we have to face the claims.

If we recall the many ancient prophecies concerning the Messiah which have been fulfilled in the person and work of Jesus, in the circumstances of his birth, in the incredible three years of his public ministry and in his sufferings and death, I believe that we must accept as true the claim of the Lord Jesus to be the messianic Saviour-King. For myself, there can be no satisfying explanation of his person and character and work other than that he was, and is the Son of God, the Messiah, the King of the Jews.

If the prophecies concerning him, spoken many centuries before he was born, were noteworthy; if the circumstances of his birth and his public ministry, and above all, the circumstances of his death were remarkable; the events which followed his death must be the most extraordinary of all. It is hard to believe that he somehow managed to survive crucifixion, revived, and was 'spirited away', and that in the end nobody ever heard about it – knowing as I do the Middle East, its inquisitiveness and curiosity in this kind of matter, and particularly the way gossip travels. If he had avoided dying, it would have been the greatest joy for his disciples. They had not grasped that he must die, let alone rise again. Furthermore, when we recognize the precautions that were taken – the guard at the tomb, the official seal on the tomb itself – and the disillusionment of those sorrowing disciples, what other explanation is there for what happened, other than that he actually arose from the dead?

The empty tomb has never been satisfactorily explained in any other way. The crushed and broken-hearted disciples could not have removed the body of Jesus from the tomb because of the watchful guard set by the authorities. The Jewish establishment had only one aim, and that was to keep the lifeless body of Jesus within the tomb. What then could have happened? – for all agree that the tomb was empty.

There are, however, further factors. There were the undisturbed grave clothes which arrested the attention of all who went to the empty tomb. They were like the empty chrysalis of a butterfly. They had not been torn from the body, nor even carefully removed. They were neither strewn about the tomb, nor neatly folded up. *The body had simply vanished out of them*, leaving them in the precise folds and crevices made when the body was wrapped in them; the turban-like cloth over the face was rolled up in a place by itself (John 20:6-7).

Another factor was the unbelieving disciples. A careful reading of the records makes it clear that at first they found the fact of his resurrection very hard to believe. It was by his appearances that they were finally convinced (see e.g. Luke 24). The manner of his appearances presents us with another factor, for they were not the appearances of a spirit. The disciples met him, touched him, ate with him. Even the rationalistic mind of Thomas was finally convinced. (See Luke 24:36-43; John 20:20, 24-28.)

A further factor is the untampered records. If the resurrection of Jesus had been a cleverly engineered fraud, one would have expected the records to have 'been adjusted'. There are some minor discrepancies, but these only go to vindicate the authenticity of the accounts. (Cf. e.g. the number of the disciples in Mark 16:14 and Luke 24:33). *No gospel writer has tried to harmonize the different eyewitness accounts.*

Another remarkable factor was the change that came over the disappointed and dispirited disciples. When the Lord Jesus died, they were numbed by shock, and scattered. Something happened which transformed them into a dynamic movement which was not only to turn their contemporary world upside down, but was cheerfully to endure organized persecution and trial. They knew beyond all doubt that Jesus was alive from the dead, and the Saviour of all who come to God by him. Down the centuries since then, countless men and women have made the same discovery: Jesus is alive! Can this be put down to hallucination, mass psychology, or fraud? Never! The fact is that God raised him from the dead, thus vindicating the claim that he was, and is both Messiah and Lord. The apostle Peter was in no doubt when he preached on the day of Pentecost:

> Men of Israel, listen to these words: Jesus the Nazarene, a man attested to you by God with miracles and wonders and signs which God performed through Him in your midst, just as you yourselves know — this Man, delivered up by the predetermined plan and foreknowledge of God, you nailed to a cross by the hands of godless men and put Him to death. And God raised Him up again, putting an end to the agony of death, since it was impossible for Him to be held in its power .... Therefore let all the house of Israel know for certain that God has made Him both Lord and Christ [Messiah] — this Jesus whom you crucified. (Acts 2:22-24, 36, NASB.)

The apostle Paul later re-stated this simply and profoundly:

> ... the gospel of God, which He promised beforehand through His prophets in the holy Scriptures, concerning His Son, who was born of the seed of David according to the flesh, who was declared with power to be the Son of God by the resurrection from the dead, according to the Spirit of holiness, Jesus Christ [the Messiah] our Lord. (Romans 1:1-4, NASB.)

Furthermore, this is not only an objective truth, but we who believe have the witness within ourselves: we have been

> born again to a living hope through the resurrection of Jesus Christ [the Messiah] from the dead. (1 Peter 1:3, NASB.)

Is it any wonder that God has made the Messiah Jesus 'King of kings and Lord of lords'? For he who was born King of the Jews and died King of the Jews is the one whom God has seated

> at His right hand in the heavenly places, far above all rule and authority and power and dominion, and every name that is named, not only in this age, but also in the one to come. (Ephesians 1:20-21, NASB.)

CHAPTER 5

WE HAVE NO KING BUT CAESAR

There are no more sad and solemn words than John 19:14-16:

> Now it was the Preparation of the passover: it was about the sixth hour, and he [Pilate] said unto the Jews: behold, your king! They therefore cried out, Away with him, away with him, crucify him. Pilate saith unto them, Shall I crucify your King? The chief priests answered, We have no king but Caesar. Then therefore he delivered him unto them to be crucified. (RV)

The Jewish world – represented by the Jewish establishment, the high priestly family, the elders, chief priests and scribes – and the Gentile world – represented by the Roman Procurator, Pontius Pilate, acting in the name of imperial Rome – joined hands to crucify the Messiah. It was one of the major turning points in Jewish history, indeed, in the history of the world. For Jesus *was* King of the Jews, and, in the final analysis, it was on this issue that he was crucified.

It was the saddest day in Jewish history when the mob cried, 'Away with him, away with him, crucify him, and the leaders of the Jewish nation said to Pilate, 'We have no king but Caesar.' From that day to this, there has never been another Jewish king. Indeed until the year 1948, the Jewish people knew no government other than 'Caesar's'. Over all those years they were under the rule of Gentiles, non-Jews, wherever they lived.

It is, of course, a gross mistake to believe that all the Jewish people, any more than all Gentiles, were responsible for the death of the Messiah. In fact, inasmuch as we are all sinners, we are all responsible for his crucifixion, for he was the Lamb of God who bore away the sin of the world; the One upon whom all our iniquities were laid. We, therefore, who have sinned are responsible for his death.

By contrast with the Jewish establishment, many of the common people seemed to be sympathetic to the Lord Jesus right to the end. For instance, we read in Mark 14:1-2,

> Now the feast of the Passover and Unleavened Bread was two days off; and the chief priests and the scribes were seeking how to seize Him by stealth, and kill Him; for they were saying, "Not during the festival, lest there be a riot of the people". (NASB)

It was Judas who provided them with the opportunity to arrest Jesus, in an isolated garden in the Kidron valley called Gethsemane. Being a suitable distance from any large population centre it presented an ideal situation for his sudden arrest. It is noteworthy that the Jewish establishment, which longed to believe that the people were not with Jesus, had to admit that he was not only popular, but so popular that had the Jewish leaders arrested him during the feast, there would have been a riot, with serious consequences for them.

Then again, in Luke 23:27-31, it is recorded:

> And there were following Him a great multitude of the people, and of women who were mourning and lamenting Him. But Jesus turning to them said, "Daughters of Jerusalem, stop weeping for Me, but weep for yourselves and for your children. For behold, the days are coming when they will say, 'Blessed are the barren, and the wombs that never bore, and the breasts that never nursed.' Then they will begin to say to the mountains, 'Fall on us,' and to the hills, 'Cover us.' For if they do these things in the green tree, what will happen in the dry?" (NASB)

Luke informs us, with his usual care, that it was 'a great multitude of the people' who followed the Lord Jesus to the place of his execution. By the way he introduces the 'women who were mourning and lamenting him', he implies that this large Jewish crowd was basically sympathetic to Jesus. On that day many Jewish faces were stained with tears, and many Jewish hearts were broken with grief. Luke further records in this chapter (verse 48):

> and all the multitudes who came together for this spectacle, when they observed what had happened, began to return, beating their breasts. (NASB)

From all of this, a more balanced picture emerges. Many of the common people were deeply moved at what had happened. It is often stated that the people who acclaimed the Lord Jesus as the messianic King on the occasion of his triumphal entry into Jerusalem were the same as those who, a few days later, called for his crucifixion. This widely held belief is expressed in a verse of one of our most beautiful hymns:

> Sometimes they strew His way,
> And His sweet praises sing;
> Resounding all the day
> Hosannas to their king.
> Then: 'Crucify!'
> Is all their breath,
> And for His death
> They thirst and cry.

Human nature may be fickle, but the evidence does not support the belief that the *same* people that acclaimed Jesus also rejected him. As we have seen, the gospels rather suggest that many of the common people knew that what was being perpetrated was evil, and the result of conspiracy and wickedness in high places, but felt powerless to stop it.

We all know from events in the world today that it is not

hard to bring together a volatile and sometimes violent group, numbering thousands, that does not necessarily represent the mind of the majority in that nation. The blood-thirsty mob which howled for the death of Jesus probably comprised a hired rabble, a number of simple but easily influenced people, and the bitter antagonists of Jesus. The Judean establishment was undoubtedly the main inspiration of the whole operation. (See Matthew 27:20; Mark 15:11) The Lord Jesus, prophesying his crucifixion, had named the 'elders and chief priests and scribes' as the main force, humanly speaking, behind his sufferings, rejection and death. (See Matthew 16:21; Mark 8:31; 10:33-34; Luke 9:22.)

If the name of the Sanhedrin, however, has been blackened in the eyes of most Christians by the corruption and evil ways of a high priestly family and clique, a kind of 'ecclesiastical mafia' (and there have been enough illustrations of this in church history also, whether Roman Catholic, Orthodox, or Protestant), it was nevertheless two members of the Sanhedrin who have for ever redeemed its reputation. These were Joseph of Arimathea and Nicodemus. Joseph was 'a prominent member of the Council' (Mark 15:43, NASB), but no party to the intrigue of the chief priests, and he had not given his vote to the sentence of death (Luke 23:50-51). These were the two men who lovingly took down from the cross the lifeless body of the Messiah, prepared it for burial, and laid it in Joseph's own newly constructed tomb.

It is often implied that the Jewish people were totally responsible for the crucifixion of Jesus. This assumption cannot be supported when we bear in mind all the facts. Some go to the other extreme and seek to exonerate the Jewish people altogether, as if there were no Jewish hand in the event. The motive behind this attitude may be laudable in that it reflects a desire to remove what many consider to be the mainspring of anti-Semitism. But it is not truth and cannot be supported by the clear evidence in the New Testament. It would be as impossible to exonerate the Jewish world as to exonerate the Gentile and Roman world.

The fact of the matter is that the Jewish establishment, deeply divided on other issues, was united in this one aim of destroying Jesus. The high priestly family of Annas and Caiaphas, dominated by the evil personality and genius of Annas, of whom even the Talmud has nothing good to say, provided the main driving force behind the whole conspiracy. The Sadducee party, the party of the chief priests and aristocratic families of Jerusalem, joined with the Pharisees, the 'fundamentalist and puritan' party in the nation at large, and with the Herodians, considered by the others to be beyond redemption because of their support for the Herods and Roman policy, in a common desire to rid the nation of the influence and work of the Lord Jesus. These conflicting parties and interests were merged, as if by an invisible hand, in order to destroy the Messiah.

The apostle Peter summed up the situation when he said:

> Him [the Messiah], being delivered up by the determinate counsel and foreknowledge of God, ye [the Jewish establishment and leadership] by the hand of lawless men [Gentiles] did crucify and slay. (Acts 2:23, RV.)

On a later occasion Peter went into more detail:

> The God of Abraham, and of Isaac, and of Jacob, the God of our fathers, hath glorified his Servant Jesus; whom ye delivered up, and denied before the face of Pilate, when he had determined to release him. But ye denied the Holy and Righteous One [the Messiah], and asked for a murderer to be granted unto you, and killed the Prince of life; whom God raised from the dead; whereof we are witnesses .... And now, brethren, I know that in ignorance ye did it, as did also your rulers. But the things which God foreshowed by the mouth of all the prophets, that his Christ [Messiah] should suffer, he thus fulfilled. Repent ye therefore, and turn again, that your sins may be blotted out, that so there may come seasons of refreshing from the presence of the Lord; and that he may

> send the Christ [Messiah] who hath been appointed for you, even Jesus: whom the heaven must receive until the times of restoration of all things, whereof God spake by the mouth of his holy prophets that have been from of old. (Acts 3:13-21, ASV.)

The day Jesus was crucified was the darkest and saddest day in Jewish history, though not simply because of his death, for that was foreordained by God. Even if the Jewish people had had nothing to do with the death of the Messiah, he would still have been crucified and have died. It would, however, have been the responsibility of the Gentiles alone. Even if the whole Jewish nation had believed on him, had recognized his claims and had accepted him as King and Messiah, he would still have been crucified, *but there would have been no Jewish hand in it.* It was the saddest and darkest day in Jewish history because the people who had been the recipients of the grace of God, the promises of God, the covenant of God, and the knowledge of God's salvation, rejected the Messiah and crucified the Lord of glory, the Prince of life.

There can be no other explanation for the second exile of the Jewish people than this. They were exiled to Babylon in B.C. 587 for seventy years because of their consistent idolatry and refusal to hear and obey the word of the Lord. What sin could have warranted an exile of 1,900 years, with its suffering and anguish unparalleled even in the long story of the Jewish people? We are told by some that it was due to transgression of the law, because of disobedience to God; by others that it was due to evil and wickedness in high places, particularly to the conspiracy, corruption and rivalry that was rife in the high priestly family. There is surely only one *adequate* explanation for the second exile of the Jewish people, however, and that is their disobedience in rejecting the Messiah. The transgression of the law, the fundamental disobedience, was their disregarding of the prophecies which had been fulfilled in him.

These other factors, the dissension and in-fighting within the nation, the rivalry and corruption in the leading religious and political families, were subsidiary to the main factor, the rejection and crucifixion of the Messiah. There is no doubt that the Gentiles bore a heavy responsibility in this matter, but that is not the question. The Gentiles were outside the covenant of God at that time. The tragedy was that the covenant people of God, that nation which was in a unique relationship to the living God, rejected and crucified the one to whom their whole history pointed, of whom all their prophets had spoken, and upon whom their whole destiny depended. For in sentencing the Messiah to death, they drove a sword through their own heart, putting to death, as it were, their own history.

We have seen that this was not the mind of the whole people, but the will of a power-hungry ruling clique caught in the coils of self-interest and self-protection. Nevertheless what the establishment did was visited upon the whole nation. This may seem strange, but it is one reason why we are commanded to pray for all in authority. It has been said that God gives a nation the leaders it deserves. National leadership, the course of a nation, and the divine blessing or judgement which falls upon it, are inextricably linked. When Ernest Bevin, British foreign secretary in the years after the second world war, withstood the flood of desperate Jewish refugees to Palestine in 1946-47, enacting severe and repressive regulations on the Jews of Palestine, and harshly interning the so-called 'illegal' immigrants, he brought the British empire he represented into collision with the purpose and word of God, and judgement came upon it. It was the same with Jewish history.

The Lord Jesus is the key to Jewish history. There is a striking comment in the Talmud (Sanhedrin 97a-97b):

> The world is to exist six thousand years. In the first two thousand years there was desolation [that is, no Law] ; two

> thousand years the Torah [the Law] flourished; and the next two thousand years is the Messianic era.

This means that the last two thousand years has been the time of the Messiah, but according to Jewish tradition the Messiah has not yet appeared. Rashi made the comment,

> ... because after the second two thousand years the Messiah must have come and the wicked kingdom should have been destroyed.

In the same place in the Talmud (Sanhedrin 97a) there is the comment of another Rabbi: 'All the predestined dates have passed.' For this reason some of the Rabbis taught that the Messiah was born in Bethlehem, or in Jerusalem, but that he was hidden by God until the time of the end. Even the mysterious reference by Daniel to the seventy weeks of years, that is 490 years, which were determined until the coming of the Messiah, arrives at the same period of time (see Daniel 9:24-27). For from whatever Persian edict we choose to date the 490 years, all end before A.D. 70 and the destruction of Jerusalem. This prophecy in Daniel clearly states that at the end of this 490-year period

> the Messiah will be cut off and have nothing, and the people of the prince who is to come will destroy the city and the sanctuary. And its end will come with a flood; even to the end there will be war; desolations are determined. (Daniel 9:26, NASB.)

There can be little doubt that this prediction was fulfilled in the destruction of Jerusalem and the Temple by Titus in A.D. 70. If that is true, then the Messiah should have come before that event, according to Daniel, and as understood by many of the Rabbis. Furthermore, he should not only have come but should have been 'cut off'.

To whom else could all this refer other than the Lord

Jesus? Everything points to Him. He was of the seed of Abraham, through Isaac, and not Ishmael; he was the star out of Jacob, the sceptre out of Israel; he was of the tribe of Judah, the branch out of Jesse, the Son of David. He was born at Bethlehem. He was cut off out of the land of the living and was numbered with the transgressors; his hands and his feet were pierced. He made his grave with the wicked and with a rich man in his death; and God raised him up on the third day. It is a fact that 'Unto him the Gentiles have sought'; 'nations have come to His light, and kings to the brightness of His rising.' Rabbi Isaak Abravanel (1437-1508), commenting on the passage in Isaiah 11:1-10, said that 'one of the signs of the true Messiah would be that the Gentiles would seek him'. The many false messiahs of Jewish history may have had Jewish followings, but none of them has had any influence upon the Gentiles. The Lord Jesus, however, has had the most profound effect and influence upon them, countless thousands of Gentiles naming themselves with his name, and experiencing the salvation of God through him.

The Lord Jesus is the key which unlocks Jewish history. He makes explicable the inexplicable. For he is the key not only to the fall of the Jewish people, but to their restoration; not only to their being cast away, but to their being received again. He is the key to the loss of their statehood and their dispersion to the ends of the earth, and the key to the re-creation of their statehood and their being regathered to the land promised to Abraham, Isaac and Jacob, and to their seed for ever. For, in spite of the fact that they rejected him, he did not reject them.

It is recorded in the gospel of John that

> the chief priests and the Pharisees convened a council, and were saying, "What are we doing? For this man is performing many signs. If we let Him go on like this, all men will believe in Him, and the Romans will come and take away both our place and our nation." But a certain one of them, Caiaphas, who was high priest that year, said to them, "You know nothing at all, nor do you take into account that it is expedient

> for you that one man should die for the people, and that the whole nation should not perish." Now this he did not say on his own initiative; but being high priest that year, he prophesied that Jesus was going to die for the nation; and not for the nation only, but that He might also gather together into one the children of God who are scattered abroad. (John 11:47-52, NASB.)

The Lord Jesus died for the Jewish nation as well as for the whole world, and the basis of all God's dealings with them in regard to their being regathered to the land, their being re-constituted as a nation and their final salvation, is the work of the Messiah on the cross. In the prophecy of Daniel it is stated that the work of the Messiah would be

> to finish the transgression, to make an end of sin, to make atonement for iniquity, to bring in everlasting righteousness, to seal up vision and prophecy, and to anoint the most holy place. (Daniel 11:24, NASB.)

In some strange and mysterious way, the finished work of the Messiah underlies the whole of Jewish history and, in particular, the events of the last period of the age.

I have called the crucifixion of the Lord Jesus the saddest and darkest day in Jewish history. But it will yet become its most glorious and radiant day. For the crucified Messiah will yet become the salvation and the glory of the Jewish people. There will come a day when the 'Spirit of grace and supplication' is poured upon them, and they will look to the one they have pierced, and mourn for him as for an only son, and be 'in bitterness for him' as for a firstborn (Zechariah 12:10). Then, and only then, will the Jewish people fully understand their history. They will recognize its significance and meaning in the light of the Lord Jesus and will understand. They will see that the age-old Jewish aspiration and hope that they would be a blessing to all the nations of the earth has been fulfilled through Jesus the Messiah, and that an innumerable company of Gentiles from 'every tongue and kindred and people and nation' has been saved through him and brought to God, and made partakers of the commonwealth of Israel.

They will understand the words of the apostle Paul in Romans 15:8-12,

> For I say that Christ [Messiah] has become a servant to the circumcision on behalf of the truth of God to confirm the promises given to the fathers, and for the Gentiles to glorify God for His mercy; as it is written, "Therefore I will give praise to Thee among the Gentiles, and I will sing to Thy name. [Psalm 18:49]

And again he says, 'Rejoice, O Gentiles, with His people.' [Deuteronomy 32:43] And again, 'Praise the Lord all you Gentiles, and let all the peoples praise Him.' [Psalm 117:1] And again Isaiah says, '...the root of Jesse, which standeth for an ensign of the peoples, unto him shall the nations seek;' (Isiah 11:10, RV).

Jesus was born King of the Jews. He died King of the Jews. He will return King of the Jews. There has never been another Jewish king since the day Jesus died, nor will there be until he, whose right it is, returns to take the throne and reign. In that day, it will be as when Joseph revealed himself to his brethren: having saved 'Egypt' and the Gentiles, Jesus will finally reveal himself to those who are his 'brethren according to the flesh'. That will be a day unparalleled in the long history of mankind. Then will that prophetic word of knowledge and wisdom which was given to the godly Simeon, shortly after the birth of Jesus, have its complete fulfilment:

> Mine eyes have seen thy salvation, which thou hast prepared before the face of all peoples; a light for revelation to the Gentiles, and the glory of thy people Israel. (Luke 2:30-32, RV.)

The Lord will yet be the glory of his people Israel. That will be the most radiant day of Jewish history, when all suffering and anguish, alienation and sorrow will finally be swallowed up in unspeakable joy – 'a morning without clouds ... like clear shining after rain'!

CHAPTER 6

KING OF KINGS AND LORD OF LORDS

Somewhere in eternity past, before the foundation of the world, before man had even fallen, the cry of God had rung through heaven, 'Whom shall I send, and who will go for us?' (cf. Isaiah 6:8). It was the heart cry of the Father as he foresaw and faced the complex problem of human sin and shame, the seemingly insoluble problem of a 'satanized' humanity. The answer to the problem was not men's destruction, although but for the love of God, that would have been a simple solution. The answer was to be their reconciliation, their being brought back into the original design and purpose of God, into eternal union with him. It was the Son who answered both the cry and the problem – 'Here am I; send me.' These wonderful words –

> Then said I, Lo, I am come; in the roll of the book it is written of me: I delight to do thy will, O my God

– were fulfilled when the Messiah Jesus came into this world. (Psalm 40:7-8, RV; cf. Hebrews 10:5-10.)

It is clear that from the beginning Jesus, as man, knew exactly what his real work was. From the moment Peter made his great confession, 'Thou art the Messiah, the Son of the living God' (Matthew 16:16), Jesus began to reveal to his disciples what his supreme service was. His whole life had been but the preparation for it. That day, upon which all history and time is focused, and upon which the saving and redeeming purpose of God depended, arrived with his crucifixion.

Nevertheless, we must never fall into the trap of thinking that because the work of our salvation was completed within the course of one short day, it was easy for the Messiah. It cost him everything! Into those few hours was contracted a world of suffering and anguish beyond all human computation. Language is totally inadequate, even when divinely inspired, to describe or interpret that kind of suffering. None of the writers of the gospels tried to describe the *real* sufferings of the Messiah. They recorded only the bare facts. Even the apostles declared only their spiritual consequences, and interpretation – that he bore our sins, that he suffered in our place, that he was made sin for us. Nowhere do they seek to describe the cost and suffering. It is as if all were aware that it was beyond the range of human language or understanding; that it was something so holy, so wonderful, so mysterious and unsearchable, so immense and eternal in its significance that the most eloquent oratory in the world would fail to describe it, and the finest theological mind would fail to define it. The real story of how the sinless One was made sin for us, of how the Lamb of God became in those dread hours the 'lifted up serpent' (2 Corinthians 5:21; John 1:29; 3:14), can never be told. All we have are clues which betray fathomless depths of anguish and suffering. We see the acts; we watch his humiliation, the torture, the derision. We hear his words, his cries; we see his reactions, the physical pain and death. We watch it all and are conscious that this is the least part of the story. For the physical sufferings of the Messiah were not the real sufferings. They were only the outward indication of an infinite and unutterable anguish. His real service was offered and fulfilled in the realm of the unseen. The Servant of the Lord passes, as it were, out of our sight into darkness; beyond this point we cannot penetrate. We have come to the limit of our finite ability to understand and can only bow our heads and our hearts.

There in that place of darkness his soul became the

offering for our sin; he was wounded, pierced through for our transgressions, he was crushed for our iniquities. There he suffered for our well-being, our peace; he was chastised, that our unhappy, tortured consciences might know peace with God. There our sorrows and griefs were borne by him; our sicknesses and ills found their home in him. (See Isaiah 52:13 – 53:12). He took upon himself both the root and the fruit of all sin, for all our iniquity was caused to fall upon him. It was the sin of the whole world which he bore away – its total evil and wickedness, all its restless hatefulness, the pain of all history. Into those few hours all of it was gathered together and loaded upon that one dear human frame.

It was not some strange coincidence that the Messiah died upon Passover. That feast commemorated God's glorious deliverance of a people in bondage and misery. Moreover at the heart of that commemoration was a slain lamb, a one-year-old unblemished male lamb, whose blood had been placed upon the lintels and doorposts of every believing family. John the Baptist said of Jesus: 'Behold, the Lamb of God, which taketh away the sin of the world!' (John 1:29, RV). It was not, therefore, by chance that the Messiah died when the lambs were being slain for the commemoration. He was the fulfilment of its age-old symbolism.

For the Satanic powers of darkness it was their hour. When at Gethsemane they had found themselves powerless to stop the Messiah's work from being fulfilled, their frenzied hate and fury knew no bounds. So terrible were those final hours that even creation shrank back in horror. It is stated in Colossians 1:17 that 'in Him all things hold together' (NASB). When the Messiah was made sin for us, and became a 'curse', it was as if the natural creation, held together in him, felt the shock. The earth shuddered, and rocks were split open (Matthew 27:51), and natural light was plunged into darkness (Mark 15:33). It was as if the being of God himself was seized by some unbearable pain and, in consequence, the universe itself was affected.

Even if we do not understand the mystery in this matter, it reveals something of the reality and depth of the Messiah's suffering. Out of those black and impenetrable depths of pain and darkness we hear ringing down through the centuries of time the awesome cry of the broken heart of the Messiah: 'My God, my God, why hast thou forsaken me?' (Mark 15:34). The Messiah had been made sin for us, and it had 'pleased the Lord to crush him'; he had put the Messiah to grief. The Lord Jesus was alone not only on the human level; he had been forsaken by God himself because of our sin.

The full extent of what he did, precisely how he suffered, how he became our sin, the immeasurable cost involved – all is beyond our ability to understand. What we do know, and know in our experience if we have truly believed on him, is that he saved us. In some way beyond our finite comprehension, a vast universe of sin, pain, and unhappiness, of suffering and death, had been concentrated upon his experience. The Lord laid on him the iniquity of us all, and he bore it away into oblivion. He paid the ultimate price at the cost of his own life, and suffered for our sins, the just for the unjust, that he might bring us to God. The Messiah tasted death for every man, and henceforth would bring many sons to glory (Hebrews 2:9-10).

Strangely enough, it is in the cruel jest of the chief priests and scribes that we are face to face with truth. They unconsciously prophesied when they said, 'He saved others; himself he cannot save' (Mark 15:31). They never spoke a truer word. His whole life had been spent in saving others from death, corruption, bondage and disease, from sin and Satan. Yet now, on the deepest level, he could not save himself. It was not that he did not have the power. He had all the power in this universe at his command, but he would use it only to sacrifice himself, not to save himself. It was his love for us which ruled out any possibility of self-preservation! It was not the nails which fastened him to the tree, nor the presence of hardened soldiers that kept him there, but divine love. That love nailed him to the cross more effectively and powerfully than anything else in this universe. Truly the love of Jesus passes knowledge. It is quite inexplicable. There were many things the Servant of the Lord could have done, but to serve God truly, love for his Father and love for us ruled them out. There is in this a deep lesson for all who would serve God. There are many things we could do, but if we truly serve God, we shall discover that we cannot do them for love of God and for love of others. Divine love will always nail us to the will of God; it will ever cause us to be willing prisoners of the Lord Jesus.

The chief priests and scribes were totally blind to what was happening on that cross. The Messiah could not save himself, because he was saving us, for he could not save himself and others as well. He had to choose either to save himself or to save fallen man; and he had chosen, in infinite love and grace, to save fallen man. Indeed, his love was so great that he was dying to save even the chief priests and the scribes, to save Annas and Caiaphas and Pilate, and the crowd who jeered and taunted him that day, if they would only have turned to God and believed on him. They thought that Jesus was finished, that his 'strange' power and influence was broken, and his lips finally silenced. They could not have been more wrong. For just where those hands and feet were nailed to the cross, where seemingly no great miracle was wrought, no dynamic power was displayed, no mighty message was preached, the miracle of miracles was wrought, the mightiest and most effective power in the history of the ages was displayed, and the greatest message ever preached on earth or in heaven was uttered. When Jesus died with that great cry, 'It is finished,' the veil of the Temple was torn in two from top to bottom (John 19:30; Mark 15:37-38). The Messiah never uttered a more powerful or a more pregnant message than that one word 'finished', nor was more effective power ever exercised than when the Messiah finished the work of our salvation, and reconciled us to God.

When Jesus died, the veil of the Temple was torn in two from the top to the bottom, for the means to reconcile fallen humanity to God had been found through the Messiah. That veil had symbolized the alienation of sinful fallen man from God, his falling short of the glory of God through sin. It represented the bolting and barring of the gates of the Eternal City, God's dwelling place, to that kind of man, to that whole world order. Now that veil was torn apart by God himself; those gates he himself unbolted and flung open. What no one else could do, the Messiah had done. He not only won for us an eternal salvation, tremendous and wonderful as that fact is alone! He closed down the old order, the old creation, the old man and nature! And, as the Servant of the Lord, he laid a solid and everlasting basis for a new order, a new creation, a new heaven and earth wherein dwells righteousness. A new man came in with him. The whole order of things brought in by the fall of man through Satan was judged in the Messiah, and finished; in him it was crucified, buried and put away for ever. Moreover in the very place of judgement, a door of hope was opened. A new day dawned when humanly speaking it had appeared the blackest of nights. For all those who feared his name the sun of righteousness had arisen with healing in its wings. For them a new and an eternal day with new life, new power and new purpose had come. For the Servant of the Lord, Jesus, the everlasting doors had lifted up their heads. He had gone in triumphantly, and with him, by the grace of God alone, all those who believe have also entered.

Every aspect of the Messiah Jesus is unique. Whether it is the mystery of his person, both God and man; or the fact of the many prophecies which have foretold his coming, his birth, his supreme work and the glory that would follow; or the beauty of his character; he is unique. And if that places him far above all, his work can only add to his uniqueness. For no one else could have done what the Lord Jesus has done. It is stated simply and profoundly in the *Encyclopaedia Judaica*:

> If, as Christians believe, the martyr Jesus was at the same time the Messiah, then his death has a cosmic importance.

In all this we see something of what it cost the Messiah to fulfil the work which God gave him to do. It was a cost beyond human computation, but he willingly paid that price, and offered himself up. Since we are so undeserving, the question arises as to why he laid down his life for us. There is only one adequate answer. He did not die for the sake of duty, nor for his own satisfaction and glory, nor even, on a higher level, for the honour and glory of God without any regard for us as people. He became the Lamb of God and bore away our sin because of his measureless and undying love. As the apostle Paul put it, he 'loved me and gave himself for me' (Galatians 2:20). Such love is as fathomless as it is inexplicable.

In this we see the heart of the King and Messiah. He is not the messianic King merely because of his pedigree, although it is both authentic and pure: he *is* the Son of David. Nor is he the messianic King because he was predestined to be the King, although that was predicted from the beginning, and divinely foreordained. He is King supremely because he is worthy to be King and to take the throne. In him we see the kind of character and nature which can do no other than reign. By his inward character he converted a crown of thorns into the most priceless and radiant crown ever worn in history, and a worthless reed into the most powerful sceptre ever wielded. In him we see a concept of royalty, of leadership, of authority, which is without peer. It is based on character, on selfless, sacrificial service, on a life laid down in its entirety for others. His kingship is founded on divine love, on absolute truth and transparent reality.

This is sufficient reason alone to call him worthy. The apostle John, seeing in vision into heaven itself, and into eternity, saw at the centre of everything the throne of

God, and in the throne he saw a 'lamb, as it had been slain' (Revelation 5:5,6). At the glorious heart of a vast triumphant and worshipping throng, in a new heaven and a new earth, is the crucified and reigning Messiah. The 'lamb, as it had been slain' is the enthroned Messiah bearing for ever the scars of his suffering, the nail marks in his hands and feet, and the spear mark in his side. John saw the Messiah take the scroll sealed with seven seals, representing the mind and will of God, which no one, Jewish or Gentile, had been able to realize, and watched him break the seals and open it. The Messiah Jesus had fulfilled the eternal purpose of God, redeeming an innumerable company from every nation on the earth, and bringing many sons to glory. No one else had ever been found worthy to inherit the throne of God, to restore all things to the Father, and to put into effect the whole mind of God for the ages to come.

In the 'little lamb as it had been slain' the key to Jewish history has finally been found, unlocking all that was inexplicable in it, and turning its sorrow into glory. For the purpose of God was not frustrated by the fall of the Jewish people, but fulfilled through it; nor did his love for them evaporate with their fall, but down through the years has proved undying. At the end all Israel, the true elect people of God, Jew and Gentile, will have been saved to sin no more, and the earth will be filled with the knowledge of the glory of the Lord, as the waters cover the sea. For God has solemnly declared this from the beginning:

> As truly as I live, all the earth shall be filled with the glory of the Lord. (Numbers 14:21, AV.)

In that day, the prophetic words of Isaiah will be fulfilled:

> Every valley shall be exalted, and every mountain and hill shall be made low: and the crooked shall be made straight, and the rough places plain: and the glory of the Lord shall be revealed, and all flesh shall see it together: for the mouth of the Lord hath spoken it. (Isaiah 40:4-5, RV.)

From the right hand of God the Messiah Jesus, Lamb of God and Lion of Judah, shall reign for ever. The King of the Jews has become the King of kings and Lord of lords, and

> of the increase of his government and of peace there shall be no end, upon the throne of David, and upon his kingdom, to establish it, and to uphold it ... for ever. (Isaiah 9:7, RV.)

For the prophetic words of King David concerning the Messiah, uttered so long ago, will have finally come to pass (see Psalm 72:17-20):

> His name shall endure for ever:
> His name shall be continued as long as the sun:
> And men shall be blessed in him:
> All nations shall call him blessed.
>
> 'Blessed be the Lord God, the God of Israel,
> Who only doeth wondrous things.
> And blessed be his glorious name for ever:
> And let the whole earth be filled with his glory;
> Amen, and Amen.

GLOSSARY

Ashkenazi-Ashkenazim
A name which in its more popular use describes those Jews originating in north-west Europe, i.e. Germany in particular, central and eastern Europe, and Russia. It then became a designation of that Jewish culture and way of life stemming from those areas, as opposed to the Sephardi (q.v.).

Balfour Declaration

Foreign Office,
November 2nd, 1917

Dear Lord Rothschild,
I have much pleasure in conveying to you, on behalf of His Majesty's Government, the following declaration of sympathy with Jewish Zionist aspirations which has been submitted to, and approved by, the Cabinet.

> His Majesty's Government view with favour the establishment in Palestine of a national home for the Jewish people, and will use their best endeavours to facilitate the achievement of this object, it being clearly understood that nothing shall be done which may prejudice the civic and religious rights of existing non-Jewish communities in Palestine, or the rights and political status enjoyed by Jews in any other country.

I should be grateful if you would bring this declaration to the knowledge of the Zionist Federation.

Yours,
Arthur James Balfour

Halukkah
The name given for the financial allowance made by Jewish communities abroad for the Jewish inhabitants of Palestine, and particularly of the four holy Jewish cities: Jerusalem,

Hebron, Tiberias, Safed. It was an organized method of support, and there were institutions which specifically supervised and channelled it. In many ways the special taxes and regulations imposed upon the Jewish communities in the Holy Land made it almost impossible for them to survive without such help. Furthermore, in religious circles it was viewed as an especial piety and good work to contribute towards Jews in Palestine. In the long run, however, the system was enervating and produced a society in Palestine largely devoid of initiative and dependent upon charity. The early Zionists, with their emphasis upon the need for self-support, and their faith in manual labour as part of Jewish recovery, came into collision with the whole system of Halukkah. At the end of the 19th century, with the rise of new communities dependent upon the labour of their own hands, Halukkah began to fade away.

Haskalah

The Hebrew term for the Enlightenment movement and ideology, the aim of which was to spread modern European culture among Jews. It was bitterly contested by orthodoxy. It began in 1770 in central Europe and spread over a wide area of Europe, including European Russia, and faded out in the early 1880s. By and large it contributed much towards the assimilation of Jews in language, dress and manners, for it saw the goal of Jewish life, in the general progress of mankind, to be a contribution to the life of the nation in which they lived. It place an emphasis upon the importance of secular studies in Jewish education. It also used biblical Hebrew for secular purposes, but although this contributed to the rebirth of Hebrew as a modern language, it was too stinted to become a powerful factor. In central and western Europe it produced a certain disintegration in Jewish life through assimilation. In Russia it remained a force until the beginning of the 20th century. There was one trend within the Russian Haskalah which sought to foster Jewish nationalism, particulary after 1870.

Hasid-Hasidism
A popular religious movement within Judaism which began in the latter part of the 18th century. At first it was bitterly contested by orthodoxy but was finally accepted and recognized. It was characterized by religious ecstasy, mass enthusiasm, a close-knit and cohesive community life, and by 'charismatic' personalities in leadership.

The Holocaust
The word is derived from Greek and means 'a whole burnt offering; wholesale sacrifice or destruction'. It is the name given to the most tragic period of the second Jewish exile. It spans a period of twelve years, from 1933 to 1945. The last six years of this period, 1939-45, were the worst. It was the Nazi-inspired 'final solution of the Jewish problem', and catered for the systematic liquidation of the Jewish people. It is conservatively estimated that at least six million Jews died in this period.

Kabbalah-Kabbalism-Kabbalist
The word 'Kabbalah' means 'received' or 'reception'. It is the most commonly used term for Jewish mysticism, especially the forms which emerged in the Middle Ages from the 12th century onwards. In fact the term covers the whole period, beginning with the destruction of the second temple in A.D. 70. It sought an apprehension of God and the meaning of life through contemplation and illumination. It did not belittle the intellect, but emphasized the fact that a real understanding of God is beyond the intellect; it has to be received through illumination. Spanish Kabbalism from the 13th century made a profound impact upon the whole movement, especially the book of Zohar, which was its finest literary achivement. Spanish Kabbalism, in fact, made it a cohesive force in Judaism. After the destruction of Jewry in Spain and Portugal during the period of the Inquisition, the centre of Kabbalism moved to Safed in North Galilee. This gave Kabbalism to the whole of Jewry and from that time messianism became its heart. It has proved to be one of the

most powerful and influential forces ever to affect the inner development of Judaism.

Maccabees-Maccabean

Additional name given to a Jewish family who led the revolt of the Jewish people against the Seleucid king, Antiochus IV Epiphanes, and especially to his third son, Judah. Thus far there has been no satisfactory explanation of the meaning or origin of the name. According to Josephus the family name was 'Hashmon', and they are thus known as 'the Hasmoneans' in rabbinic literature. Antiochus IV began a reign of terror around 171 B.C. which was to last seven years, and of which the last three-and-half years were the most severe. It was during this latter period that Mattathias, the father of the family, a godly and devout priest, led the revolt in a small town called Modi'in not far from Jerusalem, when he killed both the Greek officer and the apostate Jew who were taking part in a pagan rite. He and his five sons fled to the Judean mountains and with many others began a guerilla campaign. Many rallied to their banner. When Mattathias died later that year, his third son Judah took over the leadership and proved to be a man with the qualities of Gideon. He led the Maccabees in successive victories, all brilliantly conceived. Antiochus IV died in 164 B.C. in a military campaign in Media. In 161 B.C. Judah died on the battlefield and Jonathan, his youngest brother, took over, until he was treacherously murdered in 143 B.C. Complete independence was won by Simon, the second-eldest brother. It was the first time since before the Babylonian exile that the Jewish people were truly free, and in fact they recovered all the territory which David and Solomon ruled in the golden era of Jewish history. The Maccabean period provides us with one of the most striking eras in the history of the Jewish people. The story is told in 1 and 2 Maccabees and is commemorated in the feast of Hanukkah (the Feast of Lights).

Midrash

The word comes from a root meaning 'to seek', 'to examine',

'to investigate'. It is used of a certain type of rabbinic literature consisting mostly of homiletic interpretations of the Bible.

Proclamation of Independence

Eretz-Israel (the Land of Israel), was the birthplace of the Jewish people. Here their spiritual, religious and political identity was shaped. Here they first attained to statehood, created cultural values of national and universal significance and gave the world the eternal Book of Books.

After being forcibly exiled from their land, the people kept faith with it throughout their Dispersion and never ceased to pray and hope for their return to it and for the restoration in it of their political freedom.

Impelled by this historic and traditional attachment, Jews strove in every successive generation to re-establish themselves in their ancient homeland. In recent decades they returned in their masses. Pioneers, *ma'apilim* (immigrants coming to Israel in defiance of restrictive regulations), and defenders, they made deserts bloom, revived the Hebrew language, built villages and towns, and created a thriving community, controlling its own economy and culture, loving peace but knowing how to defend itself, bringing the blessings of progress to all the country's inhabitants, and aspiring towards independent nationhood.

In the year 5657 (1897), at the summons of the spiritual father of the Jewish State, Theodor Herzl, the First Zionist Congress convened and proclaimed the right of the Jewish people to national rebirth in its own country.

This right was recognized in the Balfour Declaration of the 2nd November 1917, and reaffirmed in the Mandate of the League of Nations which, in particular, gave international sanctions to the historic connection between the Jewish people and Eretz-Israel and to the right of the Jewish people to rebuild its National Home.

The catastrophe which recently befell the Jewish people

— the massacre of millions of Jews in Europe — was another clear demonstration of the urgency of solving the problem of its homelessness by re-establishing in Eretz-Israel the Jewish State, which would open the gates of the homeland wide to every Jew and confer upon the Jewish people the status of a fully-privileged member of the comity of nations.

Survivors of the Nazi Holocaust in Europe, as well as Jews from other parts of the world, continued to migrate to Eretz-Israel, undaunted by difficulties, restrictions and dangers, and never ceased to assert their right to a life of dignity, freedom and honest toil in their national homeland.

In the second world war, the Jewish community of this country contributed its full share to the struggle of the freedom- and peace-loving nations against the forces of Nazi wickedness and, by the blood of its soldiers and its war effort, gained the right to be reckoned among the peoples who founded the United Nations.

On the 29th November 1947, the United Nations General Assembly passed a resolution calling for the establishment of a Jewish State in Eretz-Israel; the General Assembly required the inhabitants of Eretz-Israel to take such steps as were necessary on their part for the implementation of that resolution. This recognition by the United Nations of the right of the Jewish people to establish their State is irrevocable.

This right is the natural right of the Jewish people to be masters of their own fate, like all other nations, in their own Sovereign State.

ACCORDINGLY WE, MEMBERS OF THE PEOPLE'S COUNCIL, REPRESENTATIVES OF THE JEWISH COMMUNITY OF ERETZ-ISRAEL AND OF THE ZIONIST MOVEMENT, ARE HERE ASSEMBLED ON THE DAY OF THE TERMINATION OF THE BRITISH MANDATE OVER ERETZ-ISRAEL AND, BY VIRTUE OF OUR NATURAL AND HISTORIC RIGHT AND ON THE STRENGTH OF THE RESOLUTION OF THE UNITED NATIONS GENERAL ASSEMBLY, HEREBY DECLARE THE ESTABLISHMENT OF A JEWISH STATE IN ERETZ-ISRAEL, TO BE KNOWN AS THE STATE OF ISRAEL.

WE DECLARE that, with effect from the moment of the termination of the Mandate, being tonight, the eve of Sabbath, the 6th Iyar 5708 (15th May 1948), until the establishment of the elected, regular authorities of the State in accordance with the Constitution which shall be adopted by the Elected Constituent Assembly not later than the 1st October 1948, the People's Council shall act as a Provisional Council of State, and its executive organ, the People's Administration, shall be the Provisional Government of the Jewish State, to be called 'Israel'.

The State of Israel will be open for Jewish immigration and for the Ingathering of the Exiles; it will foster the development of the country for the benefit of all its inhabitants; it will be based on freedom, justice and peace as envisaged by the prophets of Israel; it will ensure complete equality of social and political rights to all its inhabitants irrespective of religion, race, or sex; it will guarantee freedom of religion, conscience, language, education and culture; it will safeguard the Holy Places of all religions; and it will be faithful to the principles of the Charter of the United Nations.

The State of Israel is prepared to co-operate with the agencies and representatives of the United Nations in implementing the resolution of the General Assembly of the 29th November 1947, and will take steps to bring about the economic union of the whole of Eretz-Israel.

We appeal to the United Nations to assist the Jewish people in the building-up of its State and to receive the State of Israel into the comity of nations.

We appeal — in the very midst of the onslaught launched against us now for months — to the Arab inhabitants of the State of Israel to preserve peace and participate in the upbuilding of the State on the basis of full and equal citizenship and due representation in all its provisional and permanent institutions.

We extend our hand to all neighbouring States and their peoples in an offer of peace and good neighbourliness, and appeal to them to establish bonds of co-operation and mutual help with the sovereign Jewish people settled in its own land. The State of Israel is prepared to do its share in common effort for the advancement of the entire Middle East.

We appeal to the Jewish people throughout the Diaspora to rally round the Jews of Eretz-Israel in the tasks of immigration and upbuilding and to stand by them in the great struggle for the realization of the age-old dream — the redemption of Israel.

PLACING OUR TRUST IN THE ALMIGHTY, WE AFFIX OUR SIGNATURES TO THIS PROCLAMATION AT THIS SESSION OF THE PROVISIONAL COUNCIL OF STATE, ON THE SOIL OF THE HOMELAND, IN THE CITY OF TEL-AVIV, ON THE SABBATH EVE, THE 5th DAY OF IYAR 5708 (14th MAY, 1948).

David Ben Gurion

Daniel Auster
Mordekhai Bentov
Yitzchak Ben Zvi
Eliyahu Berligne
Fritz Bernstein
Rabbi Wolf Gold
Meir Grabovsky
Yitzchak Gruenbaum
Dr Abraham Granovsky
Eliyahu Dobkin
Meir Wilner-Kovner
Zerach Wahrhaftig
Herzl Vardi
Rachel Cohen
Rabbi Kalman Kahana
Saadia Kobashi
Rabbi Yitzchak Meir Levin
Meir David Loewenstein
Zvi Luria
Golda Myerson
Nachum Nir
Zvi Segal
Rabbi Yehuda Leib Hacohen Fishman
David Zvi Pinkas
Aharon Zisling
Moshe Kolodny
Eliezer Kaplan
Abraham Katznelson
Felix Rosenblueth
David Remez
Berl Repetur
Mordekhai Shattner
Ben Zion Sternberg
Bekhor Shitreet
Moshe Shapira
Moshe Shertok

Sephardi-Sephardim
A name, in its strictly correct use, referring only to those

Jews of Spanish or Portuguese origin. Sepharad means Spain. In its popular use, however, it has a far wider meaning, designating all Latin Jews and those from the Mediterranean region and describing the Jewish culture and way of life which originated in those areas.

Talmud

The word means 'Study' or 'learning'. It is used most commonly to describe that body of teaching which comprises the commentary and discussions of the scholars (3rd-5th centuries A.D.) on the Mishnah. It consists of two parts:

1. *The Mishnah,* which is the collection of the oral laws, or traditions, of the elders, as opposed to the written law of God, and was compiled and edited by Rabbi Judah Ha-Nasi (A.D. 230). It covers a period from approximately the 2nd century B.C. to the 2nd century A.D. Its object was to preserve the Law of God and to apply it to everyday life. From the time of its compilation by Rabbi Judah, it has ranked in Jewish eyes second only to the Old Testament. The word *mishnah* comes from a root meaning 'to repeat' and thus 'to teach by repetition'.

2. *The Gemara,* which is the record of the commentary and discussion on the Mishnah. *Gemara* means 'completion' or 'tradition'. There are two Gemaras, one compiled in Tiberias by Rabbi Johanan in the 4th century A.D. and the other compiled in Babylon towards the end of the 5th century A.D. Thus the Mishnah with the Tiberias Gemara is popularly called 'The Jerusalem Talmud', and the Mishnah with the Babylonian Gemara is called 'The Babylonian Talmud'. The influence of the Talmud upon Jewish life, thought and conduct is inestimable.

Targum

The word means 'translation'. It is used almost exclusively in rabbinic literature for the translation of the Bible into Aramaic, and those portions of the Bible already written in Aramaic. Alongside the translation, paraphrase-type explanation was often given. The most famous of the targums is the Targum Onkelos. Onkelos was traditionally held to be a disciple of Rabbi Gamaliel. It dates from the 2nd century A.D.. The other targums are the Targum Jonathan (4th century A.D.) and the Jerusalem Targum, also called the Targum pseudo-Jonathan (7th century A.D.).

Wadi
An Arabic word for a rocky watercourse, dry except in the rainy season. The Hebrew equivalent is 'nahal'.

Yalkut
This word comes from a root meaning 'to compile'. It is a comprehensive midrashic anthology covering the whole Bible. The best known is Yalkut Shimoni, often known as the Yalkut of Simeon of Frankfurt. It dates from the early 14th Century A.D. Yalkut HaMalchiri dates from the same period but is not so comprehensive.

Yeshivah-Yeshivot
A name given to academics or institutions for the pursuit of talmudic studies. Some of these were famous and influential centres of learning, wielding great authority in Jewish life; others were small, local 'Bible schools'. Jerusalem at the present time boasts a growing number.

The book of Zohar
The word 'Zohar' means 'splendour'. It is the central work in the literature of the Kabbalah (q.v.). It is a collection of books united under one title and comprises five volumes. It was edited and published by Moses ben Shem Tov de Leon in the late 13th century and claimed to be 'the Midrash of Rabbi Simeon ben Yohai, a teacher of the 2nd century A.D.'. The Holy Zohar, as it is sometimes called, exerted a profound influence on all 'Jewish mysticism'.

BIBLIOGRAPHY

Alon, Azaria, *The Natural History of the Land of the Bible* (Jerusalem 1969).

Avi-Yonah, Michael, *A History of the Holy Land* (London 1969).

Avi-Yonah, Michael, *The Holy Land from the Persian to the Arab Conquest, 536 B.C.-A.D. 640* (Michigan 1966).

Ben Gurion, David, *The Jews in their Land* (London 1966).

Cansdale, George S., *Animals of Bible Lands* (London 1970).

Charif, Ruth and Raz, Simcha (ed.), *Jerusalem: The Eternal Bond* (Tel Aviv 1977).

Eban, Abba, *My People: The Story of the Jews* (New York 1968).

Edersheim, Alfred, *The Life and Times of Jesus, the Messiah* (2 vols, London 1890).

Elon, Amos, *Herzl* (London 1975).

Gilbert, Martin, *Exile and Return* (London 1978).

Gilbert, Martin, *Jerusalem: A Historical Atlas* (Jerusalem 1977).

Gilbert, Martin, *The Arab-Israeli Conflict* (London 1976).

Gilbert, Martin, *The Jews of Arab Lands* (London 1976).

Gilbert, Martin, *The Jews of Russia* (London 1976).

haLevi. Yehuda, *Selected Poems* (Philadelphia 1924).

Hareuveni, Nogah in association with Frenkley, Helen, *Ecology in the Bible* (Kiryat Ono 1974).

Hertz, J. H., *A Book of Jewish Thoughts* (London 1935).

Herzl, Theodor, *The Jewish State* (trans. Sylvie D'Avigdor, London 1972).

Herzl, Theodor, *Der Judenstaat* (London 1896).

Herzl, Theodor, *Tagebücher* (3 vols, Berlin 1922).

Join-Lambert, Michel, *Jerusalem* (London 1958).

Kollek, Teddy and Pearlman, Moshe, *Jerusalem, Sacred City of Mankind: A History of 40 Centuries* (Jerusalem 1968).

Lambert, Lance, *Battle for Israel* (Eastbourne 1976).
Lowenthal, Marvin (ed.), *The Diaries of Theodor Herzl* (London 1958).
Mazar, Benjamin, *The Mountain of the Lord* (New York 1975).
Neider, Charles (ed.), *The Complete Essays of Mark Twain* (New York 1963).
Orni, Efraim and Efrat, Elisha, *Geography of Israel* (3rd ed. Jerusalem 1971).
Patai, Rapael (ed.), *The Complete Diaries of Theodor Herzl* (New York 1960).
Roth, Cecil, *A Short History of the Jewish People* (London 1969).
Roth, Cecil (editor-in-chief), *Encyclopaedia Judaica* (Jerusalem 1971).
Rosen, Dov, *Shema Yisrael* (2 vols, Jerusalem 1974).
Sachar, Howard M., *A History of Israel from the Rise of Zionism to Our Time* (Jerusalem 1976).
St John, Robert, *Tongue of the Prophets* (Hollywood 1952).
Scholem, Gershom S., *Kabbalah* (New York 1974).

LIVING BOOKS

Inspirational bestsellers from the people who brought you THE LIVING BIBLE.

THE CHASE by Richard Walsh. How could a man be so tremendously successful in business and such a failure in life? Richard Walsh was on an endless run until a mountain accident broke his neck. What follows turns tragedy into triumph in this inspiring story of courage and renewal. 07-0221 $2.95

PONTIUS PILATE by Dr. Paul Maier. This fascinating novel is about the most famous man in Roman history—the man who declared Jesus innocent but who nevertheless sent him to the cross. This is the true story of how—and why. 07-4852 $3.50

THE BEGINNING OF THE END by Dr. Tim LaHaye. What do the invasion of Afghanistan, the upheaval in Iran, the annexation of Jerusalem, and the shortage of oil in Russia have in common? This book shows how each event is part of the countdown to the end. 07-0114 $2.95

GOD'S SMUGGLER TO CHINA by Brother David. Here is an inside look behind the Bamboo Curtain by Brother David, an associate of Brother Andrew (*God's Smuggler*). You'll thrill to the stories of God's power and marvel at the perseverance and love of the Chinese Christians. 07-1083 $2.95

SONG OF ABRAHAM by Ellen Gunderson Traylor. This colorful novel portrays Abraham, whom both Arabs and Jews call "Father," as a man of strength, will, and purpose. Carefully researched and superbly told, this book can be read both for enjoyment and information. 07-6071 $2.95

BEYOND THE CLOUDS by Chip Ricks. Captain Connie Engel was the first woman ever to solo in a U.S. Air Force jet. Through all the harsh rigors and testings, she not only triumphed but maintained her identity, sense of purpose, and femininity. Not just an airplane story, not just a woman story, and not just a love story, but an inspiring combination of all three. 07-0147 $2.25

FOR FAMILIES ONLY edited by J. Allan Petersen. This book asks more than fifty of the toughest questions about family living, then provides answers from more than fifty family living experts. 07-0879 $2.95

LIFE IS TREMENDOUS by Charlie Jones. Believing that enthusiasm makes the difference, Jones shows how anyone can be happy, involved, relevant, productive, healthy, and secure in the midst of a high-pressure, commercialized, automated society. 07-2184 $2.50

WHAT WIVES WISH HUSBANDS KNEW ABOUT WOMEN by Dr. James Dobson. By the best-selling author of *Dare to Discipline* and *The Strong-Willed Child,* here's a vital book that speaks to the unique emotional needs and aspirations of today's woman. An immensely practical, interesting guide. 07-7896 $2.95